THE BUSINESS GUIDE
TO
THE PHILIPPINES

For the Friday Breakfast Brigade

Of the Benevolent Protective Order of Elks

Manila Lodge No 761

THE BUSINESS GUIDE
TO
THE PHILIPPINES

Donald Kirk

Butterworth-Heinemann Asia,
an imprint of Reed Academic Publishing Asia,
a division of Reed Elsevier (Singapore) Pty Ltd
1 Temasek Avenue
#17-01 Millenia Tower
Singapore 039192

ISBN 981-00-70810

Cover design by Fred Rose
Typeset by Pearson Publication Services (10/12pt New Century Schoolbook)
Printed in Great Britain by Biddles, Kings Lynn & Guildford

CONTENTS

PREFACE

This guide to doing business in the Philippines is a centennial edition. That is, it was 100 years ago, on 12 June 1898, that Emilio Aguinaldo, a revolutionary general then just 29 years old, proclaimed the Philippines' independence from Spain. The dream was postponed while the Americans, while conquering the Spanish colonialists in Cuba, trounced them again in the Battle of Manila Bay. They then proceeded to crush the Philippine 'insurrection,' as American history books still refer to the conflict between American forces and Philippine revolutionaries.

Still, in 1998, Filipinos are celebrating the 100th anniversary of a turning point in their country's history—as well as another turning point 100 years later. There is reason to celebrate the democratic transition of presidents after a hard-fought election in May 1998. The nation is in the midst of an economic revival that has somehow endured the economic downturn of much of the rest of the region. Foreign business people are coming to the country as they have ever since the explorer Ferdinand Magellan landed on an island off Samar in 1521.

The going has not always been easy. Magellan himself was killed on a beach in Mactan, near Cebu, after baptising a number of locals. Over more than three centuries of Spanish rule, Filipinos absorbed Spanish culture and religion while clinging to their own language and traditions. The result is a curious melange, made all the more curious by the adoption of American mores from the time the Americans arrived in 1898. US colonial rule, interrupted by the Japanese occupation from the end of 1941 until the early months of 1945, endured until 4 July 1946. After more than half a century of independence, the Philippines remains closely tied to American popular culture, even while developing its own cultural and economic strength.

No longer can foreign business interests exploit the Philippines as did the Spanish, and then the Americans, placing the land 'for 350 years in a convent and another 50 years in Hollywood'. Now, foreigners must try to work in harmony with Filipino interests, both in government and in private business. Filipinos are reciprocating by making it increasingly convenient for foreigners to thrive in their country by freeing them of many of the problems imposed by sensitive bureaucrats in the first decades after independence.

This guide, then, could hardly be more timely. It celebrates not only an anniversary but a new direction in policy. In gathering material for this purpose, I am grateful not only to the contributors whose work appears here but also to many others among both the Filipino and foreign business communities. Robert Sears and his intrepid staff at the American Chamber of Commerce in the Philippines, Dr. Alex Calata of the Philippine-American Educational Foundation and venerable historian Tom Carter all provided advice and insights, as did the gang that shows up on Fridays for the Elks Club breakfasts. To all of them, to editors Rosemary Peers and Merry Pearson, and to many others too numerous to mention I extend my deepest gratitude for helping to put together what I hope will be a useful reference for anyone thinking of joining those already doing business in the Philippines.

Donald Kirk
Manila
May 1998

ABOUT THE AUTHORS

ABOUT THE GENERAL EDITOR

Donald Kirk, author and general editor for this book, first visited the Philippines in 1968 as Asia correspondent for the old *Washington (DC) Star*. He has written numerous articles about the country for newspapers and magazines and is author of *Looted: The Philippines After the Bases*, St. Martin's Press, New York, and Macmillan, London, 1998.

ABOUT THE CONTRIBUTORS

Eric Moltzau Anderson, an economist and entrepreneur in the Philippines, has travelled widely throughout the Philippines and the rest of South-East Asia. He studied the economic implications of Clark and Subic as an independent project for the University of the Philippines.

Robert W Blume has worked for nearly 30 years as an international banker in Asia, Oceania and Latin America. During that time, he has assisted foreign investors in structuring and financing all types of businesses. These have ranged from car manufacturing in Mexico to developing a natural gas field in New Zealand and setting up a Coca Cola bottling plant in Samoa. He is now with the American Chamber of Commerce of the Philippines as investment promotion manager of the American desk in the Bureau of Overseas Investment of the Philippine's Department of Trade and Industry. Those wanting to contact him will find his office—along with those of consultants from other foreign countries—on the ground floor, 385 Buendia (Sen Gil Puyat Avenue), Makati, Metro Manila.

Emmanuel P Bonoan is an attorney and senior staff member of the tax division of SGV & Company, a member firm of the Andersen Worldwide Organisation.

Baron L Buck is the international managing director of American Security Systems International Inc (ASSI), the oldest intellectual property rights consulting firm and the only such firm in the Philippines that is 100% American-owned. An acknowledged authority on the enforcement of intellectual property rights in the Philippines, Mr. Buck was the only foreigner assigned to the technical working group on the Philippine Senate version of the Philippine Intellectual Property Rights Bill. His company was also instrumental in forming the Justice Department Task Force on

Intellectual Property Rights, as well as the presidential Inter-Agency Committee on Intellectual Property.

Cornelio C Gison, an attorney and certified public accountant, is tax-practice director, SGV & Company.

Leo Gonzaga worked for many years as correspondent of the *Far Eastern Economic Review* and also wrote for the *Financial Times* and the *Economist*. A specialist in banking, he served as editorial consultant for the American Chamber of Commerce of the Philippines for 15 years until his death, at the age of 75, on 11 February 1998. His contribution here represents the final publication of a long and distinguished career.

Raul de Guzman, managing director of Woodward-Clyde, engineering and environmental consultants, has spent the last 15 working years in policy and planning studies, environmental consulting and business development. He helped found Environmental Primemovers of Asia in 1980 and nurtured it until it was fully integrated into Woodward-Clyde. As a consultant, he was involved in a wide variety of industrial and government projects as project manager, socio-economist, financial analyst and institutional and policy specialist. He wrote this chapter with the research assistance of Angie Prelejera.

Benildo G. Hernandez has distinguished himself as an expert on labour law in the Philippines during a long career as an attorney. He is vice president/ECOP with the law firm, Sycip, Salazar, Hernandez and Gatmaitan in the Sycip Law-All Asia Capital Centre in Makati, Metro Manila.

Venvenuto Icamina has served for the past five years as chief economist for EIU (Economist Intelligence Unit) Philippines Inc.

Robert Katz has advised government as well as private-sector clients world-wide on Build-Operate-Transfer, project finance and infrastructure policy for more than 25 years. For five years he was senior manager for Price Waterhouse in Manila and had previous assignments in Mexico and Pakistan. Former president of the board of trustees of the International School Manila, Mr. Katz is on the board of directors of the American Chamber of Commerce of the Philippines. He may be reached at the Chamber or by e-mail at rkatz@webquest.com

Peter Wallace, president of EIU (Economist Intelligence Unit) Philippines Inc, has been reporting on and analysing business and finance there for more than two decades.

CHAPTER 1

CHECK IT OUT

The Philippines is a somewhat different place than it was a decade or two ago. Gone is the regime of Ferdinand Marcos—the president who imposed martial law in 1972—and then was overthrown in the People Power revolution of February 1986. Gone are many of the policies he put into place with ruinous effects for both the Philippine economy and foreign business interests. Gone too are the American bases, notably the air base at Clark and the navy base at Subic, that Marcos permitted the United States to maintain in exchange for enormous quantities of US aid funds. In their place are free ports, and their existence is one of the more visible signs of the Philippines' shifting political and economic outlook.

Some of the changes began under Corazon Aquino, the woman who led the revolt after her husband, Benigno, was assassinated as he was returning from exile in the United States in 1982. However, it was Aquino's successor, Fidel Valdez Ramos, a former general who had served Marcos as chief of the Philippine Constabulary and then helped to overthrow him, who rammed through many of the reforms that made life easier for business, Filipino as well as foreign. The growth of the Philippine economy under Ramos, however imperfect, has encouraged thousands of foreign companies and individuals to go to the Philippines, explore the possibilities and, in many cases, stake out a claim.

The puzzle, though, is how to go about it—and which of many possibilities is the most likely to work. The purpose of this book is to summarise some of the realities, as well as the many rules and regulations in a wide range of relevant areas, that will help investors on the way.

OPTIONS ON THE FAST TRACK

Once potential investors have decided, yes, the Philippines is the place, they have to make some crucial decisions. Where's the market? Are they investing for local consumption, and are they going to get their materials by import or locally? To produce for export, there are no restrictions on what is brought into the country to do the job, but that doesn't mean there's no need to worry about all the paperwork and delays associated with going through customs.

One way to avoid the hassle is to go into one of the export zones set up under the aegis of the Philippine Economic Zone Authority (PEZA). Supplies come into the zone from overseas and finished products are exported overseas, all free of tariffs or the taxes levied on sales on the open market. PEZA operates four publicly owned zones and also provides the same benefits, including both the customs benefit and preferential power rates, to those occupying a number of privately held zones. They 'make your life so much easier', as one manufacturing executive has said.

A downside of the PEZA system is that the land must be leased, and for no more than 75 years. An alternative is to set up shop elsewhere with the cooperation of the Board of Investments (BOI), which allows duty-free import of supplies and export of finished products. These factories are treated as bonded warehouses from which nothing will go onto the Philippine market.

For those thinking of ignoring the zones, the executive suggested, 'You have to weigh the size of the business versus the effort or the grief' on the outside. Operating outside of the PEZA system 'can be a nightmare', as he put it. 'There's a higher risk of theft at the port if you go the BOI route, but the bigger issue is the enormous amount of paper.' It's up to the individual investor 'to prove that everything you imported for your operation has been shipped out'. The problem gets worse when foreign businesses want to sell some assets locally to shut down or reduce operations.

Still, some executives recommend the BOI system for other reasons. 'Even if you're only exporting, you may want to go to BOI', said one. 'BOI can help set you up anywhere you like in the country, not just one of several PEZA zones. Let's say you want to have a sulphur mine, or perhaps you're exporting small items like semi-conductors. They tend to be BOI operations.' Some companies go both ways. A plant manufacturing for export may be in a

PEZA zone, while the company's research and development facility—which needs to import equipment but is not producing for export—may be set up on terms set by the BOI. 'It's a big pain; it's a hassle', said the manager of such a facility, 'but it works even if we wish they'd cut the paperwork'.

For those who want to invest in the Philippines but have no prior experience, the BOI offers what it calls a 'One-Stop Action Centre for Investments'. This is the fast-track desk that tries to get investors through the hoops of applications and other initial paperwork while eliminating travel to several offices and endless delays.

But that kind of service may not be enough. Foreign executives say investors really should go to one of the large accounting firms, such as SyCip Gorres Velayo, a member firm of Andersen Worldwide, or Joaquin Cunanan & Co./Price Waterhouse. They give the expert, reliable advice that's needed to function in a setting that may seem open and friendly on one level, but is cumbersome and full of pitfalls for the unwary on another.

'They said, "Here's how you do it," ' explained a foreign executive who set up a major manufacturing business there on the basis of recommendations and planning by one of the Big Six accounting firms in Metro Manila. 'In general, they give you a lot more contacts and make it a lot easier.'

Even if investors choose not to go to one of the top firms for advice, they still need to engage the services of a local attorney who may not be reliable or knowledgeable. 'There are plenty of legal firms out there', said the executive. 'You have to figure the risk versus the cost. The risk-free route is the Big Six. You have to provide a study for them. They'll help you write it so it sounds the right way.'

The problem with hiring an attorney to cruise through the paperwork is that the charming gentleman who offers to do the job may mislead the unsuspecting, both financially and legally. 'You go to the local, and it's a difficult way to do business,' said the executive. 'You could buy a whole bunch of stuff that's not legal. You could be in some guy's pocket for a long time and not even know it. Once you're into giving fees for this and that, you could be in it for a long time.'

He said the Big Six firm that he used was expensive, but it charged considerably less than a similar consulting firm would charge in the West. The investment worked out for both sides. 'Now we use them for everything—accounting, auditing, taxes.' In a system in which hands are constantly out expecting favours, gifts, fees and outright bribes, the executive believes in following the rules. 'We play it straight', he said. 'If you're big enough, you don't get bothered.'

A REGIONAL BASE

Investors don't need to have a factory or research facility in mind or a sales force in the Philippines to consider the country as a place for business. The government would love to establish the Philippines' credentials as a regional hub—a gathering place for regional headquarters if Hong Kong seems too pricey and uncertain under Chinese rule, Singapore too small and repressive, Thailand too depressed and overcrowded, Malaysia too unreliable under a leader who likes to blame foreigners for economic downturns, or Indonesia too corrupt and unreliable as a result of the nepotism and despotism of long-time ruler Suharto. Indeed, one compelling argument in favour of the Philippines is that the country has suffered relatively less than other South-East Asian nations in the economic downturn that hit the region in 1997 and 1998.

The attractions of Manila are sometimes difficult to sell considering that its traffic problems are almost as bad as those of Bangkok, with no real relief in sight. Nor does the record of kidnappings and 'salvagings'—the Fil-English word for assassination—impress people who might otherwise jump to Metro Manila or Cebu or Subic or Clark as central locations with lower expenses than other places. Still, over the past few years, several hundred companies have taken advantage of—or 'availed', another Fil-English term—the enticements offered by the BOI.

Getting certified as a regional headquarters leads to a host of such privileges associated with the label as preferential treatment in such crucial areas as visas and taxes. 'Go to BOI and fill out the forms', advised a foreign manager who had been through the routine. 'They'll tell you the requirements. I would never recommend guys come in and do it, but it's low cost. It's a matter of risk.' In other words, for very little money, you can take your chances on the BOI and establish yourself in a relatively friendly, economically viable environment.

As long as the Philippines sticks to the policies initiated in the past few years, the risk appears justified. Listen to Philippine leaders talk about their plans for widening the roads and building a network of rail lines linking Metro Manila to Clark and Subic and beyond, and one might think the country is about to tug itself altogether from a pit of third-world problems tinged with corruption. The country may not advance that quickly, but it's definitely worth checking out, evaluating the pluses and minuses, as so many business people have been doing with increasing intensity for the past few years. The contributions to this book are designed to help potential investors do just that—and to guide them on the way once they've decided to take the plunge.

CHAPTER 2

THE PHILIPPINES: A PLACE TO INVEST

Robert W Blume

Essentially, there are four critical areas of concern to foreign investors: a country's risk issues, or sovereign risk, its economic fundamentals, its cost dynamics, and its investment incentives. The relative weight of these concerns can be illustrated by a pyramid cut horizontally into four segments. At the bottom of the pyramid is country and sovereign risk, which provides the foundation for equity investment. Resting on that essential foundation are the country's economic fundamentals. Above that are cost factors and, finally, at the top, and of least importance, are investment incentives.

Country or sovereign risk, the basic foundation of foreign investment, is why the United States is the biggest recipient of foreign investment and why Burma, Laos and Cambodia are three of the smallest. It is also the factor that bedeviled the Philippines from the People Power revolution that overthrew Ferdinand Marcos in February 1986 until about 1991, when Marcos' successor, Corazon Aquino, had survived seven coup attempts.

How is the Philippines doing now? There's been tremendous improvement in the country's stability. The Philippines is viewed as a much safer place to invest now that a stable democracy has replaced the weak democracy that followed an era of one-man rule. What follows is an examination of how the Philippines measures up with respect to the foreign investor's four critical areas of concern.

COUNTRY RISK

The following issues relate to sovereign risk as it might affect business in the Philippines:

Perceived breakdowns in peace and order? There have been big improvements.

Perceived threat of interference and shakedowns by government officials? There have been sound improvements, but more work is needed. In general, it's not an issue except in isolated cases.

Perceived unfair treatment by regulatory authorities? There have been improvements, but the Department of Agrarian Reform and Department of Environment and Natural Resources still are problematic.

Perceived weakness in the judicial system? The time it takes for a decision and the length of the appeals process are definite concerns.

Perceived weakness in top leadership? During his six-year term that ends in mid-1998, President Fidel Ramos has been considered to be smart, energetic, committed and able to get things done in an often fractious setting. At the time of writing, there is concern about what comes next.

Perceived weakness in the bureaucracy? There are many committed people in government, but the best workers often go to the private sector because public sector salaries are low. The Philippines might follow Mexico's lead and dramatically increase the pay of government workers to attract the best. The same can be said for law enforcement.

Perceived over-regulation? The country's top leaders have won key victories to deregulate and liberalise the economy. Still more can and hopefully will be done.

Perceived weakness in the formulation of policy? The constant tinkering and fine-tuning of policy that goes on is often frustrating.

Protection of intellectual property rights? This is a big issue with many investors who bring into the country new technology, new materials, internationally established brand names, and quality images that need to be protected. The record in the Philippines—as with some of its Asian neighbours—is not good. Passage of the new intellectual property rights law is a step forward.

Perceived labour unrest? There is hardly any, which is a vast improvement and a big selling point for the country. Labour peace generally prevails.

Perceived discrimination against foreigners? There has been much improvement, but the country will benefit when the Negative Lists that exclude foreigners from certain enterprises eventually are scrapped. That will open up professions, retailing and other areas to more competition.

Perceived concentration of power in a few groups? There still are socio-economic inequities, but they are being addressed as the economy grows. However, the remaining question is: can job and income creation keep pace with population growth?

Perceived religious or philosophical unrest? The lack of religious and philosophical tensions is one of the Philippines' best selling points. The country boasts thoroughly democratic and Western thinking due to its long association with Western countries and institutions.

Finally, and most importantly, is the Philippines perceived as safe? What about threats to personal and family safety? Many recall the Manila of the 1960s as a Wild West town. Many executives carried guns in their briefcases. In the provinces, guns on the table were the order of the day. There has been definite and steady improvement to personal safety as the country matures, but certain parts of Mindanao and far northern Luzon are areas of concern.

In general, the Philippines is in good shape in terms of country risk.

ECONOMIC FUNDAMENTALS

Issues relating to economic fundamentals are straightforward, involving less gut feeling than country risk assessments. Coming into play are such factors as:

- The growth rate of the gross domestic product;
- Inflation rates;
- Availability of local capital;
- Open financial markets;
- Liberal/open investment rules;
- Availability of office and industrial space;
- Developed and well-managed industrial parks and special zones;
- Sizeable internal markets;
- Proximity to other sizeable markets;
- Developed infrastructure of roads, railways, port facilities, airports, telecommunications, electric power, and water; and

- Easy entry into and exit from the country with visas and entry/ re-entry permits.

When it comes to economic fundamentals, the general picture in the Philippines is appealing, considering the following key areas.

The availability of local capital is improving, but not strong. The total financial resources of the Philippine banking system amount to only 2.2 billion pesos (less than US$70 billion), which is less than one-third the size of Citibank in the United States. The stock market, at US$65 billion, is less than 1% of the US market.

Financial markets are open and foreign exchange can be bought and sold freely.

Investment rules in several areas—banking, insurance, telecommunications, wholesale trade, and shipping—have been liberalised in the past few years. Discussions are going on to open more areas, like retail trade. The government is actively pushing for more liberalisation and taking tough stands against the protectionists. The sugar industry is an example of protectionism keeping local producers inefficient to the detriment of consumers.

The availability of office and industrial space is good. A lot of first-class office space and many top-notch industrial parks will be in use before the end of the century. Nearly all are privately owned and operated by powerful local and international companies. Most contain export processing zones (EPZs) under the Philippine Export Zone Authority (PEZA) inside their perimeters. Foreign investors have a decided preference to operate inside the confines of industrial parks, where security, permits, waste treatment, power, water and telecommunications are assured by the park. There are now some 25 first-class business parks, with about 20 more building or planned. Most are in the Calabarzon region, stretching from Cavite through Lagunas, Batangas, Rizal and Quezon provinces, but more are being built now in Cebu, Davao and other regional cities.

With 70 million people and significant increases in personal spending power, more and more companies are attracted by the sizeable internal market as a reason to invest.

Some countries are blessed to be close to other large markets; others, like New Zealand, are not. The location of the Philippines near key South-East Asian markets to the west and Taiwan, Japan and Korea to the north is a great selling point.

Much improvement is planned for the Philippine infrastructure, but currently it is an area of much concern and frustration. Here are some areas of importance in infrastructure:

- Roads/Rail—This is an area where 'pole-vaulting'—a favourite Philippine term for leaping ahead—is being attempted. The question is, can the government meet its goals with its management resources and can they find enough Build-Operate-Transfer (BOT) proponents to provide funds since so many projects are being planned for that type of financing.
- Port facilities—One bright spot is the new Batangas Port Project, financed with Japanese aid money, but most port facilities throughout the country are in need of attention. The National Port Plan lists about 80 ongoing and about 350 proposed locally funded projects, requiring an immediate influx of 10 billion pesos (more than US$300 million).
- Airports—The Philippines badly needs a new international airport to serve the Metro Manila Gateway, but the project seems to be moving slowly. The major airport is one reason for scant interest in moving regional headquarters to the Philippines from Singapore or Hong Kong.
- Telecommunications—With the most liberalised industry in South-East Asia, much work is under way. Lots of phone lines are being put in and costs coming down.
- Electric power—This is the shining light of the BOT program. The proposed privatisation of Napocor could reduce power costs by 25 to 35%, which could attract a lot of new manufacturing interest.
- Water—Privatisation of the Metro Manila water supply should lead to 90% coverage, up from the current 60%, as well as a price reduction of up to 50%. This also is a big potential attraction for investors.
- Ease of entry into and exit from the country—The private sector and various foreign chambers of commerce are working with the Philippine Government to liberalise visas. To date this remains a trouble spot, with a perception of too much paperwork and visas that are good for only one year.

COST ISSUES

This is the kingdom of the bean counters, who show up after the top executives have put their 'chop', or OK, on the issues of country risk and economic fundamentals. Cost factors are straightforward, but vitally important. The most frequently asked questions about costs have to do with: taxes and licenses, office space, housing, factory space, compensation of local officers and engineers, compensation of local clerical staff and factory workers, utilities such as electric power and telecommunications, and tariffs. Here's how the Philippines rates:

- Taxes and licences—The 35% corporate and personal tax rates will be reduced to 30% under the new tax reform act.
- Office space, factory space and housing—Much is available, but the costs are increasing at a rate of 25 to 35% per year.
- Manpower (staff and officers)—The Philippines doesn't have the cheapest labour in Asia, but both staff and professional manpower is considered to be very productive for the price.
- Utilities—Utilities are considered to be average in the region, but further economies are needed.
- Tariffs—The goal is to bring all tariffs down to a uniform 5% by 2005. Tariffs now are considered to be moderately high.

Overall, the 'big-bang-for-the-buck' factor in the Philippines is labour. Other factors are considered to be in line with or more costly than those of its South-East Asian neighbours.

SPECIAL INCENTIVES

Special incentives are viewed as the frosting on the cake because no amount of government incentives can make up for a weak country-risk profile. A good example of this would be North Korea. They opened an industrial park near Pyongyang with great incentives but had no takers.

The most common and attractive incentives for investors in the Philippines are income tax breaks, or tax holidays; tariff breaks on the import of capital equipment and raw materials; special tax deductions such for developmental expenses as infrastructure and employee training; special visas for easy entry and exit; and government-sponsored training for workers. Naturally, investors also welcome continuity and reasonable fairness in the granting and administration of incentives.

Four Philippine authorities are allowed by law to grant investment incentives:

- Board of Investments (BOI);
- Philippine Economic Zone Authority (PEZA);
- Clark Special Economic Zone /Clark DevelopmentCorporation; and
- Subic Bay Metropolitan Authority.

In the case of BOI, the main incentives are an income tax holiday of up to six years and a 3% duty on imported capital equipment and spare parts. Under the authority of PEZA, Clark and Subic, investors pay a 5% income tax on adjusted gross income, and all equipment and raw materials are duty free and free of value-added tax.

THE PHILIPPINES VERSUS THE REGION

How does the Philippines rate among the countries of the Association of South-East Asian Nations (ASEAN) as a place to invest? The Philippines offer incentive packages that are considered to be in line with and competitive with those of its South-East Asian neighbours.

In terms of the fundamental issue of country risk, Laos, Burma and Cambodia, which are not members of ASEAN, are not in the running. Vietnam, which joined ASEAN in 1996, is a borderline case. That leaves Singapore, Malaysia, Thailand, Indonesia and Brunei. Singapore and Malaysia rank higher than the Philippines; Thailand and the Philippines are roughly equal; and the Philippines ranks ahead of Indonesia and Brunei.

In terms of economic fundamentals, the Philippines also ranks in the middle of the pack. Its big drawback in this regard is infrastructure.

In the area of costs, the Philippines does well. That is why regional headquarters in Singapore and Hong Kong are giving the Philippines a second look despite the problems associated with the international airport and the road system. The productivity of Philippine labour, at reasonable cost, is the Philippines' top selling point.

On investment incentives, the Philippines is competitive with its ASEAN neighbours.

Overall, the Philippines is considered increasingly to be a good, safe and sound place to invest (see tables 1 and 2). It's in the middle of the pack and has the potential to gain on its neighbours. Sovereign risk isn't a large concern, but there is some uneasiness. And although the inefficient infrastructure is a serious issue, the country has a key strength in its large quantity and quality of labour at reasonable cost. Tables 1 and 2 compare the Philippines with its neighbours in terms of factors affecting foreign investment.

Because of these factors, the Philippines is attracting investment in the area of hi-tech assembly: electronics, semiconductors, appliances, and light manufacturing in specialty areas. Investors also are tending to insulate themselves within the protective walls of the many fine industrial parks or PEZA zones. One new area for investment is that of manufacturing such products as concrete pipe, building materials and copper transmission wire to supply large BOT projects.

Assuming a continuing stable country-risk platform, much of the Philippines' future success depends on timely completion of the many ongoing and planned infrastructure projects, the successful upgrading of the Metro Manila water system and the successful privatisation of the nation's power system. None are guaranteed, and each project will require a lot of government tough-mindedness to complete. But if reasonable success is achieved, the country stands a good chance of 'pole-vaulting' into the next century.

Table 1. The Philippines compared with other ASEAN countries and three major powers in terms of economic and social factors

Country	GDP PPP, US$ billions	GDP PPP per capita, US$	Growth, %	Population, millions	Exports, US$ billions	C/A Balance, US$	Reserves, US$ billions	Literacy, % of population	Urban population, %
Indonesia	724	3,705	7.8	200	50	-9	29	84	34
Thailand	454	7,535	6.4	61	57	-15	33	94	46
Philippines	199	2,935	5.0	70	22	-4	10	94	46
Malaysia	191	9,470	8.2	21	78	-5	27	89	47
Vietnam	97	1,310	9.5	77	8	-3	0.6	92	21
Singapore	70	23,565	3.8	3	125	14	77	92	100
Burma	35	753	6.0	48	1	-0.3	0.2	82	26
Cambodia	12	1,266	6.0	10	0.6	-0.2	0.3	38	14
Laos	8	1,670	6.9	5	0.3	-0.3	0.2	57	22
Brunei	6	18,900	2.0	0.3	2	2	30	90	61
USA	7,575	28,515	5.9	268	614	-165	55	86	76
China	3,587	2,935	9.4	1,228	145	2	116	82	30
Japan	2,782	22,200	2.6	126	411	71	218	100	78

Source: *Asia Week*

Table 2. Investment attraction ranking

Sovereign risk, 40%	*Economic fundamentals, 30%*	*Cost factors, 20%*	*Incentives, 10%*	*Overall, 100%*
Singapore	Singapore	Indonesia	Malaysia	Singapore
Malaysia	Malaysia	Thailand	Thailand	Malaysia
Philippines	Philippines	Philippines	Philippines	Philippines
Thailand	Thailand	Malaysia	Indonesia	Thailand
Indonesia	Indonesia	Brunei	Singapore	Indonesia
Brunei	Brunei	Vietnam	Brunei	Brunei
Vietnam	Vietnam	Burma	Vietnam	Vietnam
Burma	Burma	Laos	Burma	Burma
Laos	Laos	Cambodia	Laos	Laos
Cambodia	Cambodia	Singapore	Cambodia	Cambodia

Source: Robert W Blume

CHAPTER 3

RECESSION: A BALANCE SHEET

Peter Wallace and Venvenuto Icamina

The year 1997 saw the Asian tigers catch the flu, and the epidemic spread to cubs like the Philippines.

It started in Thailand. Fund managers, sensing imminent disaster from years of overbuilding and over-investment in sub-par industries using cheap dollars, took their funds out of Thailand. This led to a Thai stock market crash and a 'blood baht'. Then the fund managers turned their eyes to the rest of the region, believing that what happened in Thailand could happen in other South-East Asian countries that were driven by the same stimuli. One such stimulus was liberalised capital accounts, including opening up of dollar deposits and withdrawal of dollars with no questions asked and easier entry and exit of portfolio investments without prior central bank approval. Others were fixed currencies pegged to the dollar, massive portfolio inflows, low-cost dollar loans and property booms. So the stock-market collapse/currency free fall spread across the region.

More trouble surfaced with the withdrawal of foreign funds. With the dollar supply drying up, some local companies, including property developers who were already suffering from poor profits or even losses, lost a vital lifeline and defaulted on their loans. This dragged banks down, forcing closure of 58 banks and financing companies in Thailand and 12 in Indonesia. To control the damage, Thailand, Indonesia and Korea entered into a growth-constricting rescue program with the International Monetary Fund (IMF), while the rest implemented austerity measures. A regional growth of 8 to 10% per year during the previous decade decelerated to 3 to 5% in 1997. In Thailand, growth was 1% growth.

The Philippines, barely recovered from a poor start in the first quarter of 1997, slipped again after July as the peso depreciation and high interest rates raised production costs and narrowed profit margins. Increasing competition forced companies to keep most of the cost increases to themselves, resulting in tumbling profits. Output growth suffered and expansion plans came under review.

The government tried but failed to exit from the IMF Extended Fund Facility Program in 1997. Three final conditions were required for the exit:

- Implementation of the expanded value-added tax;
- The oil deregulation law; and
- The completion of the remaining components of the Comprehensive Tax Reform Package (CTRP).

The CTRP was finally approved in early December 1997, but in a form that failed to meet the intent. The Supreme Court rejected the oil deregulation law, which was subsequently passed in different form in February 1998. These failures have meant the IMF has had to rethink its strategy for the Philippines. It was originally intended and expected that the IMF would issue a 'seal of good housekeeping' report as the Philippines exited the program. Failure to meet two of the key objectives means the IMF may have to delay the exit and just let the agreement expire—and say nothing. It's an unfortunate lost opportunity for the Philippines that the politicians could have avoided.

Authorities imposed some additional restrictions on foreign currency deposit unit (FCDU) loans and property sector loans; closely monitored consumer loans; imposed a stricter definition of past due loans (90 days or one quarter of non-payment versus the six months it had been previously); raised the 'liquidity reserves' to as high as 8% of deposits before bringing them down again to 4% in November; and imposed an additional 2% general loan-loss reserve on banks.

These measures were a reaction to growing concerns over rising bank exposure to the property sector and other risky accounts and to financial collapses occurring in the region. They were intended to minimise the vulnerability of the banking system to defaults. The central bank also reduced the dollar oversold and overbought limits from 10% to 5% of the bank's unimpaired capital. As well, it disallowed the deduction of cancelled non-deliverable-forward contracts arising from 'suspicious' orders of goods from overbought and oversold limits to minimise dollar speculation. Tests were provided to identify whether the cancelled non-deliverable-forward contracts were legitimate or not.

Globalisation also caught up with local industries, with textiles and garments, paper, steel, rubber and metal-working losing out to imports and forcing a review of the tariff reform program. Encouragingly, however, the government stood by its plan to lower tariff rates and simply corrected the distortions in the structure by reimposing a tariff differential between finished and semi-finished products. (That is something the Supreme Court didn't allow them to do on oil products.) Some companies started upgrading, but the peso fall cut modernisation plans short as the peso cost of imports of new equipment became prohibitive.

Apart from regional contagion, the Philippine economy also had to grapple with the onset of an El Niño drought that affected major crops like rice and sugar. The government constructed new irrigation facilities covering 25,000 hectares of farmland and rehabilitated existing irrigation for 120,000 hectares to mitigate the effects of El Niño. Cloud seeding was resorted to in some parts of Mindanao and Central Luzon (in part to replenish the dwindling water supply in Metro Manila), while some 350,000 tons of rice were imported.

Meanwhile, the government programmed a record 60% increase to 150 billion pesos in infrastructure spending in an attempt to complete a large number of flagship projects. Build-Operate-Transfer (BOT) projects like the Metro Manila Skyway, EDSA MRT 3 rail line, the Cavite Express Tollway and the privatisation of water distribution in Metro Manila were also accelerated.

ECONOMIC GROWTH

Competition from imports as well as from rising labour costs adversely affected key local industries, especially textiles and garments, steel products, metal-working and rubber products. Weak demand hurt car manufacturing, while petroleum was affected by low returns and the relatively weak industrial activity. Price adjustments weren't enough to push profits to decent levels. A few industries—electronics and electrical machinery, furniture and wood products, and cement—emerged as winners and partly mitigated the poor results elsewhere. Manufacturing managed a growth of only 2.3%, although the slowdown may have been caused in part by statistical under-reporting of production outside Metro Manila. But this was offset by the sustained improvement in transport and communications, banking and finance, and construction.

Overall, real gross domestic product (GDP) still managed a 5% growth in the first quarter of 1997, only slightly below its 5.1% increase in the first quarter of 1996. Real gross national product (GNP) grew by only 5.8% versus 6.9% in the first quarter of 1996, due mainly to the slowdown in the remittance of profits by Filipino residents abroad. For the most part, these are yields from proceeds of corporate foreign bond floats and other dollar loans temporarily deposited or invested in short-term instruments abroad.

On the demand side, it was the 45% decline in peso conversions of FCDU deposits that prevented an acceleration of the economy. This decline too might have been a result of statistical distortion. Double-counting in FCDU withdrawals has been minimised with a better reporting system in which FCDU conversions of exporters and recipients of overseas Filipino workers' remittances were taken out. However, the same adjustments could not be applied to the previous year's data because of the difficulty of tracing back the errors.

Price cuts on air travel, beverages, some consumer products, and telecommunications and better marketing, coupled with the full operations of such major export-oriented firms as Toshiba, Hitachi, Acer, and Intel, led to improved sales and the economy's rally in the second quarter. Industries like wood products, pulp and paper, and metal-working also started recovering. And with increases in export-generating capacity—particularly in electronics, computer parts and auto parts—exports accelerated. In real terms, the growth of export of goods increased from 9.3% in the first quarter to 14.4% in the second quarter—up from 17.9 to 26.1% in dollar terms. Infrastructure spending also increased 23.1%. This was good enough to counterbalance the slowdown in private construction (up only 10.1% in the second quarter) that was caused by a pause in new high-rise projects as the government implemented a record number of high-impact projects in Metro Manila and other growth areas. GNP rose by 6.4%, while GDP gained 5.8% in the second quarter.

Then the Thai debacle occurred in July 1997, dragging the rest of the region, including the Philippines, down with it. The fall of the peso was exacerbated by the fact that the third quarter was a period of high import demand for the build-up of inventory in anticipation of heavy Christmas spending. The initial reaction of the Bangko Sentral ng Pilipinas was to 'burn all speculators' and keep most of the dollars from leaving. It tightened up on liquidity, raising liquidity reserves to up to 8%, and brought its overnight borrowing rate to as high as 35%. Interest rates soared. Industries were hit by a double whammy—the rising cost of imported inputs and high interest rates. Unable to pass on the full cost increases due to competition and falling consumer confidence, sales targets were reduced. That caused a chain reaction that affected suppliers, subcontractors and the rest of the industries. Interest-rate-sensitive property development—especially condominiums and other prime residential units—was hit most severely. Low- and middle-income housing demonstrated some resilience as overseas Filipino workers with more pesos bought houses, but this segment also started to slow down in the fourth quarter.

Agriculture started to feel the effects of the El Niño drought, with rice output falling by 15.4% and sugar dropping by 63.2% in the third quarter. Poultry and livestock, in part faced with poor corn harvests and the higher peso cost of supported corn, posted slower growth of 2.8% and 3.3%, respectively, barely a third of their increases in the first half.

Hence, GNP growth weakened to 5.7%, while GDP growth slowed to 4.9% in the third quarter.

Economic growth decelerated further in the fourth quarter with GNP growing by 5.2% and GDP by 4.7%. Exports were still strong, and agriculture managed to maintain a decent pace of growth despite El Niño, but the other remaining growth stimulus—government spending—slowed after a budget cut of five to six billion pesos was imposed by fiscal officials to avoid a deficit. Fourth-quarter tax and tariff collections, which were slightly below year-earlier levels, were also an indication that corporate output, sales and profits were down. Some companies reportedly started laying off workers, although the numbers were not yet significant. And based on the speed and number of retail shops putting up bargains right after Christmas, holiday spending was probably weaker than expected. Duty-free shops reported a 40 to 70% decline in sales in 1997.

COST OF BUSINESS

Exchange rate

The peso lost 13.6% to the US dollar from an average of 26.2 pesos to the dollar in 1996 to 29.77 to the dollar in 1997. The depreciation was much worse on a year-end to year-end basis, at 54%, as the peso slid from 26.3 to the dollar in December 1996 to 40.5 in December 1997.

Fund managers taking their dollars out of the country and the jitters caused by debate on amending the constitution to permit a president to run for re-election were the main factors bringing the peso down until September 1997. After September, a different set of factors sustained the depreciation: a peso moving in sympathy with other currencies in the region, companies purchasing their dollar requirements several months in advance, debtors paying off or preterminating their dollar debts, and banks unwilling to sell dollars or selling only at high prices. Even the inflow of dollars from *balikbayans* (homecoming Filipinos) in December failed to stabilise the exchange rate.

Interest rates

The peso depreciation created pressure on interest rates, with the prime lending rate rising from pre-July levels of about 14% to as high as 35% in October–November 1997 before settling down to a still prohibitive 25 to 26% in December. The average T-bill rate also moved up, albeit more slowly than prime rates, from 11% throughout most of the first half of the year to 18% by December. This occurred as the government started incurring a budget deficit—which meant heavy borrowings—and as authorities tried to narrow the gap between T-bill rates and prime rates to attract banks back into T-bill auctions.

The Bangko Sentral ng Pilipinas' initiatives to stabilise the exchange rate were largely responsible for the initial increase in interest rates. But eventually the Bangko Sentral shifted to a strategy of balance between interest rates and the exchange rate because businessmen, economists and even the government's economic managers complained of the damage it was doing to the economy. It loosened up on liquidity by reducing liquidity reserves to 4% in mid-November and lowered its overnight borrowing rate to 13%. But regional uncertainties and the banks' concern that the Bangko Sentral might suddenly tighten the lid on money supply again kept interest rates high. This forced a joint agreement between the Bangko Sentral and the Bankers Association of the Philippines to bring prime rates down to 18 or 19%.

The target wasn't attained. In December 1997, demand for peso loans rose from companies needing the pesos for the purchase of dollars—to service future requirements or maturing dollar debts, etc.—and the unwillingness of banks to accommodate this demand meant interest rates stayed high.

Inflation

Despite the currency and interest rate volatility, inflation remained under control in 1997. Although on an upward trend since September, the highest it reached was 6.5% in November; it was down to 6.1% in December. The whole-year inflation average of 5.1% was the lowest since 1987.

Companies feared that passing on their full cost increases to consumers would depress demand and erode their market shares, so their minimal price increases kept inflation low. Timely rice imports also kept the prices of that commodity stable. Wage restraints also helped; there had been no minimum wage adjustment since May 1997. To a certain extent, the freezing of oil prices in August eliminated another excuse for further price escalations, but this was at the expense of oil companies' profitability and the consequent difficulty of maintaining the required import levels and hence buffer stock. It also meant postponement or cancellation of their expansion plans.

EXTERNAL SECTOR

Balance of trade (goods)

Dollar receipts from the export of goods reached US$20.7 billion, up 23.1% during the first 10 months of 1997:

- Electronics, the top export at US$10 billion (48% of total exports), was also one of the fastest-growing at 30%, with boosts from new and additional investments by major Japanese, American and Taiwanese companies.
- Machinery and transport equipment, mostly auto parts like ignition wiring sets, with earnings of US$2 billion, has replaced garments as the number two export. It grew by 115.6%, thanks to the recent expansion of Yazaki-Torres and other top manufacturers.
- Garments, now relegated to third place, finally stopped their skid in the third quarter and managed to stay flat at US$1.9 billion. This was due in part to a low base in 1996 and a supplementary quota granted by the United States, partly in exchange for Philippine withdrawal of its plan to file action in the World Trade Organisation against new US rules of origin.
- Coconut oil recovered as favourable weather and new high-yield varieties planted in the early 1990s started to bear fruit. It posted a growth of 55% to US$525 million.

In contrast, dollar payments for the import of goods grew by only 11.1% to US$27 billion during the 10-month period. High import costs weakened the demand for raw materials except those needed by exporters derailed purchases of capital equipment by upgrading local industries and reduced consumer appetites for imported goods. Raw material imports rose by only 8.16%, while consumer goods imports were down 6.6%. Only purchases of electronics, electrical and telecommunications equipment (up 50% to US$5.2 billion) and computers and office machines (up 62.6% to US$1.1 billion) remained strong.

Hence, the merchandise trade deficit narrowed by 8.6% to US$9.3 billion for 1997.

Balance of Payments

Despite the narrowing trade gap and some improvement in the current account position, the balance of payments slipped into a deficit of US$1 billion as of October 1997. This was a 13-year low. For the most part, an estimated US$3 billion net outflow in portfolio investments and the decline in 'change in assets of commercial banks'—including FCDU loans, which were down 62% as of July—caused the balance-of-payments deficit.

The decline in the Bangko Sentral's gross international reserves from US $11 billion at the end of 1996 to barely US$9 billion at the end of 1997 confirmed that the balance of payments was indeed in the red. The change in the gross international reserves (in this case US$11 billion less US$9 billion, or US$2 billion) is roughly equivalent to the balance-of-payments position. (This is a deficit if the change in gross international reserves is negative and a surplus if the change is positive.) The decline in the gross international reserves was due in part to the Bangko Sentral's sale of dollars to defend the peso, especially during the late June–early July period when it reportedly sold US$2 billion. To an extent, some of the dollars sold were replaced by a US$700-million drawdown from the existing IMF extended fund facility, a soft loan of US$400 million from Japan Eximbank, and deposit to the BSP from ING Bank amounting to US$500 million. However, as much of the debt will have to be paid from peso resources, the peso cost has risen significantly.

Foreign Debt

At the end of June 1997, data indicated a total foreign debt of US$44.8 billion, up US$2.9 billion from US$41.9 billion at the end of 1996. Of this total, 19% was short-term debt. The government managed to reduce its debt exposure by US$900 million to US$22 billion. Private banks (up US$1.6 billion to US$7 billion) and companies (up US$41.7 billion to US$10.9 billion) were mainly responsible for the increase in the country's indebtedness. At least one-quarter of the liabilities were from Japan, while another 24% came from bond floats.

Except for the July–August boosts to the gross international reserves, a handful of loan packages obtained by local companies and drawdowns of official developmental assistance already in the pipeline, there was probably a minimal increase in foreign debt after July as creditors avoided higher exposures in a region suffering from financial turmoil. Again, as much of the debt will have to be paid from peso resources, the peso cost has risen significantly.

OUTLOOK

The sharp fall in the Korean won in December 1997, followed by a 90% decline in the Indonesian rupiah in early January 1998, caught South-East Asian currencies in a negatively reinforcing spiral. These developments indicate that regional contagion still reigns and the currency volatility that started in 1997 has not abated.

The currency pressure now appears to bear no relation to basic economic values; South-East Asian currencies today may be the world's most undervalued (by 60 to 70%) versus the US dollar. Moreover, with the region's economy at a virtual standstill, it's hard to see where the pressure could be coming from. Imports are down, while there are no more portfolio funds to influence currency movements.

It's possible the regional demand for dollars is still rising sharply because a number of large companies are still heavily exposed to dollar debts and are buying dollars with any cash they can raise. Other firms want more dollars to preterminate their debts. But, most of all, confidence is down; nobody wants to hold on to local currencies longer than they have to, and those with dollars are not willing to part with them.

With currency shifts in one country, others are forced to make a realignment to keep the prices of their exports competitive and to avoid having their markets become a dumping ground for cheaper goods from the rest of the region. Thus a downward spiral is sustained.

PROSPECTS FOR CURRENCY STABILITY

The IMF support packages in Thailand, Indonesia and Korea were supposed to help stabilise the regional currency situation, but those countries found it hard to follow the IMF's strict growth-constricting regimen of reforms. In general, the IMF programs are better suited to countries with debt-ridden governments that are heavily domestic market-oriented and are highly inflationary. However, Asian countries generally have well managed fiscal positions, are export-oriented and have low inflation rates. Asia's problem is its heavily-indebted and relatively poorly performing private sector, so an IMF program that tends to raise interest rates and constrict government spending causes many private companies to fail. This just increases uncertainty and prolongs recession in these countries. That's why Thailand, Indonesia and Korea were asking for greater flexibility.

Admittedly, fixing some of the distortionary government policies still extant in these countries is necessary and that is where the IMF's strength lies. The policy conflicts between the IMF and the Asian governments eventually were minimised. Thailand, for example, has accepted the reality that it will have to deflate its economy to bring it back on track. These countries have to begin serious efforts to implement the needed adjustment measures so that currencies can stabilise. However, the cost of stability to these countries will be at least two or three years of economic paralysis.

Risks on the political scene are exacerbating the crisis. Indonesia is of particular concern, with President Suharto as Asia's longest-running national leader and with a poorly regarded research and technology minister, BJ Habibie, as his vice president. Although President Suharto signed an agreement with the IMF, there's good reason to doubt that he will adhere to its conditions. Add to this his uncertain health and rising social unrest, and Indonesia becomes a time bomb just a few ticks away from explosion. Some Indonesian Chinese are already leaving the country.

However, one major uncertainty is reduced with China's announcement that it won't devalue its currency this year. According to Chinese authorities, it doesn't need to because the country is still benefiting from its 40% devaluation two years previously and has some US$90 billion in reserves to defend the renmimbi. China is also well aware not only of the disastrous realignment its currency adjustment would cause in other Asian countries but of the negative effects such action would have on its heavily foreign-technology- and foreign-debt-dependent state-owned enterprises. But whether it can hold out, particularly beyond the end of 1998 and particularly if regional currencies drop even more, is a serious concern.

Moreover, the US market is expected to remain buoyant. The US Federal Reserve Bank didn't raise its rate in February 1998 so as not to cause a slowdown. It doesn't have to; US inflation remains at a tolerable 2 to 3%, so tightening up on liquidity is still uncalled for. Hence, the United States should continue to provide a market for Asia's export-driven recovery unless the worsening balance-of-trade gap generates a protectionist response there.

The Philippines, a relatively small country and easily influenced by outside forces, will be affected by regional shocks that might occur later. Conversely, if the region achieves some semblance of stability, the Philippine currency will also become stable. The fall of the won in December 1997, for example, disrupted what could have been a fourth quarter of peso stability.

The sharp drop of the rupiah in January 1998 induced a 35% fall in the peso–dollar rate in just three days, but it eventually regained 12% as the rupiah also recovered. Then it fell again as the rupiah dropped in the third week of January. Given that the region's currencies are already undervalued and the IMF support packages will eventually calm down markets, currencies were likely to grow less volatile.

PHILIPPINE POLICY RESPONSES

Philippine policy thrusts for 1998 are for maintenance of economic stability, the peaceful turnover of government and continuation of structural reforms.

One of the last acts of the Congress before it adjourned in February 1998 was the revision of the oil deregulation law with features acceptable to the Philippine Supreme Court, though not necessarily to the industry. The situation at the time of writing was such that once the amended law was passed and the transition period completed, the country was to exit from the IMF Extended Fund Facility Program. But to ensure stability amid regional turbulence, the country was to enter a new precautionary agreement with the IMF. The program was designed to provide early warning signals and a defence against potentially destabilising regional developments—through such measures as prudent government spending and bank lending policies and closer monitoring of the financial system—and quick access to supplementary financing in case of need. The precautionary arrangement might even graduate into a regular IMF support program if the regional situation gets out of hand, with the government looking for US$2 to 3 billion in financial assistance. The other key aspect of stability would be to ensure an adequate food supply in the critical period of an El Niño dry spell. Heavy investments in irrigation that started in 1997 were being sustained, and imports of rice—an estimated one million tons in 1998—and corn were continuing.

However, continuation of structural reforms is questionable. It's doubtful the country's new president, elected in May 1998, will be able to identify priority policies and to get the support of the congress promptly. 'Muddling through' has been the operative term for the near future.

ECONOMIC GROWTH

The regional currency turmoil's inevitable impact on business confidence led to some rethinking by managers in the Philippines. The initial business response was two-fold:

- With the value of the peso lower, interest rates higher and wages up, local industries had no choice but to raise their selling prices beyond the 5 to 7% adjustments of 1997 to avoid losses. The immediate effect of the price adjustments was a slowdown in demand, so firms also cut production and costs and retrenched workers.
- Rising costs, weak markets and uncertainties in the near-term also led to postponement or cancellation of business expansion and upgrading and a decline in private construction activity.

Beyond that, companies had to reassess their businesses, with the crisis providing sound rationale for major change. Only infrastructure projects that had already been started but were not yet completed would be a source of investment growth. But this too would eventually weaken as most of the projects were completed. There would be few to replace them until after the new government settled in and assigned its own priorities. A difficulty for the new government would be the need to scale down or cancel projects in the proposed national budget for 1998, given downsized revenue projections due to the economic slowdown reducing the taxable base.

A number of the private-sector-funded BOT infrastructure projects might also be deferred because of the downgrade in the region's credit rating and the hesitancy of creditors to increase their exposure in a region plagued by financial troubles. Standard & Poor and Moody's lowered the Philippine debt outlook from 'positive' to 'stable', while maintaining 'speculative grade' ratings on existing debts. The failure of the country to get a good report from the IMF as it exits doesn't help. A number of proposed BOT projects have Indonesia, Malaysian and Thai proponents who might find it difficult to secure foreign borrowings. Hence, fixed investment growth could slow down markedly in the near term from 1997.

Although wages and salaries were likely to increase (the minimum wage in Metro Manila was raised by 7% in January 1998), this would be offset by lay-offs and reduced working hours, so consumer spending would be slow. However, the softening in household spending would be mitigated by election campaign spending and the higher peso value of remittances in hard currency from Filipinos working overseas. Even in the unlikely event that the remittances didn't grow from the estimated 1997 level of US$6 billion, peso depreciation alone would raise their value by 90 billion to 270 billion pesos. That would add an extra 5% boost to consumption if spent on local products. So consumer spending should grow, but at a slower, albeit decent, rate of 4%.

Exports should also benefit from peso depreciation, although this would be limited by the fact that the country's main competitors also depreciated their currencies. Another limiting factor is the fact that more than 70% of the country's exports are import-dependent. Only 30 to 40% is local value-added. But a significant proportion of exports are market-linked and these won't be affected by the currency movements in the rest of South-East Asia. Mainly the products sold within the region and products that other South-East Asian countries are also selling will cause the drag. Export of goods and services were projected to post a real growth of 12% in 1998; dollar export of goods was projected at 20%. At the same time, cancellation of expansion plans and the higher peso cost of imports would slow purchases of goods abroad. Hence, import of goods and services would grow by 12.2%, with the dollar import of goods growing by only around 10%. This would lower the balance-of-trade deficit to slightly below US$9 billion versus almost US$10 billion in 1997.

Overall, real GDP growth was expected to decelerate to 3.5% in 1998. GNP growth would be cut to 4% from 5.8% in 1997. At worst, GDP growth could slow down further to 1.8% and GNP would only manage a 2.5% increase if, for instance, the regional contagion, currency volatility and El Niño were worse than expected and the results of the elections did not inspire a quick revival of business confidence.

PHILIPPINE GROWTH PERFORMANCE

The 3.5% GDP growth for 1998 may mean the end of a four-year economic boom, but it doesn't suggest a crisis. In fact, for the first time, the Philippines would outgrow its neighbours and a number of other Asian countries. This indicates that the Philippines would be one of the countries least affected by the regional currency crisis—and the first to come out of it. The Philippines' resilience was brought about by a combination of factors:

- Because dramatic investment-driven, dollar-funded growth only started in the Philippines in the mid-1990s, there was limited time and access to cheap foreign funds to build up the excesses. Thus there was less vulnerability to the dollar crunch. Most South-East Asian countries had been recklessly overbuilding and over-investing for a decade or more, funded by foreign creditors who were more than willing to extend cheap dollars to these countries.
- In the Philippines, a third of a century of IMF-imposed discipline has helped it complete most key structural reforms. Other countries have yet to do so, and now have to do so more drastically and painfully.
- A low export base and the right basket of new exports will enable the country to penetrate markets abroad, even during cyclical downturns (as in the case of electronics in 1996), without creating a disturbance.
- A two- to three-million-strong army of overseas workers regularly and consistently remit dollars, even during the worst of times. This

has amounted to US$4 to $6 billion per annum in recent years and is rising.

- A grossly underserved demand for infrastructure means that heavy spending is borne out of real need and provides private BOT investors with an opportunity to earn good returns. Elsewhere in Asia, spending on buildings, structures and major industrial projects like indigenous brand car manufacturing and aerospace has become an increasing source of prestige. These mostly unnecessary projects are the first ones to go during a period of crisis. The Philippines already have in place one of the better BOT laws in the region.
- The Philippines has weathered several economic—and political—crises before, so it has the experience and pragmatism to handle this one.

Compared to the 1983–85 crisis experience, the Philippine economy wouldn't fail this time. At that time, the country had a serious foreign debt problem; debt was as high as 80% of GNP, whereas now it's 50%. Debt servicing ate up 30% (now 10%) of receipts from export of goods and services that the dwindling dollar supply couldn't cover. The gross international reserves were down to US$700 million, or less than one month of imports. That crisis was a result of a narrow export base, heavily-protected inefficient local industries, government guarantees on debts of undeserving crony companies, state-run monopolies and large-scale corruption. The government was forced to make drastic adjustments; the GNP declined by 7 to 8% and inflation shot up to 30 to 50%. No creditor was willing to lend to the country and, worse, short-term debts became due and demandable after the country declared a moratorium on debt payments. It took the People Power revolution of 1986 to restore normalcy. Interestingly, these same weaknesses are now becoming apparent elsewhere in Asia.

COST-OF-BUSINESS FORECAST

Although the exchange rate might become less volatile, at the time of writing it was still expected to depreciate as the current account deficit created pressure on dollar supply. Also, the need to remain competitive would force the peso to move in tandem with the rest of the currencies in the region. However, the alignment of the peso with the rest of the regional currencies probably would occur only up to a point. The peso wouldn't match the drops in Indonesia because it doesn't need to; even if the rupiah plunged drastically, investors still wouldn't come to Indonesia and buyers still might not order more Indonesian goods because of political uncertainties that could disrupt production schedules. The peso might follow the Thai baht more closely, but the situation in Thailand was stabilising. A further sharp weakening of the baht was not likely and the existing differential shouldn't need to be narrowed.

Purchasing-power parity estimates put the realistic average exchange rate for the Philippines at nearly 42 pesos to one US dollar—a 41% fall from the average of 29.9 pesos to the dollar in 1997. A new dollar-forward hedging facility of the central bank would also help keep the peso hovering near the 42-peso mark. Given that the exchange rate was already at 40 pesos to the dollar at the end of 1997, this meant that the peso would continue to depreciate somewhat, possibly to the level of 45 pesos to the dollar.

A peso weakening—or a strengthening—beyond the central-forecast value wasn't ruled out entirely. If import-dependent producers, dollar-debt holders and speculators still saw the region as an uncertain place, currency drops elsewhere would lead them to buy more dollars than they needed to, which could drive the exchange rate down further, possibly to 50 pesos to the dollar. But if the regional situation stabilised beyond expectations and everyone realised that no matter what happened to the Indonesian rupiah, Philippine products would not be affected and dollars might be dumped into the market, bringing the rate to between 35 and 40 pesos to the dollar. However, the Thai baht would also have to appreciate significantly to between 40 and 45 from 53 baht to the dollar for that to happen.

Forecasting has become a guessing game because it's no longer an economic model that is being followed, but the whim of the regional markets. Given the peso depreciation, coupled with local food shortages induced by the El Niño phenomenon, inflation could accelerate to between 9 and 10%. A relatively soft market demand and a likely lower liquidity growth ceiling under the IMF precautionary program would assure that inflation did not vastly exceed 10%. But if fiscal and wage discipline are abandoned, which means violating some covenants under the precautionary program, sharper than expected peso depreciation and a more damaging El Niño could still drive inflation to as high as 15%.

The peso's relative calm plus some loosening up on liquidity to support election-related spending should bring interest rates down slightly. The average prime lending rate should fall to 20 to 25%, as opposed to 24 to 26% in the latter part of 1997. It wasn't expected to drop below 20% because banks would be unwilling to extend a substantial volume of loans to companies under the prevailing uncertainties. The need to siphon off election-induced excess liquidity could raise the rate as high as 28%, but when the peso restabilised the prime rate should fall again to between 16 and 20%. That's a good enough basis for economic recovery by the year 2000.

CHAPTER 4

MAKING THE COMMITMENT

Robert Katz

The Philippine government is totally committed to private-sector participation in its development initiatives and recognises that a friendly
business environment and investor confidence are critical factors in
achieving the status of a newly industrialised country. Private-sector participation in implementing national infrastructure projects and in performing services traditionally provided by government is now legally recognised
as the engine of economic growth and the key to improved efficiency in
delivering public services. Even the government's regulatory interventions
are being rationalised to allow the private sector maximum flexibility in
harnessing their creativity and expertise in entrepreneurial initiatives. The
government's policy environment, which is strongly supportive of this
strategy, has two fundamental cornerstones.

First, structural adjustments have been geared towards opening the economy to competition and levelling the playing field for international investors, developers and service providers. Macroeconomic reforms to promote this goal include liberalisation of:

- Entry and pricing of public utilities;
- The regulatory environment;
- Foreign exchange;
- International trade and import of capital goods; and
- International investment and banking rules.

Second, a clear policy and institutional framework has been put in place to permit the unencumbered flow of private resources into the government's development program, particularly in the infrastructure sector. The salient features of the policy framework for privatising project financing include:

- A wide scope of sectors/activities that may be privatised, as well as a wide range of options for contractual arrangements;
- Market-based tariff/rate setting;
- A broad range of government support; and
- Flexibility in the procurement process, namely, in addition to public tenders, some contracts may be negotiated under carefully proscribed conditions.

In 1986, the Philippine government embarked on a privatisation program that has evolved in three waves:

- In the first wave, the government began to privatise government-owned-and-controlled corporations.
- In the second wave, the government invited the private sector to develop new infrastructure under the Build-Operate-Transfer (BOT) scheme, first in power generation, then light rail, toll roads, water supply, shipping terminals, airports and other projects including information technology.
- In the third wave, the government encouraged public–private partnerships to provide municipal services and such traditional public services as solid waste management, public health, education, pension funds and the post.

WHY INVEST IN PHILIPPINE INFRASTRUCTURE?

Democracy and the free-enterprise system

The Philippines has demonstrated to the world that there is a democratic path to development and that peace can be attained and will continue to hold in an environment of dialogue and consultation. Once referred to as the 'sick man of Asia', the country now boasts a reputation as 'Asia's newest tiger'. This is in spite of the currency attacks on some of its neighbours that also nipped the Philippine peso, resulting in a depreciation of about 27% in relation to the dollar by the end of 1997.

The Philippine solution to the power brownouts of the late 1980s and 1990s became the model for private-sector participation in virtually all major infrastructure projects. The decades-old conflict in Mindanao ended in 1996 with the signing of a peace agreement between the government and the Moro National Liberation Front. This peace process has been a remarkable success and is now a model for other countries faced with internal armed conflict.

The internationally acclaimed Asia Pacific Economic Cooperation summit in Manila in November 1996 focused world attention on the Philippines as an international business and convention centre. It also signalled the country's readiness to compete aggressively in the global economy while opening its own markets to international competition. This transformation in a span of just four-and-a-half years is the most reliable indicator of the Philippines' potential for hard work and achievement, and it is part of what makes the country so attractive to the international investor.

When Fidel V. Ramos was elected president in 1992, the question of leadership succession in a democratic setting was largely settled in the minds of the Filipinos, although outside observers consider democracy in the Philippines to be a fragile experiment. However, the smooth transition in leadership from former President Cory Aquino to Ramos was a strong signal that democracy has taken root and political stability was at hand. In spite of public rallies and political posturing, the 1998 elections and transition to power of a new administration have been proceeding smoothly and reinforce international confidence. While sceptics remain, investors who share the Filipino confidence in their country's democratic and economic future see the months leading up to and immediately following the election as a period of opportunity.

In the political arena, Ramos promoted a close working relationship with the legislature by forming a majority coalition. The peace in Mindanao is holding and the arrangements called for in the peace agreement are being implemented. The declaration of a Special Zone of Peace and Development and the establishment of the Southern Philippines Council for Peace and Development has created a new and exciting hub of economic activity.

The talks about amending the constitution were evidence of a healthy democracy. Referring to this activity as 'cha-cha' (short for CHArter CHAnge) was typical of the Filipinos' light-hearted approach to even the most serious of issues. Serious observers do not anticipate a return to an authoritarian form of government.

Economic liberalisation

For a country that has experienced economic boom-and-bust cycles for the past 20 years, ambitious economic reforms had to be implemented aggressively. This was necessary not only to achieve the desired economic status but also to ensure that those economic gains will be sustained for the foreseeable future. These reforms embrace a program of economic liberalisation and, where possible, full deregulation and privatisation. Significant reforms to date include:

- Liberalisation of foreign investment;
- Liberalisation of trade;
- Reforms in the financial and fiscal sectors;
- Deregulation of foreign exchange; and
- Privatisation of infrastructure.

SUSTAINED ECONOMIC GROWTH

The structural policy adjustments in the areas of trade and investment, capital and financial sectors and telecommunications for the purpose of opening up the economy have contributed to economic growth in the last two years. Investor-friendly policies adopted to make the country an attractive investment site included:

- The Long-Term Lease Act allowing foreign investors to lease lands for up to 75 years;
- Access to the Multilateral Investment Guarantee Agreement, providing insurance cover for political and non-commercial risks;
- Simplification and streamlining of investment rules and procedures;
- Enhancement of the one-stop shop concept to serve investors, exporters and foreign buyers;
- Implementation of the expanded BOT law to provide attractive benefits and incentives to private investors in BOT infrastructure projects; and
- The Export Development Act.

The success of reforms has been reflected in improved performance in a number of economic areas.

Economic growth

The country's gross national product (GNP), the growth of which languished at less than 2% from 1991 to 1993, expanded to 5.3% in 1994 even though the most optimistic projection had been 4.5%. The 1995 GNP growth rate of 5% was followed by a rate of 6.9% in 1996. This growth was led by improved performance in agriculture and manufacturing. On the demand side, exports and investments continued to sustain the economy. Economic growth during the first six months of 1997 was 5.9%. This was scaled down to 5.5% for the year due to the adverse effects of the peso depreciation that accompanied the region-wide currency destabilisation.

Inflation

The economy was growing even as the rate of inflation was declining. From 18.7% in 1991, inflation dropped to 8.1% in 1995. For 1996, inflation rates averaged 8.4% and for 1997 the rates were moving gradually toward the Association of South-East Asian Nations (ASEAN) average of 5% until the peso depreciated. That put upward pressure on prices in peso terms, while local prices in hard currencies obviously declined.

Interest rates followed the decline in inflation, from 23.4% in 1990 to 11.3% in 1995. The 91-day treasury bill rates—the benchmark of commercial interest rates—was as low as 14.2% at the time of the currency depreciation, lower than the 16.1% average in 1992.

Both declining inflation and interest rates were made possible by stability in the monetary environment as the Philippines ensured easier access and freer flow of cheaper funds.

Foreign exchange rate

The country achieved a degree of predictability in the foreign exchange market, though the exchange rate vis-à-vis the US dollar depreciated to nearly 40 pesos to the dollar during the regional economic turmoil of late 1997 and 1998 from 26.22 pesos in 1996. The country's success in establishing a stable exchange rate has boosted confidence in the liberal use of foreign exchange in financial transactions.

The decline in monetary values was a region-wide phenomenon. As of August 1997, the peso value had fallen by 16%, the Malaysian ringgit by 14% and the Indonesian rupiah by 23%. By December 1997, the peso was hovering at about 40 to the dollar. Most international economists were predicting the 1998 exchange rate to stabilise at about 40, although fluctuations in the band of 37 to 43 were likely in the short run.

Fiscal surplus

One of the most important factors contributing to Philippine financial stability is an improved fiscal position. For 1996, after two decades of continuing deficits, the country posted a budget surplus of 6.3 billion pesos. The consolidated public sector financial position also registered a surplus of 5.7 billion pesos for the first semester of 1997.

International reserves

Better economic fundamentals bolstered the country's balance-of-payments position, which has led to a continuing rise in the international reserves. International reserves have risen from only US$2 billion in 1990 to US$11.7 billion at the end of 1996. That is sufficient to cover two to seven months of merchandise imports and represents a 15.8% improvement over the government's target of US$10.1 billion. At the end of May, international reserves stood at a healthy $11.4 billion, representing three months of imports, but this dropped back to about $9 billion by December.

BOT LEGAL FRAMEWORK

The landmark Republic Act 7718, commonly known as the Amended BOT Law, was enacted in May 1994. Subsequently, the necessary implementing rules and regulations were drafted to clarify procedures and give operational dimension to its legislative vision.

The Amended BOT Law opened new investment opportunities to the private sector by offering a greater range of credit enhancements and BOT investment incentives, by streamlining the approvals process and by liberalising the entire regulatory framework. In the Philippines, 'BOT' has become very broadly defined and describes any of the project implementation schemes authorised under the BOT law.

Infrastructure projects may be constructed, rehabilitated, improved, expanded, modernised, operated, financed and maintained under any of the following schemes of contractual arrangements:

- Build-Operate-Transfer (BOT)
- Build-Transfer (BT)
- Build-Own-Operate (BOO)
- Build-Leave-Transfer (BLT)
- Develop-Operate-Transfer (DOT)
- Build-Transfer-Operate (BTO)
- Develop-Operate-Transfer (DOT)
- Rehabilitate-Operate-Transfer (ROT)
- Contract Add-and-Operate (CAO)

- Rehabilitate-Own-Operate (ROO)

To the credit of the Philippine government, the Amended BOT Law is now so highly regarded internationally that other countries have requested copies for possible replication in their own privatisation efforts. Multilateral agencies such as the World Bank have referred to it as a model for similar programs throughout the developing world, inspiring the Philippines to constantly monitor progress and maintain its competitive edge in the region.

The infrastructure privatisation policies and plans that have been crafted since 1994 are finally bearing fruit. There are 86 national infrastructure projects with an estimated cost of $27 billion.

PROJECT IMPLEMENTATION MODES

Public tenders

In general, priority projects that have been identified by the concerned implementing agency or local government unit and approved by appropriate approving bodies are put out to tender.

Negotiated contract

Direct negotiation is applied when there is only one complying tenderer, as in the following instances:

- If, after advertisement, only one proponent applies for prequalification and meets the prequalification requirements, after which a tender/ proposal is submitted that is deemed compliant by the agency or local governing unit;
- If, after the prequalification of more than one project proponent, only one submits a tender that is found by the agency or local governing unit to be complying; or
- If, after prequalification, more than one proponent submits a tender, but only one is found by the agency or local governing unit to be complying.

Unsolicited proposals

An agency or local governing unit may accept unsolicited proposals on a negotiated basis provided that the project meets the following conditions:

- The project involves a new concept or technology and/or is not part of the list of priority projects;
- The new technology must possess at least one of the following attributes: a recognised process, design, methodology or engineering

concept that can significantly reduce construction costs, extend economic life, reduce costs of facility maintenance and operations, or reduce negative environmental impact or social/economic disturbances or disruptions during either the project construction or operation phase;

- The project involves a process for which the proponent possesses exclusive rights, either worldwide or regionally;
- The project involves a design, methodology or engineering concept for which the proponent possesses intellectual property rights;
- The project requires no direct government guarantee, subsidy or equity; and
- The agency or local governing unit concerned has solicited proposals by publication but received no comparative or competitive proposals to challenge the price proposal of the original proponent.

Other implementation modes

Joint Venture

Approved joint-venture projects such as the Metro Manila Skyway and Manila Cavite Expressway proceed in accordance with Memorandum Order No. 266, which sets the guidelines for government-owned-and-controlled corporations to participate in joint ventures. The joint-venture agreement between the government-owned-and-controlled corporation and a private proponent must be approved by the president upon recommendation by the Government Corporate Monitoring and Coordination Committee. That committee is chaired by the executive secretary and supported by the presidential management staff as technical secretariat.

Local government units (LGUs) include municipalities and provincial governments. Under the Local Government Code, these political jurisdictions are also authorised to enter into joint-venture arrangements. The procedure for LGU joint ventures are not as clearly specified as those for project implementation under the BOT law. Public tenders are not specifically required for joint-venture projects. Consequently, this process is perceived to be less transparent than the BOT process and is believed to be more susceptible to legal challenges and court delays. Many LGUs believe that the joint venture route is faster than the BOT process and tend to encourage joint ventures for this reason, but there appears to be no substantive evidence to support that conclusion. In fact, the principal of harmonisation processes, when one law is specific and one law is silent regarding public tendering, suggests that the BOT option is the fastest and surest route to project implementation.

Equity participation

In many projects, the government brings something to the table, providing land or rights of way, relocation of squatters, etc. In most projects to date, this support has been provided free of charge. This results in lower tenders and, consequently, in lower tariffs to the public for the infrastructure and/ or service provided. In some cases, the implementing agency may wish to be compensated more directly for the support it provides by becoming an equity partner with the project proponent, receiving a fixed percentage of the return on equity. This provides the implementing agency with the benefits of joint ventures while assuring that all of the procedures of the BOT law are followed and all the benefits of the BOT law, including transparency of public tendering, are realised.

Rules of the game/credit enhancements

The Philippine BOT program started with the power sector. To ensure the private power program's success, the government established an enabling environment that required such bold steps as restructuring the government's energy sector policy, departments and regulatory agencies, as well as removing constraints to broader participation of the independent power producers in the BOT scheme. This included providing comprehensive guarantees as documented in the performance undertakings issued in favour of the independent power producers under power purchase agreements with the National Power Corporation (Napocor).

The provision of performance undertakings to back Napocor's power-purchase and fuel-supply obligations began as a response to an emergency situation in the power sector when macro and sectoral events prompted government to provide critical credit enhancements.

With the power crisis almost a distant memory, the government has deemed it reasonable to re-evaluate the power-sector policy and to consider appropriate policies for other sectors. Expectations have been raised based on the guarantees issued during the emergency period and it will be necessary to change these expectations as the government's policy evolves. The government is drafting a policy framework for providing government support to BOT financing schemes. The draft framework seeks to balance the government's interest in prudent fiscal management; the public's need for adequate, efficient and affordable amenities; and the private sector's gain of reasonable return on its investments.

Government guarantees need to be managed more prudently now that they have benefited from a better functioning business environment and widespread public acceptance of private sector involvement in areas traditionally monopolised by inefficient government-owned enterprises.

The government is now exploring ways to unbundle risks and refine its guarantee policy. It is moving away from its earlier provision of comprehensive guarantees, including the coverage of market risks. The fundamental approach now incorporates a more appropriate allocation of risks between the proponent and government based on the relative ability of each to bear such risks.

For example, in tollways and rails, commercial risks either are being shared or fully shifted to the private sector. The principal guarantee provided is that parametric adjustments in toll rates will be implemented. Where this is frustrated by political pressures and judicial judgments, there is compensating indemnity for the private proponent. By and large, the traffic-volume risks are borne by the private proponent.

Even risks that are better handled by government are being unbundled so that those rendered insignificant by improvements in the country's creditworthiness have a sunset clause. Examples of these are agreed provisions on exchange convertibility risks that are mandated to expire when the country achieves investment-grade rating.

The government is beginning to cost such guarantees and reckon them more explicitly in fiscal and balance of payments management. In a tender for a major power project (the Ilijan Natural Gas Project), tenders were requested that would provide both full and partial guarantee to obtain a measure of the value of such guarantees to the private sector.

SETTING UP IN THE PHILIPPINES

Ownership requirements

Generally, 100% foreign equity may be allowed in all areas of investment except financial institutions and those included in the Negative Lists of the Investment Law. Foreign equity in industries and activities is limited as follows:

- List A—areas reserved for Filipinos under the Philippine constitution and other laws such as mass media, retail trade, and small-scale mining where foreign ownership is prohibited, and advertising, land ownership and public utilities where minority foreign ownership is allowed; and
- List B—areas that are defence-related, those with adverse effects on public health and morals, and domestic market enterprises with paid-in capital of less than $200,000, unless they involve advanced

technology or directly employ at least 50 people, in which case the paid-in capital can be as little as $100,000.

Before a foreign corporation can open an office in the Philippines, it must first secure the necessary licences or registration certificates from the appropriate government bodies. A foreign firm can set up either a representative office, a branch, a domestic corporation or a regional headquarters. Generally, the registration process starts with incorporating or registering with the Philippine Securities and Exchange Commission (SEC).

The processing of papers with the SEC takes about 15 working days from filing to approval. To incorporate a Philippine company, a majority of the incorporating directors, from a minimum of five to a maximum of 15, must be Philippine residents. The company secretary must be a resident Filipino. For firms where foreign ownership is restricted, the maximum number of foreign directors must not exceed the proportion of actual foreign equity in the firm and all its executive and managing directors must be Filipino.

At least 25% of the authorised capital stock of a domestic corporation must be subscribed and at least 25% of the subscribed capital must be paid-in; however, subscriptions by alien individuals or foreign entities must be fully paid. For joint ventures, the SEC will allow foreign equity greater than 50% of the equity provided the area of activity is not restricted under the Negative Lists under the Investment Law. Table 1 summarises the differences between representative and branch offices, domestic corporations and regional headquarters.

Board of Investments incentives

The Philippine Board of Investment (BOI) provides information services to prospective investors and a range of incentives for those who move ahead with projects.

Investments Priorities Plan

'Pole-vaulting', a term often heard in the Philippines for leaping ahead economically, is the theme of the Investments Priorities Plan (IPP) that was introduced in the latter part of 1997. In spite of the regional currency crisis, the Philippine economy is still fundamentally sound. Despite a slowdown in 1998, the economy's long-range outlook is still quite positive. Reforms are continuing and more investment-enhancing measures are being pursued. The regional downturn may put the Philippines in a position to fast-track priority economic activities to pole-vault the economy's development relative to its current position.

Table 1. Comparison of forms for a presence in the Philippines

	Representative office	Brance office	Regional headquarters	Philippine corporation
Characteristics	Legal entity is merely an extension of the foreign company. It is legally not a separate entity and has no legal personality distinct and separate from the foreign corporation.	Legal entity is merely an extension of the foreign company. It is legally not a separate entity.	Legal entity is merely an extension of the foreign company. It is legally not a separate entity.	It is a separate legal entity from the foreign corporation, with its own legal personality. Thus liability is limited to Philippine subsidiary.
Activities	May not engage in business in the Philippines. However, it may conduct activities that are non-income-generating, such as marketing and market research, collecting and distributing information, advertising and promotion and in general acting as a liaison for the head office of the foreign corporation.	May engage in any lawful activities. May engage in business and/or income-generating activities.	Limited to acting as a supervisory, communications and coordinating centre for its affiliates, subsidiaries and branches in the Asia-Pacific region. It should not participate in the management of any subsidiary or branch office it may have in the Philippines. Likewise, it should not derive any income from the Philippines.	May engage in any lawful business and/or income-generating activities.

Tax consequences	Not subject to corporate income taxes as long as it does not engage in transactions or do business in the Philippines	Subject to income tax rate of 35% with respect to income from sources in the Philippines. Advantages of a branch vis-à-vis a domestic subsidiary: 1) A branch is taxed only on net income from sources within the Philippines; 2) Fewer formalities involved in opening a branch; 3) A branch may require less staff (i.e., can operate with only a resident agent, who may also act as general manager; 4) Able to claim as deduction allocated head office expenses subject to certain requirements.	Not subject to corporate income taxes as long as it does not engage in transactions or do business in the Philippines. It is exempt from income tax and all kinds of local licences and fees.	Subject to income tax rate of 35% with respect to its world-wide income. Advantage of subsidiary vis-a-vis a branch is that the foreign company is protected from contractual and other liabilities incurred by Philippine industry.
Procedure for establishment	Minimal registration, filing or reporting requirements to establish and maintain representative office. Registration with the Securities and Exchange Commission is required.	Registration with the Securities and Exchange Commission is required.	Registration with the Board of Investments and the Securities and Exchange Commission is required. There is an initial requirement to remit $30,000 into the Philippine banking system.	Registration with the Securities and Exchange Commission is required.

Some of the goals of the 1997 IPP are to set up and upgrade infrastructure and support facilities and continue new infrastructure development. Priority investment areas in the infrastructure modernisation program include: development of industrial estates; modern service cities; telecommunications; ports; water supply; waterways and sewerage systems; toll roads/highways; power generation and transmission; and distribution facilities for refined petroleum products/LPG, including depot/bulk handling.

Proponents/investors applying for incentives at the BOI should provide the following documents:

- An endorsement from the concerned government agency, corporation or local government unit with certification that BOI incentives have been considered in the supply contract;
- A copy of the supply contract; and
- An environmental compliance certificate.

Incentives to registered firms

Investment incentives under Executive Order 226 as amended by Republic Act 7918 include:

- Tax exemptions
  - –duty of 3% on imported capital equipment and its accompanying spare parts;
  - –income taxes;
  - –taxes and duties on imported spare parts; and
  - –wharfage dues and export tax, duty, import and fees.
- Tax credits
  - –domestic capital equipment and accompanying spare parts; and
  - –raw materials and supplies.
- Additional deductions from taxable income
  - –labour expense; and
  - –necessary and major infrastructure works.
- Non-fiscal incentives
  - –employment of foreign nationals;
  - –simplification of customs procedures; and
  - –importation of consigned equipment for an unlimited period subject to posting of a re-export bond.

Multinational regional bonded warehouses

Multinational regional bonded warehouses may be owned by multinational companies; have their regional headquarters in the Philippines; are used as supply depots for distribution to the Asia-Pacific market; and have a storage period of two years. Application requirements before such a facility may be operated include:

- A copy of the certificate of SEC registration certified by the corporate secretary;
- Photocopies of articles of incorporation, by-laws or articles of partnerships;
- Evidencing of absolute ownership or lease contract of the proposed warehouse;
- Proof of investment or inward remittance by foreign investors bank certification;
- Plant layout including the size and type of construction of the proposed warehouse;
- Plant location showing access to the property;
- Mayor's occupancy permit for the building;
- Audited or interim financial statement for the two years immediately preceding the date of application;
- Applicant's income tax return for the preceding two years;
- List of machinery and equipment;
- Project feasibility study; and
- Post clearance having jurisdiction over the warehouse.

VISAS

An alien coming to prearranged employment is normally issued a visa by the Philippine consulate abroad. However, a petitioning company may request that an alien previously admitted in the Philippines under a different non-immigrant status be permitted to change to that of a prearranged employee. This will be granted provided the company can show that no person in the Philippines is willing and competent to perform the labour or service for which the non-immigrant is hired and that the non-immigrant's admission would be beneficial to the public interest. Prearranged employment visas are granted for a period coterminous with the employment contract, but in no case may they exceed two years. They may be extended yearly, but the total extensions may not exceed three years, except in very exceptional cases in which extensions not to exceed five years may be granted.

The following is a checklist of requirements for applying for a visa for prearranged employment:

- Letter of request from the petitioning company;
- Completed and notarised application form;
- Certified true copy of any written contract or agreement entered into for the immigrant's service;

- Bio-data of employee;
- Articles of incorporation of the petitioning company;
- SEC certificate of registration of the petitioning company;
- Alien employment permit from the Department of Labor and Employment;
- Affidavit of support/guarantee;
- True copy of the passport of the employee;
- Income tax return of the petitioner.

Other documents may be deemed necessary for an adequate evaluation of the petition.

TARIFFS

The Philippines has agreed to gradual implementation of the General Agreement of Trade and Tariffs (GATT) terms, but the actual dates for full compliance for sensitive industries may be several years off.

In a press release dated 28 November 1997, the United States lamented the Philippine Government's efforts to delay the tariff revision schedule mandated under Executive Order No. 24, noting that this would send the wrong signals to the international business community.

Under the Tariff Reform Program (Executive Order No. 264), tariff rates in most products will be lowered to between zero and 5% by 2004 in accordance with the country's commitment in the ASEAN Free Trade Agreement.

For now, the government has adopted a four-tiered structure, imposing tariffs of 3%, 10%, 20% and 30% depending on the product. Basically, the Philippines has a decade in which to conform to the terms of the General Agreement of Trade and Tariffs. However, the private sector has sounded alarms on the fast pace of tariff reductions, which they claim have been hurting local industries. The Inter-Agency Tariff and Related Matters Committee has agreed to slacken the pace of the tariff cuts from a steep 10 percentage point drop to only 5%.

The Federation of Philippine Industries believes that the priority areas of automobiles, petrochemicals, iron, garments and textiles should be among those protected first from the rapid tariff cuts. Petitions have been included in the ongoing tariff review to produce intermediate rates, freeze existing rates for some products, and delay reductions for other products next year.

CHAPTER 5

TAKING THE PLUNGE

For the benefit of potential investors who may have bitter memories of properties lost to government policies in the Philippines or elsewhere, the Board of Investments (BOI) has come up with a bill of 'basic rights and guarantees of foreign investments'. However, like all such documents, it may not be enforceable in a crisis. Nor is it easy to wade through the paperwork needed to make all the guarantees really happen, or happen very quickly. Still, the document stands as a sign of shifting thinking when it comes to the kind of welcome foreign interests receive.

The list of rights includes those of repatriation of investments, remittance of earnings, foreign loans and contracts, freedom from expropriation and non-requisition of investment.

An investor is entitled 'to repatriate the entire proceeds of the liquidation of the investment in the currency in which the investment was originally made at the exchange rate prevailing at the time of repatriation'. One has 'the right to remit earnings from the investments in the currency in which the investment was originally made and at the exchange rate prevailing at the time of remittance'. One has 'the right to remit, at the exchange rate prevailing at the time of remittance, such as may be necessary to meet the payment of interest and the principal on foreign loans and foreign obligations arising from technological assistance contracts'.

The next right may be the most critical at some politically unforeseen moment. 'There shall be no expropriation by the government of the property represented by the investments or of the property of enterprises except for public use or in the interest of national welfare and defence and upon payment of just compensation.' And if such a dread occurrence should happen, the document promises that, 'foreign investors or enterprises shall have the right to remit sums received as compensation for the expropriated property in the currency in which the investment was originally made and at the exchange rate prevailing at the time of remittance'.

Finally, only 'in the event of war or national emergency and only for the duration' will there by any 'requisition of the property presented by the investment or of the property of enterprises'. And 'just compensation for the requisitioned property may', again, 'be remitted in the currency in which the investment was originally made and the exchange rate prevailing at the time of remittance'. Considering some of the problems encountered by foreigners in the Marcos era, such words are more than mere rhetoric. They represent a serious policy shift.

GETTING STARTED

The basic rights of foreign investors are backed up by chapter and verse of conditions designed to ease operations. *Philippines 2000*, an annual publication of the Securities and Exchange Commission (SEC) that lists the 2,000 top companies in the Philippines, offers a checklist of 'The Basics' that go considerably further than basic rights—right down to the basic things you have to do to get out of the starting gate.

'Establishing business in the Philippines is not as difficult as it seems', the book points out. 'An investor needs only to undertake the applicable combination of activities. Some can be done simultaneously. Specific requirements may vary depending on several key factors like foreign equity, nature of business, locations, among others.' For starters, the book definitely recommends stopping at the BOI's One-Stop Action Centre, the Bureau of Trade Regulation and Consumer Protection, the PEZA and the SEC.

The following is *Philippines 2000*'s list of requirements to comply with in setting up business in the Philippines:

- Registration of corporations and partnerships with the SEC;
- Registration of business name/single proprietorship with the Bureau of Trade Regulations and Consumer Protection;
- Registration for incentives with the BOI;

- Registration of export firms (for those locating in any of the country's export processing zones and availing of incentives) with the Philippine Export Zone Authority;
- Securing a tax identification number from the Bureau of Internal Revenue (BIR);
- Securing building permits and licences to do business from city halls and municipal offices in the localities where the business will be set up;
- Securing an employer's number from the Social Security System;
- Securing membership in the government health care benefits system from Medicare;
- Securing electric services connection from Manila Electric Company (MERALCO) for business in the MERALCO franchise area or from local electric utility firms for companies locating in non-MERALCO franchise areas; and
- Securing water services from the Metropolitan Waterworks and Sewerage System for firms locating in Metro Manila or from the Local Water Utilities Administration for firms locating outside Metro Manila.

Operational requirements

An enterprise must comply with additional requirements in operation and/ or diversification. These include:

- Reportorial requirements for amendment of articles of incorporation with the SEC;
- Reportorial requirements for registration of business/expansion for incentives with the BOI;
- Regular tax payments with the Bureau of Internal Revenue;
- Registration of a customs-bonded warehouse with the Bureau of Customs;
- Opening of letters of credit with authorised agent banks;
- Certificate to import duty-free from the BOI;
- Authority to load/certificate of origin from the Bureau of Customs Export Coordination Division;
- Information sheet for first-time exporters from the Bangko Sentral ng Pilipinas; and
- payment of wharfage fees/exemption from payment from the Philippine Ports Authority.

The following is a list of required special permits, clearances and registrations:

- Expatriates' visas from the Bureau of Immigration;
- Alien employment permits from the Department of Labor and Employment;
- Clearance for garment exporters/quota allocation from the Garments & Textile Export Board;
- Registration for operation of a customs-bonded manufacturing warehouse from the Bureau of Customs;
- Environmental compliance certification from the environment Management Bureau of the Department of Environment and Natural Resources;
- Approval of projects involving land use/conversion from the Housing & Land Use Regulatory Board, the National Housing Authority and the Department of Agrarian Reform;
- Permits to construct/operate pollution-control devices from the Department of Environment and Natural Resources;
- Trademarks/patents registration with the Bureau of Patents, Trademarks and Technology Transfer;
- Registration of power generation projects with the National Power Corporation;
- Philippine standard quality marks to ensure that locally manufactured consumer products conform to Philippine Standards from the Bureau of Product Standards;
- Import commodity clearance quality marks to ensure that imported consumer products conform to Philippine standards from the Bureau of Product Standards;
- Clearance for projects that involve food, chemicals and others from the Bureau of Food and Drug;
- Registration of tourism projects with the Department of Tourism;
- Franchises for mass transit operation from the Land Transportation, Franchising and Regulatory Board;
- Approval from the National Telecommunications Commission for telecommunications projects;
- Licence/clearance for defence-related projects from the Department of National Defence and the Philippine National Police;
- Clearance for oil exploration activities from the Office of Energy Affairs; and
- Mining rights acquired from the Bureau of Mines and Geo-Sciences.

Special permits/clearances for selected export businesses

Export products require the following clearances and permits prior to every shipment:

- Clearance for plant export from the Bureau of Plant Industry;
- Clearance for export of food, drugs and chemicals from the Bureau of Food and Drug;
- Clearance/quota for coffee exports from the International Coffee Organisation Certifying Agency;
- Commodity clearance for natural fibres export from the Fibre Industry Development authority;
- Clearance for quota allocation of garment exports from the Garments and Textile Export Board;
- Clearance for export of fisheries and other aquatic products from the Bureau of Fisheries and Aquatic Resources;
- Special documentation certificate for preferential treatment of handicrafts export from the Department of Trade & Industry, National Capital Region; and
- Export clearance for coconut products from the Philippine Coconut Authority.

THE ABCS OF SEZS

To assist in deciding where to locate a factory or firm, the commercial section of the American embassy in Manila has come up with the following recommendations.

Any person, partnership corporation or business organisation, regardless of nationality, control and/or ownership, may register as a free-trade-zone enterprise with the Philippine Economic Zone Authority or PEZA (formerly Export Processing Zone Authority, or EPZA). To qualify for duty and tax incentives, all production must be exported, although there are provisions under which up to 30% of the output—not merely assembly or packaging of materials—may be allowed for domestic consumption, subject to applicable taxes and duties.

PEZA manages the country's four government-owned export processing zones. It also manages 25 or so privately owned and developed sites in strategic parts of the country that have been designated as special economic zones (SEZs). An additional 30 or so proposed sites have been approved as SEZs. PEZA is also responsible for promoting tourism and providing trainable labour inside the economic zones.

With minimum government intervention, ecozones may be developed in privately owned industrial sites, through local government and/or private sector initiatives under any of the schemes allowed under the Build-Operate-Transfer (BOT) law. These may be decentralised, self-reliant and self-sustaining industrial, agro-industrial, commercial/trading, banking, financial, investment and tourist centres.

SyCip Gorres Velayo & Co., one of the Big Six accounting firms, has listed the types of ecozones as follows:

- Industrial estates (IEs) are tracts of land developed for the use of industries. They have basic infrastructure, such as roads, water and sewage systems, pre-built factory buildings and residential housing for the use of the community.
- Export processing zones are special IEs whose locator companies are export-oriented. EPZ incentives include tax- and duty-free importation of capital equipment, raw material and spare parts.
- Free-trade zones are areas near ports of entry, such as seaports and airports. Imported goods may be unloaded, repacked, sorted and manipulated without being subjected to import duties. However, if these goods are moved into a non-free-trade zone, they will be subject to customs duties.
- Tourist and recreational centres contain establishments to cater for both local and foreign visitors to the ecozones. Such businesses include hotels, resorts, apartelles (Fil-English for apartment hotels that rent by the week or month) and sports facilities.

The following is a short description of each type of ecozone enterprise:

- An export enterprise manufactures, assembles or processes products that are 100% exported, unless a lower percentage is approved by PEZA.
- A free-trade enterprise imports and markets tax- and duty-free goods within the free-trade area in the ecozone. Goods taken outside the free-trade area are subject to customs and tariff duties.
- A service enterprise is engaged in any one or a combination of the following activities: customs brokerage, trucking/forwarding, janitorial, security, insurance and/or banking, consulting, or any such service approved by PEZA.
- A domestic-market enterprise is a manufacturer, assembler or processor of goods that sells at least 50% of its products on the local market if majority-owned by Filipinos and at least 70% locally if majority-owned by foreigners.

The following are some other categories cited by SyCip that are key parts of the ecozone program:

- A pioneer enterprise is one that meets any of the following conditions
  –manufactures, processes or produces goods not produced on a commercial scale in the country;
  –uses a design, formula, scheme, method or process that is new and untried in the Philippines;

–produces non-conventional fuels or manufactures equipment that utilises non-conventional sources of energy; or
–develops areas for agro-export processing development or is given such a status under the Investment Priorities Plan.
- A utilities enterprise is contracted to provide light and power, water supply and distribution, communications and transportation systems in an ecozone.
- A facilities enterprise is contracted to build and maintain such necessary infrastructure as warehouses, buildings, road networks, ports, sewerage and drainage systems and other facilities considered necessary by PEZA to develop and operate an ecozone.
- A tourism enterprise operates tourist accommodation facilities, restaurants and sports and recreational facilities in an ecozone.
- An ecozone developer/operator develops, operates and maintains the ecozone, all component sectors (i.e., IEs, EPZs, free-trade zones and tourist/recreational centres) and all related infrastructure (roads, light and power systems, drainage facilities, etc.)

Incentives granted by PEZA apply only to registered ecozone companies and only during the period of their registration with PEZA. Export enterprises registered under the Export Processing Zone Authority continue to enjoy their current incentives. However, PEZA enterprises for which the income tax holiday has already expired will be subject to the special 5% tax rate as provided under the ecozone act.

Export and free-trade enterprises registered with PEZA can avail themselves of a range of fiscal and non-fiscal incentives, as cited by SyCip. These include:

- Tax- and duty-free import of capital equipment, raw materials, spare parts, supplies, breeding stocks and genetic materials;
- An income tax holiday of four to a maximum of eight years for non-pioneer and pioneer projects, respectively;
- A special tax rate of 5% of gross income in lieu of all national and local taxes after the income tax holiday;
- A tax credit for import substitution;
- exemption from wharfage dues, export tax and import fees;
- A tax credit on domestic capital equipment, breeding stocks and genetic materials;
- Unrestricted use of consigned equipment;
- Permanent resident status for foreign investors and family members;
- Employment of foreign nationals; and
- Remittance of earnings without prior approval from the Bangko Central.

Ecozone developers and operators, facilities, utilities and tourist enterprises and domestic-market enterprises can avail themselves of the following incentives as well:

- A special tax rate of 5% of gross income in lieu of all national and local taxes;
- Additional deduction for training expenses;
- Permanent resident status for foreign investors and family members;
- Incentives under the revised BOT law; and
- Other incentives as may be decided on by the PEZA board.

Of the 5% tax paid by PEZA enterprises, 3% goes to the government, 1% to local government units where the ecozone is located, and 1% to a fund for development of communities surrounding the ecozone. Gross income is defined as the gross revenues of any business activity less sales discounts, sales returns and allowances, and allowable deductions.

Deductions common to ecozone enterprises are: direct salaries, wages or labour expenses; goods in process; finished goods; supplies and fuels; depreciation of plant, property and equipment; rent and utility charges for building equipment; warehouses and handling of goods; and financing charges associated with fixed assets. However, administrative expenses and incidental losses are not deductible from gross revenues.

In addition, certain deductions are allowed specifically for ecozone export, free-trade and domestic-market enterprises. These include production-supervision salaries and raw materials used in manufacturing. Deductions applicable to facilities, utilities and tourism enterprises include service-supervision salaries and direct materials and supplies.

Registration and filing fees with PEZA amount to US$300, while registration with the Securities and Exchange Commission (SEC) costs 0.1% of the authorised capital. The minimum daily wage for non-agricultural workers is about US$5.30 per day. Rental rates for industrial land range from US$27 to US$45 per square metre per month. The construction cost for a self-designed factory building is about US$200 per square metre.

As the American embassy's country commercial guide points out, investments in foreign trade zones—whether government-run export processing zones, special ecozones, industrial estates or free-trade zones—fall under the jurisdiction of PEZA. Without prior Bangko Sentral approval, after-tax profits and other earnings from foreign investment in foreign-trade-zone enterprises may be remitted outward in the equivalent foreign exchange, provided that such foreign investments have been previously registered with the Bangko Sentral ng Pilipinas.

Enterprises located in the free-trade zones are allowed to import capital equipment and raw materials free from duties and taxes. PEZA manages and operates foreign-trade zones and ecozones as separate customs territories. Machinery and equipment, raw materials, supplies and other inputs brought into these zones for the exclusive use of registered enterprises enjoy simplified import procedures. These include exemption from pre-shipment inspection, assessment and payment of duties and taxes, and other import restrictions. However, movement of these imported goods from the free-trade area to a non-free-trade area within the country is subject to tariffs and taxes.

PEZA firms also are entitled to other incentives granted to BOI-registered companies as provided under the Omnibus Investments Code, plus such additional benefits as exemption from local and national taxes (except for real estate taxes). In lieu of paying other taxes, as noted, 5% of the gross income earned by a PEZA-registered establishment is remitted to the government. Foreign companies investing in the Philippines may lease land for 75 years, with a 25-year renewal on their original 50-year lease. This is an improvement over the previous limit of 50 years.

OTHER WAYS TO INVEST

It is not necessary to go the PEZA route to invest. The American embassy's commercial guide notes that the Philippine government has taken important steps since the turn of the decade to welcome foreign investment. The 1991 Foreign Investments Act (FIA) lifted the 40% foreign-ownership ceiling previously imposed on domestic enterprises as long as no incentives are sought and the activity does not appear on a foreign investment Negative List.

May 1994 amendments to the country's banking law have since allowed 10 foreign banks to establish branches in the Philippines. This had been restricted since 1948. In October 1994, after decades of protection, the government has also opened up the insurance sector to majority foreign ownership. Legislation passed in March1996 abolished one of three Negative Lists under the FIA—List C, which protected 'adequately served' sectors—and lowered the minimum capital requirement at which majority foreign ownership would be allowed from US$500,000 to US$200,000.

Other investment-friendly proposals are in various stages of congressional deliberation, indicating a growing receptiveness to foreign investment in the Philippines. Some of these are net-operating-gross carryover, accelerated depreciation of capital equipment, and larger foreign equity stakes in retail trade companies, investment houses and financing firms.

Foreign investment Negative Lists

While investment liberalisation has been substantial, certain barriers to foreign entry remain. Depending on the industry or activity, the FIA's foreign investment Negative Lists fully or partially restrict foreign ownership under two broad categories.

List A restricts foreign investment in certain sectors because of constitutional or legal constraints. For example, such industries as mass media, retail trade, small-scale mining, private security agencies and the practice of licensed professions are fully reserved for Philippine citizens. Varying foreign ownership ceilings are imposed on enterprises engaged in, among others, financing, advertising, domestic air transport, public utilities, construction, pawnshop operations, education and employee recruitment.

Land ownership is also constitutionally restricted to Filipino citizens or to corporations with at least 60% Filipino ownership. In general, companies engaged in exploring and developing natural resources—which must be undertaken under production-sharing or similar arrangements with the government—should be at least 60% Filipino-owned, except for such high-cost and high-risk activities as oil exploration and large-scale mining.

List B restricts foreign ownership generally to 40% for reasons of national security, defence, public health, safety and morals. This list also seeks to protect small and medium-sized firms by restricting foreign ownership to no more than 40% in non-export firms capitalised at less than US$200,000.

The FIA's foreign investment Negative Lists do not include sectors regulated by Bangko Sentral where foreign ownership restrictions must also apply. Rural banking, for example, is completely closed to foreigners. A 60% foreign ownership ceiling applies to domestically incorporated commercial banks. Currently, investment houses must be majority foreign-owned by Philippine nationals.

Barriers to foreign investors seeking incentives

Under Book I, 'Investments with Incentives', of the 1987 Omnibus Investment Code, the Board of Investment offers incentives to investors in preferred pioneer or non-pioneer activities listed in an annual Investment Priorities Plan (IPP). As a general rule current regulations limit foreign participation in BOI-registered firms to 40% by imposing the following more stringent conditions for foreign-owned enterprises to qualify for incentives:

- In general, foreign-owned firms producing for the domestic market must engage in a pioneer activity to qualify for incentives. Non-pioneer activities generally are opened up to foreign equity beyond

56

40% only if domestic capital proves inadequate to meet the desired industry capacity after three years.

- Subject to certain conditions, such as the type of products/services exported and/or export markets, export-oriented companies may also qualify for BOI registration and incentives. The export requirement is higher for foreign-owned companies (at least 70% of production should be for export) than for domestic companies (50% of production for export).
- Foreign-owned companies that meet the conditions for BOI registration must agree to attain Filipino status (i.e., divest to maximum 40% foreign ownership) within 30 years or such longer period as the BOI may allow, taking into account the benefits/potential of the project. Foreign firms that export 100% of production are exempted from this divestment requirement.

Privatisation and BOT projects

The government has expanded the privatisation program launched by former President Corazon Aquino in 1986. There are no separate regulations or practices that discriminate against foreign buyers, except for foreign ownership ceilings that may apply under the FIA and other laws. Proponents of BOT and similar projects valued at over one billion pesos may register for incentives with the Board of Investment. The BOT and similar schemes generally are open to both domestic and foreign contractors/operators. The exceptions are projects that involve operating such public-utility franchises as railways/urban rail mass-transit systems, electricity distribution, water distribution and telephone systems. These must be awarded to enterprises that are at least 60% Filipino-owned. American firms have already won contracts under BOT and similar arrangements, several of them for power generation.

One-stop action centres have become fashionable in government circles for simplifying procedures—and not just at the BOI. *Philippines 2000* lists them all:

- One-Stop Action Centre for Investments at the BOI;
- One-Stop Export Documentation Centre at the International Trade Centre Complex;
- One-Stop Import Processing Centre at the Bureau of Import Services;
- One-Stop Shop Tax Credit Centre at the Department of Finance; and
- One-Stop Action Garments Export Assistance Centre at the Garments and Textile Export Board.

There are other sources of help as well. For technical services and quality control, *Philippines 2000* suggests contacting any of the following organisations:

- Cottage Industry Technology Centre;
- Philippine Shippers Council;
- Product Development and Design Centre of the Philippines;,
- Philippine Textile Research Institute; or
- National Manpower & Youth Council of the Department of Labor and Employment.

When in need of export marketing support, an investor can consult various agencies for free assistance:

- Export Assistance Network (Exponet) for advice on matching exporters with buyers/raw material suppliers;
- Bureau of Export Trade Promotion for market information, strategy production research and foreign-trade assistance;
- the Garments and Textile Export Board One-Stop Action Centre for garments-export assistance;
- the Philippine International Trading Corporation for trading with socialist countries;
- the Centre for International Trade Fair Exposition and Missions for advice on trade fairs and exhibitions;
- the Product Development and Design Centre of the Philippines for advice on product development and improvement; and
- the National Subcontractors Exchange (Subconex) for subcontracting facilitation between contractors and sub-contractors.

RIGHT TO PRIVATE OWNERSHIP AND ESTABLISHMENT

The Philippine Government welcomes free enterprise, provides incentives to needed investments, and respects the private sector's right to freely acquire or dispose of its properties or business interests. However, acquisitions, mergers and other combinations of business interests involving foreign equity must comply with foreign nationality caps specified in the Constitution and other laws.

Few activities are completely closed to private enterprise, except for reasons of security, health and public morals. While statutes prohibit unfair trade practices, the Philippines currently does not have comprehensive antitrust legislation.

Private and government-owned firms generally compete equally, although there are exceptions. For example, government-owned banks corner the bulk of public sector deposits. The National Food Authority, a government agency, is the sole importer of rice. In some cases, government procurement guidelines—specifically for rice, medicines and infrastructure projects—favour Philippine over foreign-controlled firms.

The free ports and SEZs within the former US military bases at Clark and Subic operate under the management and control of the Bases Conversion Development Authority. They are exempt from the PEZA mandate.

The ASEAN Free Trade Area (AFTA) calls for a common effective preferential tariff (CEPT) of 0 to 5% by 2003. The Philippines started to phase in the CEPT scheme on 1 January 1996. The 1 July 1995 completion of the Philippines five-year tariff reduction program has made the ASEAN region the fastest growing market for Philippine-made products. The scheduled implementation of the CEPT scheme makes AFTA a building block for the program of APEC, the Asia Pacific Economic Cooperation group of 18 countries and 'economies', including Hong Kong and Taiwan, on both sides of the Pacific.

As a member of APEC, the Philippines is committed to the region's move toward free trade. While developed economies are expected to establish free trade by 2010, developing economies like the Philippines will get an extension of 10 years. The Philippines hosted the November 1996 APEC summit of leaders of the 18 members in Subic Freeport, a major American naval base turned over to Philippine authority just four years before. It was a crowning symbolic achievement for President Ramos, as well as for the chairman of the Subic Bay Metropolitan Authority, Richard Gordon, who is the grandson of an American marine and former mayor of Olongapo, the city beyond the gates of the port.

CHAPTER 6

PAYING YOUR TAXES

Cornelio C Gison and Emmanuel P Bonoan

Philippine taxation is governed primarily by the National Internal Revenue Code (the Tax Code). The Tax Code recently underwent substantial revisions with the passage of the Tax Reform Act of 1997, which took effect on 1 January 1998. Special laws also provide for tax incentives and the special tax treatment of various classes of taxpayers.

Primary responsibility for the administration and enforcement of the Tax Code rests with the Bureau of Internal Revenue (BIR), which is part of the Department of Finance. The BIR is headed by a commissioner who has exclusive and original jurisdiction to interpret the provisions of the code and other tax laws. The commissioner also has the power to decide disputed assessments; grant refunds of internal revenue taxes, fees or other charges, or penalties imposed; compromise the payment of any internal revenue tax; and abate or cancel a tax liability. An unfavourable decision of the commissioner with respect to such assessments and refunds can be appealed by the taxpayer to the Court of Tax Appeals.

Transfer pricing issues—how much tax to impose on the estimated value of goods transferred from one entity to another in the same group—are encountered sometimes by foreign corporations doing business in the Philippines. Although no regulations fix specific formulas to meet these issues, the Tax Code authorises the Commissioner of Internal Revenue to allocate income and deductions between related parties. The commissioner uses the arm's-length principle, assuming that the parties would have adopted a more realistic estimate of the value of goods if they are entirely unrelated to one another.

The national internal revenue taxes imposed by the Tax Code are:

- Income tax on individuals and corporations;
- Estate and donor's taxes;
- Value-added tax;
- Percentage taxes; and
- Documentary stamp tax.

TAX INCENTIVES

Aside from the Tax Code, a number of special laws grant tax incentives to foreign investors. For example, under the Omnibus Investments Code (Executive Order No. 226, as amended), enterprises that have registered with the Board of Investments and which qualify under an annually published Investments Priorities Plan may avail themselves of an income tax holiday of four or six years. These firms may also enjoy tax- and duty-free importation of capital equipment and spare parts until 31 December 1999 if they are located outside the National Capital Region. In addition, they are granted tax credits on purchases of domestic capital equipment and tax credits for taxes and duties on raw materials used in the manufacture, processing or production of export products.

More than 30 special economic zones (SEZs), where export-oriented manufacturing concerns can set up their operations, are located in different parts of the country. Under the Philippine Export Zone Authority Law (Republic Act No 7916, as amended), an export zone-registered enterprise can, in lieu of all other national and local taxes, pay a tax of 5% of its gross income. This incentive is enjoyed with the tax incentives granted by the Omnibus Investments Code. Thus, for the first four or six years of its operations a zone-registered enterprise may opt to avail itself of the income tax holiday. Once this has expired, it will be subject to the 5% tax. The exemption from national taxes covers all internal revenue taxes such as value-added tax (VAT) and the excise tax.

Separate laws have created two of the largest special economic zones in the former US military bases of Clark and Subic Bay. Enterprises located in these economic zones also enjoy the income tax holiday and 5% preferential tax.

TAX TREATIES

To minimise the effects of double taxation, the Philippines has tax treaties with a number of countries. They essentially follow the models of the Organisation for Economic Cooperation and Development (OECD). In the event that a treaty conflicts with a domestic tax law, Philippine constitutional law upholds the precedence of the treaty over the domestic law. The Philippines has tax treaties with Australia, Austria, Belgium, Brazil, Canada, Denmark, Finland, France, Germany, Indonesia, India, Israel, Italy, Japan, Korea, Malaysia, Netherlands, New Zealand, Norway, Pakistan, Poland, Romania, Russia, Singapore, Spain, Sweden, Thailand, United Kingdom and the United States.

The concept of the permanent establishment becomes relevant in relation to these treaties as the Tax Code itself does not speak of permanent establishments. Typically, business profits of a resident of another state with which the Philippines has a tax treaty are taxable in the Philippines only if the resident has a permanent establishment in the Philippines to which the profits are attributable. The treaties also reduce the rates of certain passive incomes derived from the Philippines by residents of treaty countries. Thus tax treaties provide a viable means by which residents of other countries may minimise their Philippine tax liabilities.

INCOME TAX

Individual income tax

All aliens, whether they are residents or not, are taxed only on their income from Philippine sources. Resident aliens and non-resident aliens engaged in trade or business are taxed on their net income (that is, after deductions and personal exemptions) according to a schedule of rates ranging from 3% to 34%. The maximum rate will be reduced to 33% effective 1 January 1999 and to 32% on 1 January 2000.

Items of income that are subject to the sliding schedule pertain either to compensation income arising from an employer–employee relationship or to income derived from conducting a trade or business. The Tax Code provides a different set of rates for capital gains and passive income from interest, royalties, dividends and prize winnings.

The test of whether or not an alien is a resident depends on a variety of factors, the most important of which is one's intention with regard to the length of time and the nature of the stay in the Philippines. In the absence of definite intentions, resident alien status can be imposed. Aliens who come to the Philippines for a definite purpose but whose work requires them to reside for an extended period may also be considered as resident aliens.

Non-resident aliens not engaged in trade or business are taxed a flat rate of 25% on all income from Philippine sources, including passive income. However, they are subject to the same rates of tax imposed on resident aliens and non-resident aliens engaged in trade or business on capital gains from the sale of shares of stock and of real property. (See discussion on capital gains of shares of stock.) The Tax Code fixes a simple criterion for determining whether a non-resident alien is engaged in trade or business: if a non-resident's stay in the Philippines exceeds an aggregate period of 180 days in any calendar year, that person shall be deemed to be doing business in the Philippines.

A special tax rate is enjoyed by aliens who work for regional or area headquarters and regional operating headquarters of multinational companies; off-shore banking units (OBUs); and petroleum service contractors and subcontractors. These individuals are taxed 15% on their gross income and at the usual rates on all passive income and capital gains tax from the sale of shares of stock and real property.

Allowable deductions from gross income

In the same manner as citizens, resident aliens who receive a salary from their employment in the Philippines—unless their salaries are subject to final tax, as with individuals employed in regional or area headquarters, operating headquarters or OBUs—are allowed basic personal exemptions in the following amounts:

- 20,000 pesos for single individuals or married individuals judicially decreed as legally separated and with no qualified dependents;
- 25,000 pesos for head of family (defined as an unmarried or legally separated man or woman with one or both parents, or with one or more brothers or sisters or with one or more legitimate, recognised, natural or legally adopted children living with and dependent upon that individual for their chief support, where such brothers or sisters or children are not more than 21 years of age, unmarried and not gainfully employed or where such children, brothers or sisters, regardless of their age, are incapable of self-support because of mental or physical defect); and
- 32,000 pesos for each married individual; however, in the case of married couples with only one source of income, only the income earner shall be allowed the personal exemption.

An additional exemption of 8,000 pesos for each of up to four dependents may also be claimed. For married individuals, this exemption may be claimed by only one of the spouses. In the case of legally separated spouses, additional exemptions may be claimed by the spouse who has custody of the child or children. This exemption may be claimed only if the dependent lives with taxpayer, is not more than 21 years of age, or is incapable of self-support because of mental or physical defect. The additional exemption covers legitimate, illegitimate and adopted dependents.

Non-resident aliens engaged in trade, business or the practice of a profession in the Philippines are entitled to the personal exemptions only if the country of which they are citizens grants similar privileges to Philippine citizens who are not residents of that country. The amount of allowable exemption is the same as that granted by their country to non-resident Philippine citizens up to the maximum allowed in the Tax Code. Furthermore, such non-resident aliens may deduct from their gross income those business-related items that the Tax Code allows corporations to deduct.

Non-resident aliens not engaged in trade or business in the Philippines are not allowed the personal exemptions as they are taxed a flat rate on their gross income from Philippine sources.

Taxation of Passive Income

Interest

In general, a final tax of 20% is imposed on interest from any currency bank deposit and yield or any other monetary benefit from deposit substitutes and from trust funds and similar arrangements. This tax is withheld at the source. However, interest income from a depository bank with a foreign currency deposit unit (FCDU) is subject to a final tax at the rate of 7.5%.

Interest income of non-residents derived from OBUs and FCDUs in the Philippines is exempt from tax.

To encourage long-term investments, interest from time deposits or investment in the form of savings, common or individual trust funds, deposit substitutes, investment management accounts and other investments with a maturity period of not less than five years is exempt from tax. However, if the investor preterminates the deposit or investment before the fifth year, a final tax is imposed on the entire income based on the length of time that the investment instrument was held by the taxpayer, as follows:

- Four years to less than five years, 5%;
- Three years to less than four years, 12%; and
- Less than three years, 20%.

Dividends from Philippine corporations

A final tax of 6% is imposed on:

- Cash or property dividends from domestic corporations or from joint stock companies, insurance or mutual fund companies and regional operating headquarters of multinational companies;
- The share of an individual in the distributable net income after tax of a partnership (except a general professional partnership); or
- The net income after tax of an association, a joint account or joint venture, or consortium taxable as a corporation of which an individual is a member of a co-venturer.

The rate of tax on dividends will be increased to 8% beginning 1 January 1999 and to 10% beginning 1 January 2000.

Prior to the passage of the Tax Reform Act, dividends received by citizens and resident aliens were taxed at a rate of 0%. Thus the rates of tax now imposed on dividends will not apply to income forming part of retained earnings as of 31 December 1997 even though it is declared or distributed on or after 1 January 1998.

Royalties

Generally, royalties are taxed at a rate of 20% unless they are from books, literary works and musical composition, in which case the tax is 10%.

Prize winnings

In general, the tax on prize winnings is 20%. However, prizes derived from the Philippine Charity Sweepstakes and Lotto winnings are exempt.

Capital gains from sale of shares of stock.

The Tax Code imposes a final tax of 5% on the net capital gain realised during the taxable year from the sale, barter, exchange or other disposition of shares of stock in a domestic corporation, when the net capital gain does not exceed 100,000 pesos and 10% on any amount greater than 100,000 pesos. These rates of tax apply to shares of stock not traded on the local stock exchange. If the stock is listed and traded on the exchange, a transaction tax of 0.5% of the gross selling price or gross value in money is imposed on the transferor or seller of the share of stock in lieu of income tax.

Fringe Benefits

A fringe benefit is any good, service or other benefit furnished or granted in cash or in kind by an employer to employees exercising supervisory or managerial functions. Fringe benefits may consist of housing; expense accounts; vehicles; household personnel, such as maids and drivers; membership fees, dues or other expenses borne by the employer for the employees in social or athletic clubs or other similar organisations; expenses for foreign travel; holiday and vacation expenses; educational assistance to the employees or their dependents; and life or health insurance and other non-life insurance premiums in excess of what special laws allow. Interest on loans at less than market rate to the extent of the difference between the market rate and the actual rate granted is also considered a fringe benefit.

The fringe benefits tax is payable by the employer, who is responsible for withholding and remitting it to the government. If the fringe benefit is required by the nature of or is necessary to the trade, business or profession of the employer, or when the fringe benefit is for the employer's convenience, the fringe-benefits tax shall not apply.

The fringe benefits tax is 34% (33% effective 1 January 1999 and 32% effective 1 January 2000) of the grossed-up monetary value of the fringe benefit furnished or granted to the employee. The grossed-up monetary value of a fringe benefit is determined by dividing the actual monetary value of the fringe benefit by 66% (67% effective 1 January 1999 and 68% effective 1 January 2000).

For example, if, in 1998, an employer pays 100,000 pesos for its executives' sports club dues, the tax of 51,515 pesos is computed as follows:

- Grossed-up monetary value: 100,000/66% equals 151,515pesos;
- Tax on the grossed-up value: 151,515 x 34% equals 51,515.

In the case of non-resident aliens not engaged in trade or business within the Philippines, the tax is 25% of the grossed-up value of the fringe benefit, which is determined by dividing the actual monetary value of the fringe benefit by 75%.

In the case of individuals employed by regional or area headquarters and regional operating headquarters of multinational companies and individuals employed by OBUs, the tax is 15% of the grossed-up benefits, which is determined by dividing the actual monetary value of the fringe benefit by 85%.

Fringe benefits that are not taxable are: those that are authorised and exempted from the tax under special laws; contributions of the employer for the benefit of the employee to retirement, insurance and hospitalisation plans; and *de minimis* benefits.

Tax on corporations

Domestic and resident foreign corporations

Persons wishing to do business in the Philippines may do so by either setting up a domestic corporation or obtaining a licence to do business from the Securities and Exchange Commission (SEC). Generally, a Philippine corporation may be wholly owned by aliens except where the constitution and special laws impose a limitation on foreign ownership.

For tax purposes, a corporation may maintain an annual accounting period based on a fiscal or a calendar year. With the approval of the BIR commissioner, a corporation may change from one accounting period to another subject to the filing of separate adjustment returns. Generally, gross income must be reported in the taxable year in which it is earned or the payment is received, and deductions in the year in which they are incurred or paid. In the case of building, installation or construction contracts covering a period of more than one year, gross income must be reported on the basis of percentage of completion, but gross deductions therefrom must be of expenses paid or incurred in the taxable year.

Foreign corporations are classified as either resident or non-resident. Resident foreign corporations are those engaged in trade or business in the Philippines and are generally taxed in the same manner as domestic corporations at a rate of 34% on their net income. These rates will be reduced to 33% effective 1 January 1999 and to 32% effective 1 January 2000.

In arriving at net income, a corporation's gross income is reduced by the deductions allowed by the Tax Code. Furthermore, gross income is equivalent to gross sales less sales returns, discounts and allowances and cost of goods sold, which includes all business expenses directly incurred to produce the merchandise and to bring them to their present location and use.

Effective 1 January 2000, the Tax Code leaves open the option for corporations to be taxed at a rate of 15% on their gross income if the president of the Philippines so allows it. If this feature of the Tax Code is implemented, the option to exercise it shall be available only to firms whose proportion of cost of sales or receipts from all sources does not exceed 55%. Furthermore, this method of tax, once elected, shall be irrevocable for three consecutive taxable years during which the taxpayer is qualified under the scheme.

Minimum Corporate Income Tax

The Tax Reform Act introduced an innovation in the way domestic and resident foreign corporations are taxed with the introduction of the Minimum Corporate Income Tax (MCIT). Beginning on the fourth taxable year from the time that the corporation commenced its business operations, a minimum corporate income tax of 2% of the gross income as of the end of the taxable year shall be imposed when the MCIT is greater than the regularly computed tax. Furthermore, any excess of the minimum corporate income tax over the normal income tax can be carried forward and credited against the normal income tax for the three immediately succeeding taxable years.

The following scenario is an example of how the MCIT works: Z company set up shop in 1998. Four years later, in 2002, Z Company had a gross income of one million pesos, but claimed deductions in the amount of 950,000 pesos. The regular corporate income tax for that year is 32%; thus Z company will be liable for 16,000 pesos on its net income of 50,000 pesos (50,000 x 32%). However, this is less than the MCIT of 20,000 pesos (2% of one million), so Z Company must pay the MCIT.

If, in 2003, Z Company again earns a million pesos, but is liable for a tax of 25,000 pesos on its taxable income (an amount larger than 2% of its gross income for that year), it can credit the 4,000-peso difference between the MCIT owed for 2002 and that year's normal income tax against the 2003 tax. However, if Z Company's MCIT is still greater than its normal income tax in 2003, it must again pay the MCIT and receives no credit from the previous year's MCIT.

Special tax rates for other resident foreign corporations

International carriers

International carriers are subject to a rate of 2.5% on their gross Philippine billings. For international air carriers, gross Philippine billings are defined as the amount of gross revenue from the carriage of persons, excess baggage and mail originating from the Philippines in a continuous and uninterrupted flight, irrespective of place of sale of ticket or passage document. Tickets which are re-validated, exchanged and/or endorsed to another international airline form part of the gross Philippine billings if the passenger boards a plane in a port or point in the Philippines. For a flight that originates from the Philippines on another airline, only the portion of the ticket corresponding to the leg flown from the Philippines to the point of trans-shipment shall form part of the gross Philippine billings.

In the case of international sea carriers, gross Philippine billings means gross revenue for passenger, cargo or mail originating from the Philippines up to final destination, regardless of the place of sale or payments of the passage or freight documents.

Regional or area headquarters

Regional or area headquarters are Philippine branches of multinational companies that act as supervisory, communications and coordinating centres for their affiliates, subsidiaries or branches in the Asia-Pacific Region and other foreign markets. Although considered as a resident, the regional or area headquarters does not engage in trade or business in the Philippines and does not earn income. They are thus tax-exempt.

On the other hand, regional operating headquarters are branches established in the Philippines by multinational companies that are engaged in any of the following services: general administration and planning, business planning and coordination; sourcing and procurement of raw materials and components, corporate finance advisory services; marketing control and sales promotion; training and personnel management; logistics services; research and development services and product development; technical support and maintenance; data processing and communication; and business development. On their net taxable income, they are required to pay a tax of 10%.

Offshore banking units (OBUs)

OBUs are subject to a final income tax at the rate of 10% of income from foreign currency transactions with local commercial banks, including branches of foreign banks that may be authorised by the Bangko Sentral ng Pilipinas (BSP) to transact business with OBUs, and interest income from foreign loans to residents.

Branch profits remittance tax

Under the Corporation Code a foreign corporation may obtain a licence to engage in business in the Philippines without having to incorporate anew. The resultant entity, called a branch, is an extension of the foreign corporation and does not constitute a separate entity. Being resident, the branch is subject to the corporate income tax on its income from Philippine sources. Furthermore, under a two-tiered system of taxation, any profits remitted by a branch to its head office shall be subject to a tax of 15%, based on the total profits applied or earmarked for remittance without any deductions for the tax component. Casual gains and profits, capital gains and all manner of passive income received from sources within the Philippines are not considered as branch profits unless they are effectively connected with the conduct of the enterprise's trade or business in the Philippines.

Improperly accumulated earnings tax

Philippine corporation law prohibits a corporation from retaining surplus profits greater than 100% of its paid-in capital, except in the following instances:

- The retention of such profits is justified by corporate expansion projects;
- The corporation is prohibited under a loan agreement from declaring dividends without the consent of its creditors; or
- Other special circumstances, such as when there is need for a special reserve for probable contingencies.

Otherwise, such retained earnings are considered to be improper when permitted to accumulate beyond the reasonably anticipated needs of the business.

The Tax Code imposes a tax of 10% on the improperly accumulated earnings of a corporation except in the case of publicly held corporations, banks and other non-bank financial intermediaries, and insurance companies. For the purpose of the tax, a rebuttable presumption exists that a holding company or investment company is set up to avoid a tax on its shareholders or members.

Tax on passive income

Interest and royalties

Generally, a final tax of 20%, which is withheld at the source, is imposed on royalties derived from Philippine sources and on interest from any currency bank deposit and yield or any other monetary benefit from deposit substitutes and from trust funds and similar arrangements. However, interest income of domestic and resident foreign corporations from a depository bank under the foreign currency deposit system is subject to a final tax at the rate of 7.5%. In the case of a depository bank, any income derived by it under the expanded foreign currency deposit system from foreign currency transactions with local commercial banks and other entities authorised by the Bangko Sentra ng Pilipinas is subject to a rate of 10%.

Dividends from a Philippine corporation

Dividends received by domestic and resident foreign corporations from another domestic corporation are exempt from the dividend tax.

Capital gains

Sale of shares of stock

The Tax Code imposes a final tax of 5% on the net capital gain realised during the taxable year from the sale, barter, exchange or other disposition of shares of stock in a domestic corporation when the net capital gain does not exceed 100,000 pesos and 10% on any amount greater than 100,000 pesos. These rates of tax apply to shares of stock not traded on the local stock exchange. If the stock is listed and traded on the exchange, a transaction tax of 0.5% of the gross selling price on gross value in money is imposed on the transferor or seller of the share of stock.

Sale or disposition of land or buildings

A final tax of 6% is imposed on the gain from the sale or disposition of lands or buildings that are treated as capital assets. This is based on the property's fair market value or on the fair market value of the property as indicated by schedules maintained by provincial or city assessors, whichever is higher.

Non-resident foreign corporations

Generally, a foreign corporation not engaged in business in the Philippines is liable for a tax of 34% of the gross income received from Philippine sources. Effective 1 January 1999, the rate will be reduced to 33% and on 1 January 2000 to 32%.

On other types of income, non-resident foreign corporations are taxed at different rates. On foreign loans the rate is 20%. On cash or property dividends received from a domestic corporation, the tax rate is 15% provided that the corporation's country of domicile shall allow a credit against the tax due from the corporation taxes deemed to have been paid in the Philippines equivalent to 19% for 1998, 18% for 1999 and 17% thereafter. This represents the difference between the regular income tax of 34% in 1998, 33% in 1999 and 32% thereafter.

Deductions from gross income

Subject to the qualifications set by the Tax Code, domestic corporations, resident foreign corporations and resident aliens engaged in trade or business or in the exercise of profession are allowed to deduct a number of business-related items.

Ordinary and necessary trade, business or professional expenses

There are reasonable allowances for the following ordinary expenses, which must be related to the taxpayer's trade, business or profession and which must be substantiated with sufficient evidence, such as official receipts or other adequate records:

- Salaries, wages and other compensation for personal services actually rendered, including the grossed-up monetary value or any fringe benefits granted by the employer to the employee, provided that the employer has paid the fringe benefits tax;
- Domestic and foreign travel expenses;
- Rental or lease expense; and
- Entertainment, amusement and recreation expenses subject to ceilings which the Tax Reform Act has allowed the secretary of finance to fix.

Interest

Interest expenses paid or incurred during the taxable year provided that the allowable deduction is reduced by an amount equal to the following percentages on the interest income subjected to final tax: 41% beginning 1 January 1998; 39% beginning 1 January 1999; and 38% beginning 1 January 2000.

However, deduction of interest expense is not allowed in the following cases:

- If an individual taxpayer reporting income on a cash basis who incurs indebtedness wherein interest is paid in advance through discount or otherwise. In this case, deduction shall be allowed only in the year the indebtedness is paid. If the indebtedness is payable in periodic amortisations, the amount of interest which corresponds to the amount of the principal amortised or paid during the year shall be allowed as a deduction in that taxable year.
- If the taxpayer and the person to whom the payment has been made or is to be made are related.
- If the indebtedness is incurred to finance petroleum exploration.

Furthermore, at the option of the taxpayer, interest incurred to acquire property used in trade, business or practise of a profession may be allowed as a deduction or be treated as a capital expenditure.

Taxes

On taxes paid to a foreign country, the Tax Code allows domestic corporations either to credit the amount of taxes paid or incurred during the taxable year to any foreign country against the Philippine tax due or to treat such taxes paid to a foreign country as a deduction.

Alien individuals and foreign corporations are not allowed to credit taxes paid to a foreign country against their Philippine taxes.

Losses

Ordinary Losses

Losses actually sustained during the taxable year that have not been compensated for by insurance or otherwise are allowed as deductions if incurred in trade or business. Losses can also be treated as deductions if property lost due to *force majeure* is connected with the taxpayer's trade, business or profession. In the case of individuals, a loss that has been claimed as a deduction for estate tax purposes cannot be claimed for income tax purposes.

The Tax Reform Act introduced the concept of the net-operating-loss carryover to benefit enterprises whose allowable deductions for a taxable year exceed their gross income. The net operating loss of the business or enterprise for any taxable year immediately preceding the current taxable year that had not been previously offset as a deduction from gross income may be carried over as a deduction from gross income for the next three consecutive taxable years. However, no carryover is allowed if a net loss was incurred in a year for which the taxpayer was exempt from income tax.

If the business is in the name of a corporation, the net-operating-loss carryover may not be applied unless there has been no substantial change in the ownership of the enterprise such that either no less than 75% in nominal value of outstanding issued shares is held by or on behalf of the same persons or no less than 75% of the paid-up capital of the corporation is held by or on behalf of the same persons.

There are special rules for applying the net-operating-loss carryover for mines other than oil or gas wells.

Capital losses

Losses from sales or exchanges of capital assets are allowed only to the extent of the gains from such sales or exchanges.

Bad debts

Debts due to a taxpayer that are actually ascertained to be worthless and charged off within the taxable year may be taken as a deduction if they are connected with a profession, trade or business and they are not entered into between related parties. However, the recovery of bad debts previously allowed as a deduction in any preceding year can be included as part of gross income in the year of recovery to the extent of the income tax benefit of the deduction.

Depreciation

According to the Tax Code, a 'reasonable allowance' may deducted from gross income for obsolescence of property used in trade or business using the straight-line, double-declining balance, or sum-of-the-years-digit methods, or any other method approved by the Commissioner of Internal Revenue. A change in the depreciation method requires the commissioner's prior approval. In the case of resident foreign corporations and non-resident aliens engaged in trade or business, depreciation of property is allowed only when it is located in the Philippines. Special rules exist for depletion of oil and gas wells and mines.

Charitable and other contributions

Contributions or gifts actually made to the Philippine Government for public purposes or to certain religious, charitable, scientific, youth development, cultural or educational associations may be deducted from gross income. The amount may not exceed 10% in the case of an individual, or 5% in the case of a corporation, of the taxable income derived from trade, business or profession as computed before the deduction is made. However, certain contributions (as when the recipient charitable or educational organisation conforms to approved criteria established by regulations) may be deductible in full.

Research and development expenses

Generally, research and development expenses that have not been charged to a capital account may be allowed as deductions during the taxable year in which the expense was paid or incurred.

However, the taxpayer may choose to treat research and development expenses as deferred expenses if they are chargeable to a capital account but not chargeable to property that is subject to depreciation or depletion. If treated as deferred expenses, the deductions must be ratably distributed over a period elected by the taxpayer of no less than 60 months (beginning with the month in which the taxpayer first realises benefits from such expenditures).

Optional standard deduction

In lieu of all the deductions allowed by the Tax Code, resident alien individuals who do not earn purely compensation income may elect a standard deduction in an amount not exceeding 10% of their gross income. The optional standard deduction does not include the personal exemptions allowed to individuals. Non-resident aliens may not use the optional standard deduction.

Declaration and payment of the income tax

Except for non-resident aliens not engaged in trade or business in the Philippines, all individuals must file an income tax return and pay the income tax covering income for the preceding taxable year on or before 15 April of each year. Employers are required to deduct and withhold the tax on compensation income. An election may be made to pay the tax in two equal instalments, in which case the first instalment must be paid at the time the return is filed and the second instalment on or before 15 July following the close of the taxable year.

Individuals who receive self-employment income, whether this constitutes the sole source of income or is in combination with salaries, must make and file a declaration of their estimated income for the current taxable year on or before 15 April of the same taxable year. The estimated tax is the amount the individuals declared as income tax in their final adjusted and annual income tax return for the preceding taxable year minus the sum of the credits allowed by the Tax Code against the income tax. The estimated tax must be paid in four instalments, with the first instalment due at the time of the declaration and the second and third instalments due on 15 August and 15 November of the current year, respectively. The fourth instalment must be paid on or before 15 April of the following calendar year upon the filing of the final adjusted income tax return.

Corporations must file a quarterly summary declaration of gross income and deductions on a cumulative basis for the preceding quarters upon which the income tax is paid. The computed tax is decreased by the amount of tax paid or assessed during the preceding quarters and must be paid no later than 60 days from the close of each of the first three quarters of the taxable (calendar or fiscal) year. The income tax due per quarter must be paid when the quarterly return is filed. As with self-employed individuals, corporations must file a final adjustment return.

If the sum of the estimated quarterly income tax payments made by a corporation exceeds the total tax due for the year, the corporation may carry over the excess amount and credit it against the estimated quarterly income tax liabilities for the succeeding taxable years. Alternatively, the corporation may apply for a tax refund or tax credit certificate for the excess amount.

VALUE-ADDED TAX (VAT)

A value-added tax is imposed on any entity that sells, barters, exchanges, or leases goods or properties or renders services in the course of trade or business. 'In the course of trade or business' means the regular conduct or pursuit of a commercial or economic activity by any entity, whether or not the entity engaged in that activity is a non-stock, non-profit private organisation. The importation of goods is also subject to VAT, whether or not the importation is in the course of trade or business.

The VAT is equivalent to 10% of the gross selling price or gross value in money of the goods or properties sold, bartered or exchanged. Any excise tax on the goods is also part of the gross selling price. In the case of imported goods, the VAT is based on the total value of the goods as determined by the Bureau of Customs plus customs duties, excise taxes and all other incidental charges. Where the customs duties are determined on the basis of the quantity or volume of goods, the VAT is based on the landed cost plus excise taxes, if there are any. With respect to sales or exchanges of services, including the use or lease of properties, the VAT is based on the gross receipts from those sales or leases.

Generally, the term 'goods or properties' includes all tangible and intangible objects for which there can be an equivalent monetary value, such as:

- Real properties held primarily for sale to customers or held for lease in the ordinary course of trade or business;
- The right or privilege to use a patent, copyright design, model plan, secret formula or process, goodwill, trademark, trade brand or other property or right;
- The right or privilege to use in the Philippines any industrial, commercial or scientific equipment;
- The right or privilege to use motion picture films, tapes and discs; and radio, television, satellite transmission and cable television time.

The VAT is an indirect tax in that, while the obligation to collect and remit the tax rests with the seller of goods or services, the cost of the tax may be passed on to the buyer, transferee or lessee of goods, properties or services.

A VAT-registered entity may credit the VAT paid on purchases of other goods and services against the tax on its sales of goods or services. For example, if Y Company, a VAT-registered entity, sells one million pesos worth of razor blades, it is liable for VAT in the amount of 100,000 pesos. However, if Y Company paid VAT of 90,000 pesos on the purchase of steel and importation of machinery, it may credit that amount (called an 'input tax') against the VAT it collected from the sales of razor blades (i.e., the 100,000 pesos, which is called an 'output tax'). Thus, Y Company must remit VAT of 10,000 pesos (100,000 minus 90,000).

If the amount of input tax is greater than the amount of output tax, the excess may be credited against succeeding output VAT or, upon approval of the Commissioner of Internal Revenue, may be claimed as a refund or credited against other company internal revenue taxes.

Certain transactions of VAT-registered entities are subject to a rate of zero, in which case that entity may claim the amount of VAT paid on the purchase of goods or services as a refund or credit against other internal revenue taxes. Zero-rated transactions include:

- Export sales; foreign-currency-denominated sales to a non-resident of goods (except automobiles and non-essential goods) assembled or manufactured in the Philippines for delivery to a Philippine resident;
- Sales of goods or services to entities that have exemptions under special laws or international agreements to which the Philippines is

a signatory (e.g., embassies, diplomatic personnel, United Nations organisations, etc.);

- Processing, manufacturing or repacking of goods for other persons doing business outside of the Philippines;
- services rendered to vessels engaged exclusively in international shipping; and
- Services performed by subcontractors or contractors in processing, manufacturing or converting goods for an enterprise for which export sales exceed 70% of total annual production.

The Tax Code exempts from VAT certain transactions such as the sale of services subject to percentage tax, services rendered by individuals pursuant to an employer–employee relationship, and export sales by persons who are not VAT-registered.

The difference between a zero-rated transaction and an exempt transaction is that, while the former is subject to VAT (albeit at a rate of zero), the latter is not. A zero-rated seller of goods or services is entitled to a refund or tax credit of the input tax paid on the purchase of goods and services. On the other hand, in an exempt transaction, the seller cannot bill any output tax to his customers because the transaction is not subject to VAT. Consequently, the seller is not entitled to a refund or credit of the input tax paid on the purchase of goods and services. Likewise, the VAT-registered purchaser of goods or services that are VAT-exempt is not entitled to a refund or credit of the input tax paid on the purchase of goods and services, in which case the VAT becomes an added cost of operations.

VAT-registered entities are required to issue an invoice or receipt for every sale and, in addition to the regular accounting records required, must maintain subsidiary sales and purchase journals in which daily sales and purchases are recorded.

Entities that are liable for VAT must file a quarterly return of the amount of gross sales or receipts within 25 days following the taxable quarter prescribed for each taxpayer. However, the VAT must be paid on a monthly basis.

PERCENTAGE TAXES

Percentage taxes at varying rates are imposed on:

- Certain entities exempt from VAT;
- Domestic carriers and keepers of garages;
- International carriers and government-granted franchises;
- Overseas communications originating from the Philippines;

- Gross receipts of banks and other non-bank financial intermediaries and finance companies;
- Life insurance premiums;
- Agents of foreign insurance companies;
- Amusement taxes; and
- Sale or exchange of shares of stock listed and traded through the local stock exchange or sold through initial public offering.

EXCISE TAX

Generally, goods manufactured or produced in the Philippines for domestic sales or consumption and goods that are imported into the Philippines are subject to an excise tax. Excise taxes may be based on weight or volume capacity or on any other physical unit of measurement (i.e., specific tax) or on the selling price or other specified value of the goods (*ad valorem*).

DOCUMENTARY STAMP TAX

Generally, the Tax Code imposes a documentary stamp tax on documents, instruments, loan agreements and papers and upon acceptances assignments, sales and transfers of the obligation, right or property incident thereto. This must be collected and paid for by the person making, signing, issuing, accepting or transferring the same wherever the document is made, signed, issued, accepted or transferred when the obligation or right arises from Philippine sources and the property is situated in the Philippines at the same time the act is done or the transaction had.

An instrument, document or paper that is required by law to be stamped cannot not be recorded unless it has been stamped. Nor can it be used as evidence in any court until the stamp tax has been paid and the stamp affixed on the document and cancelled. Likewise, notary publics and other officers authorised to administer oaths cannot certify any document subject to the stamp tax unless the proper documentary stamps are affixed thereto and cancelled.

ESTATE AND DONOR'S TAXES

The Tax Code imposes on a decedent's heirs a tax on the net estate at rates ranging from zero to 20%. In the case of citizens and resident aliens, the gross estate includes the value of all property, real or personal, tangible or intangible, situated in the Philippines or abroad, while the net estate refers to the remaining value after deduction of certain expenses and obligations incurred in settling the estate.

A schedule of rates ranging from zero to 15% is imposed on net gifts made during the taxable year. However, the rate is 30% if the gift is made to a stranger.

REMEDIES

As a rule, internal revenue taxes must be assessed by the Bureau of Internal Revenue within three years after the last day prescribed by law for filing of the return. Where a return is filed after the period prescribed by law, the three-year period is counted from the day the return was filed. However, in the case of a false or fraudulent return with intent to evade a tax or of failure to file a return, the Tax Code allows the Bureau 10 years from the time of the discovery of the fraud, falsity or omission to assess the tax or file a proceeding in court without assessment. An internal revenue tax that has been assessed within the 10-year period may be collected by distraint or levy or by a court proceeding within five years after its assessment.

The three-year period within which the Bureau may conduct an assessment may also be extended by written agreement between the Bureau and the taxpayer before the period expires. The extended period may be extended again by subsequent written agreement before the expiration of the period previously agreed upon. Any internal revenue tax which has been assessed within the extended period may be collected by distraint or levy or by a court proceeding within five years following the assessment of the tax.

The running of the three- or 10-year statute of limitations on making the assessment may be suspended for:

- The period when the commissioner is prohibited from making the assessment or beginning distraint or levy or a proceeding in court and for 60 days thereafter;
- When a reinvestigation requested by the taxpayer is granted by the commissioner; or
- When the taxpayer cannot be located at the address given in the return filed upon which a tax is being assessed or collected.

A taxpayer may protest an assessment by filing a request for reconsideration or reinvestigation within 30 days from receipt of the assessment. Within 60 days from the filing of the protest, the taxpayer must submit all relevant documents; otherwise the assessment becomes final. If the protest is denied in whole or in part, or is not acted upon within 180 days from the submission of documents, the taxpayer adversely affected by the decision or inaction may appeal to the Court of Tax Appeals. This must be done within 30 days of the receipt of the decision or of the lapse of the 180-day period; otherwise the decision becomes final and executory. Decisions of the Court of Tax Appeals may be appealed by either the taxpayer or the commissioner to the Court of Appeals and, hence, to the Philippine Supreme Court.

The Commissioner may collect delinquent taxes either by distraint of personal property or levy on real property or by filing a civil or criminal action. These courses of action may be pursued simultaneously.

CHAPTER 7

ENVIRONMENTAL LEGISLATION

Raul de Guzman

The Philippines, considered a tiger economy in ASEAN countries, is facing growing demands for extraction and use of its natural resources. This means degradation of the natural environment is becoming more evident as development accelerates, and that further deterioration is inevitable without vigorous decisions to plan for, monitor and regulate the environment. Hence, legislation and regulations should be followed strictly by the decision-makers in both private and public business sectors.

The Philippines has no lack of legislation and provisions with regard to the environment. But environmental research as well as debates and revisions on pending bills in both houses of the Congress are concurrent with the implementation of development projects. In spite of the government's efforts to come up with a sound environmental program, industrialisation, technological development and the consequent depletion and exhaustion of natural resources are progressively threatening the country's resource base and life-support system.

Interdisciplinary research and development now is encouraged in any environment-related development project. That is why environmental law may be defined, according to Amado Tolentino Jr, formerly with the Department of Environment and Natural Resources, as 'a set of legal rules addressed specifically to activities that have the power to affect the quality of the environment, whether natural or man-made'. Environmental law involves various natural and social sciences, technologies ranging from technical-engineering ones to policy research and development, resource management and public administration, as well as the principles and techniques of law.

In 1977, the Philippines initiated Presidential Decree 1151, otherwise known as the Philippine Environmental Policy (PEP), subsequently followed by Philippine Environmental Code (PEC), which laid down the basic environmental policies of the government. Its mandate is to:

- Create, develop, maintain and improve conditions under which man and nature can thrive in productive and enjoyable harmony with each other;
- Fulfil the social, economic and other requirements of present and future generations; and
- Ensure the attainment of an environmental quality that is conducive to a life of dignity and well-being.

The PEC seeks to establish management practices and quality standards for such environmental areas as air emissions, waste discharge, land-use management, waste management and natural- resource management.

Subsequent laws and regulations covering those areas have been enacted. The Pollution Control Law (1976, regulations 1978, revised 1993) seeks to prevent and control pollution of water, air and land. The Environmental Impact Statement (EIS) System (1978, subsequent regulations and amendments, 1984, 1992), seeks public and private projects that significantly affect the quality of the environment. The Water Quality Management Regulations (1978, revised 1990) includes provisions for water management within the environmental code standards. The Effluent Regulations (1982, revised 1990) establishes measures for effluent control. The Toxic Substances and Hazardous and Nuclear Waste Act (1990) restricts, regulates, and prohibits the importation, manufacture, processing, sale, distribution and disposal of chemical substances and mixtures that present unreasonable risk and/or injury to health or the environment. It also prohibits the entry and transit of nuclear and hazardous wastes for whatever purpose. The National Integrated Protected Areas System Act

(NIPAS Act, 1992) provides for the establishment and management of a national integrated protected areas system and defines its scope and coverage. The Special Economic Zone Act (1995) provides the legal framework and mechanism for the creation, operation, administration and coordination of special economic zones, creating for this purpose the Philippine Economic Zone Authority (PEZA). The Mining Act (1995) provides incentives to investors engaging in exploration, development and utilisation of mineral resources and allows 100% foreign-owned companies to operate.

ENVIRONMENTAL IMPACT STATEMENT SYSTEM

Among the laws and regulations, the EIS system is the most controversial because it involves a lot of social and bio-physical assessment of the developmental projects. EIS mandates that all government agencies, government-owned or controlled corporations and private companies prepare an environmental impact assessment for any project or activity that affects the quality of the environment. These are to be conducted in accordance with the Philippine EIS System Guide: Policies and Procedures, 1994. An environmental impact assessment is required to obtain an environmental compliance certificate (ECC), which is issued by the president of the Philippines or his duly authorised representative certifying that the project under consideration will not bring about an unacceptable environmental impact and the proponent has complied with the requirements of the EIS system.

Securing an ECC

An ECC should be secured for most development projects at the conceptualisation stage. Various government agencies also require an ECC before they issue project-related permits and approvals. Accordingly, the Department of Environment and Natural Resources (DENR) has stated that securing an ECC is the most critical step in developmental projects. DENR has delineated the ECC requirements for 'environmentally critical projects' and for 'environmentally criteria areas'. The EIS system involves six steps: scoping, environmental impact assessment, report preparation and submission, additional information requirements, EIS evaluation and a public hearing.

Scoping is the initial stage in preparing an EIS in which the information and assessment requirements are established to provide the proponents with the scope of the work. It is the most critical step in EIS preparation since it is the stage where the key actors—the proponent, environmental impact assessment preparer, Environmental Management Bureau (EMB), DENR regional office, the community and provisional environmental resources officers, local government units (LGUs) and other non-governmental agencies, Environmental Impact Assessment Review Committee and stakeholders—discuss and clarify the scope of the project. Scoping is done by invitation and is not open to the public. Scoping sessions can take the form of community meetings, technical meetings and public meetings.

Public participation and social acceptability are considered to be the most controversial part of environmental impact assessment preparation. That is where the battles over ideology take place. Extensive studies, public education and information dissemination are carried out, especially for immense projects like dams and power plants. The public, more often than not, reacts emotionally; others politicise, and numerous academic differences occur over the social acceptability of development projects.

EIS preparation and submission follows scoping. The proponent needs to submit an EIS that conforms to the agreement made in the scoping report. The proponent can hire an EIS preparer or use its own technical staff provided they are EMB-accredited as required by Department Administrative Order 37 (DAO 37). Procedures on the preparation of the environmental impact assessment can be found in the DENR's procedural manual for DAO 96-37, initial version of 1997.

Once the EIS has been prepared and submitted, a review process is initiated by the EMB. This is where the decision to grant or deny the ECC takes place. EMB convenes the Environmental Impact Assessment Review Committee within 15 days from the date of submission of the documents.

BUSINESSES/PROJECTS UNDER THE EIS SYSTEM

Kalakalan 20 Projects

The Kalakalan 20 Projects are business enterprises established through Republic Act 6810 in the countryside and in the *barangay* or *barrios*, the lowest unit of governance. They must meet the following criteria:

- They are not located in the four cities and 13 municipalities of Metro Manila or other highly urbanised cities;
- They are business entities, associations or cooperatives engaged in producing, processing or manufacturing products, commodities or other productive services;
- They have total assets of 500,000 pesos or less at the time of registration; and
- They are not existing businesses that have collapsed and/or been transferred from an ineligible area to an eligible area.

Kalakalan 20 Projects may receive an exemption from the EIS systems if they are non-polluting or the wastes they produce are manageable.

Environmentally critical areas (ECAs)

The definition of environmentally critical areas is provided in Presidential Decree 1586, which authorises the president to declare projects that are critical. Proclamation 2146 technically defined critical projects to be:

- All areas declared by law as national parks, watershed reserves, wildlife preserves and sanctuaries (NIPAS Act);
- Areas set aside as aesthetic potential tourist spots;
- Areas that constitute the habitat of an endangered or threatened species of indigenous Philippine wildlife, whether flora or fauna;
- Areas of unique historic, archaeological or scientific interest;
- Areas that are traditionally occupied by cultural communities or tribes (indigenous cultural communities);
- Areas that are frequently visited and/or hard-hit by natural calamities (geological hazards, floods, typhoons, volcanic activity);
- Areas with critical slopes;
- Areas classified as prime agricultural lands;
- Recharged areas or aquifers;
- Bodies of water;
- Mangrove areas; and
- Coral reefs.

Environmentally critical projects

Environmentally critical projects are defined as any of the following project types, whether they are new or an expansion in production (output) or physical area:

- Heavy industries (i.e., non-ferrous metal industries, iron and steel mills, petroleum and petrochemical industries, smelting plants);
- Resource extractive industries (i.e., large-scale mining and quarrying projects, forestry projects, dykes and/or fish-pond development projects);
- Infrastructure projects (i.e., major dams, power plants, reclamation projects, roads and bridges); and
- Golf courses.

EIS-EXEMPT PROJECTS

Projects are exempted from the EIS system if they are:

- Environmentally critical projects that began operation before 1982, except where their operations are expanded in production or output or entail new construction and/or new facilities; or
- Projects not located in environmentally critical areas that are considered non-polluting, have a capitalisation of less than 500,000 pesos, and employ no more than 20 persons.

ENVIRONMENTAL LEGISLATION VIOLATIONS AND PENALTIES

There are three types of enforceable violations in the EIS system: environmentally critical projects that are operating without an ECC or ECC exemption, projects within an environmentally critical area that are operating without an ECC and projects violating ECC conditions.

The EMB, DENR regional offices and LGUs have the authority to impose a fine, require corrective action, or both for projects found in violation of the EIS system. A fine not exceeding 50,000 pesos is imposed for a single violation. Repeated violations result in the issuance of a cancellation/suspension order and/or revocation of the ECC. However, the proponent has the right to submit motions for reconsideration.

ROLE OF THE LEADING AGENCIES

The Department of Environment and Natural Resources (DENR) is the primary government agency responsible for environment protection. The board has considerable power, enabling it to issue mandatory requirements for immediate compliance with environmental laws and immediate halt to pollution-causing activities. It also issues and renews permits for the prevention and abatement of pollution-causing activities.

The Environmental Management Bureau (EMB) is the leading government agency responsible for reviewing the completeness of an EIS based on the procedural checklist of DAO 37.

Under the New Local Government Code of 1990, the provincial government or LGUs are now responsible for processing ECCs for Kalakalan 20 Projects.

The Laguna Lake Development Authority is the leading agency for the promotion and acceleration of development and balanced growth in the Laguna de Bay basin. It issues permits to construct, operate and expand, which are included in the documents to be attached upon submission of an EIS. These are for the manufacturing plants situated around the Laguna de Bay basin and include those in portions of Manila, Quezon City, Pasay, Taguig, Pateros, Marikina, Caloocan City and Muntinlupa.

PENDING LEGISLATIVE WATCHLIST

The following environmental laws are pending in the Congress: a proposed national environmental management authority, a new environmental and land-use code and a revised forestry and fisheries code.

THE OUTLOOK

Philippine environmental concerns, just like global environmental concerns, vary in magnitude, nature, involvement, and concept. While development is ongoing in both country and urban areas, research and development on the effectiveness of legislation should be taken seriously. Several factors affect the development and implementation of the environmental legislation, including the demands of the international market, the competitiveness of quality Philippine products, the availability of such resources as space and natural resources, and the country's ability to cope economically with El Niño and other natural disasters.

At the moment, it is hard to gauge the effectiveness of environmental legislation since many people are involved in implementing developmental projects. Ideally, environmental laws would be proven effective only if developmental projects have no adverse effect on the environment. But opinions differ and many will claim to be experts. Business and industry will have their own definition of development, while fishing and other grassroots communities will have theirs. Now is the time to pay more than lip service to the importance of environmental research and streamlining a concept of development, as well as to conduct research on the effectiveness of Philippine environmental legislation.

CHAPTER 8

DEREGULATION IN JEOPARDY

Peter Wallace

In early 1998, the Philippine Congress enacted a new oil deregulation bill after the Philippine Supreme Court struck down the earlier law, and President Fidel Ramos signed an executive order fully deregulating the oil industry. Congressman Enrique Garcia, who had battled against the previous version, challenged the new law as well. He argued that the law favoured the major oil companies and was contrary to the constitutional prohibition against monopolies and oligopolies. While awaiting a lengthy court process on the new law, Mr. Wallace offered this analysis of the debate surrounding the court decision on the original version—and its significance in terms of doing business in the Philippines. Venvenuto Icamina and Arturo Fidelino of the Economist Intelligence Unit Philippines provided research material for this analysis.

The Philippine Supreme Court's November 1997 decision to declare the law deregulating the oil industry unconstitutional was a very serious setback for the Ramos administration's reform program. The decision's adverse impact on investments and its wide-ranging economic ramifications risked aggravating the expected economic slowdown in 1998 arising from the significant depreciation of the peso and the rise in domestic interest rates. With investors already nervous about Asia, it couldn't have come at a worse time. The continuity of economic policies is now at risk with the threat of a reversal of economic reforms coming from a Supreme Court that is now also interpreting economic policy.

Voting 9 to 2, the court ruled that Republic Act 8180, which provided for the full deregulation of the oil industry, violated the constitutional provision which states that 'the State shall regulate or prohibit monopolies when the public interest so requires' and that 'no combination in restraint of trade or unfair competition shall be allowed'. The court specifically cited as 'substantial barriers to the entry and exit of new players' in the oil industry three provisions of the law which:

- Set a four-percentage point tariff differential between imported crude oil and imported refined petroleum products, i.e., a 3% tariff on crude oil and a 7% tariff on refined petroleum products;
- Requires both refiners and importers of petroleum products to maintain a minimum inventory equivalent to 10% of their annual sales or 40 days of supply, whichever is lower; and
- Prohibits 'predatory pricing' defined in the law as 'selling or offering to sell any product at a price unreasonably below the industry average cost so as to attract customers to the detriment of competitors'.

Briefly, these provisions were intended by Congress to achieve certain policy objectives:

- First, the tariff differential was intended to encourage investments in domestic refineries and avoid a situation in which the country would end up being too dependent on imported finished petroleum products. Without the differential no one will produce locally, as they can buy from more efficient producers overseas without the high cost of investment.
- Second, the inventory requirement was aimed at ensuring security of supply and discouraging the entry of fly-by-night importers. This may go against truly free trade, but it is a sensible precaution to protect consumers.
- Third, the ban on predatory pricing was designed precisely to prevent the three existing major oil companies from engaging in price-

cutting to prevent the entry of new players. This is of doubtful benefit and could have been scrapped without negating the whole law.

The court swept aside the weight of these policy considerations by asserting that the tariff differential 'works to the immense benefit' of Petron, Shell and Caltex since importers 'will suffer the huge disadvantage of increasing their product cost by only 4%'; that the inventory requirement 'will entail a prohibitive cost' to prospective investors; and that the 'predatory pricing on the part of the dominant oil companies is encouraged by the provisions of the law blocking the entry of new players'.

The court's finding on the three points was a clear case of the judiciary substituting its own policy judgement for that of the Congress. Without conceding that the provisions tended to favour Petron, Shell and Caltex, the court still had no right to interfere. The separation of powers is clear in the constitution, and the court should have recognised that these policy decisions are the prerogative of Congress. In this case, the policy considerations involved balancing the twin objectives of encouraging competition from imports and ensuring the security of domestic supply.

Additionally, the Congress can be presumed to be as equally concerned about the poor as the court professes to be, and it is the judgement of Congress of what is best for the poor that should dominate. Without a clear showing that the provisions promote oligopolistic behaviour per se, the court should have respected the policy decisions as a matter that is not within the competence of the judiciary to determine.

If the law imposed impossible conditions that left no doubt that the intention was to keep out new players, then the court would be right in ruling that the law violates the constitutional proscription on monopolies and restraint of grade. It could, for instance, have imposed a tariff rate of 80% on imported finished petroleum products as is done presently with sugar, or an inventory requirement of one year's supply applicable only to new players, or even a provision prohibiting new players from setting prices lower than those of existing players. As it was, it imposed its own judgement on the issues and, in doing so, failed to understand the nuances of business.

In a pure open economy, those restrictions should not apply. But the Philippines is in transition to that stage, and it is general government policy to provide some interim protection (until 2004) to encourage domestic production.

Most disturbing was the kind of reasoning that went into the court's findings. The way the court explained its position on predatory pricing was confusing, to say the least. In the petition filed by Congressman Enrique Garcia et al., it was argued that the prohibition on predatory pricing works to the disadvantage of new players. As newcomers, they may be expected to 'lower prices, even to the extent of selling at a loss in the initial stages, to gain a foothold in the market and increase their market share, a situation that would be beneficial to the Filipino people'. Stated another way, Mr. Garcia and company argued that the prohibition would prevent new players from undercutting Petron, Shell and Caltex. In responding to the charge, the Department of Energy (DOE) contended that, on the contrary, the prohibition was designed to stop the three companies from undercutting new entrants, thereby detering them from entering.

Yet in expressing agreement with Mr. Garcia's contention that the prohibition on predatory pricing was 'anti-competitive', the court noted that 'considering these significant barriers...and the lack of players with the comparable clout of Petron, Shell and Caltex, the temptation for a dominant player to engage in predatory pricing and succeed is a chilling reality'. A closer reading of the court's reasoning would show that it actually ruled in favour of Mr. Garcia's contention on the basis of DOE's counter-argument. Expressing apprehension that the three majors could engage in predatory pricing to kill the competition, the court proceeded to strike down the prohibition against predatory pricing as unconstitutional. This is an impossible logic to follow. And it is not a 'chilling reality'. It hasn't happened.

Faced with the solicitor general's submission that the law has in fact resulted in 30 new entrants to the industry, of which eight had already started operations at the time of writing and the rest are scheduled to operate by 2000, the court argued that 'not one (among the entrants) belongs to the class and category of Petron, Shell and Caltex' and that 'in any event, it cannot be gainsaid that the new players could have been more in number and more impressive in might if the illegal entry barriers in Republic Act 8180 were not erected'.

One difficulty with the court's contention is that it didn't state exactly how many players it would take for it to conclude that entry requirements are not deterring entry. 35? 40? 50? 100 new entrants? In a small domestic market like the Philippines? Thailand, where the industry is deregulated, has 19 participants. Thirty would seem more than a reasonable number, and that in a short seven months. In addition, one is kept guessing as to what it would take for the court to consider a new entrant as being in the 'class and category' of the three major oil companies. One suspects that Total Petroleum, Getty, Mobile and the Petroleum Authority of Thailand might well be insulted by this assertion.

Apparently unaware that it is practically contradicting its stand against a 4% tariff differential, the court supported its belittlement of the new entrants by noting that 'indeed there is no showing that any of these new players intends to install any refinery and effectively compete with these dominant oil companies'. It apparently didn't occur to the court that the low 4% tariff protection was most likely one of the factors to have discouraged potential investors from planning to put up a domestic refinery. If there is no differential, there will certainly be no encouragement. Nor did it occur to the courts that sensible business practice would be to test the market first, before expending over a billion dollars on a refinery. As far as we can determine, it didn't actually ask these 30 entrants what their intention was. It substituted its guesses for fact.

This is, in fact, one of the most disturbing points about the decision. It was made in a matter of a few days, with almost no hearings, no call for expert witnesses, no research of the implications of any proposed decision on a matter even the court agreed was of supreme national importance.

So, what the court's conclusions amount to at most are their subjective, even speculative, findings over those of Congress and the executive department. As dissenting Associate Justice Jose Francisco correctly observed in arguing against the court's finding on the minimum inventory requirement (i.e., that the requirement exacts a 'prohibitive cost' on new entrants), 'Whether or not the requirement is advantageous, disadvantageous or conducive for new oil companies hinges on presumptions and speculations which is [sic] not within the realm of judicial adjudication.' Disputing the court's conclusion on predatory pricing, Mr. Francisco argued that 'in the absence of any concrete proof or evidence, the assertion that it will not be the new oil companies which will lower oil prices remains a mere guess or suspicion'.

OIL INDUSTRY INVESTMENTS

As to the 4% tariff differential that the Supreme Court rejected, this was meant to provide incentives for new investors to put up refining facilities in the country. Compared with other industries, it is a very small margin and the oil deregulation law mandated it to be further narrowed until a uniform rate was reached in four years. With the differential, a balance hopefully would be achieved between import of finished products and new investments in oil refineries that the country sorely needs. This would tend to create a downward pressure on prices in case local manufacturers overprice while new players were still in the process of putting up their facilities.

There is absolutely no incentive for a firm to spend a billion dollars or so on a refinery in the Philippines if they can just import at equal or lower cost from existing refineries overseas. In fact, one major new player had already decided to import and distribute refined products because the 4% differential doesn't provide enough cushion for a needed investment of

$1.2 billion, equivalent to a daily capacity of 150,000 to 200,000 barrels, in a small market like the Philippines.

The use of a tariff differential has been a cornerstone of government policy for years. It is one of the essential policies in promoting investments and exists in all industries. In car manufacturing, for example, fully built-up cars have tariffs of 30 to 40% while parts and knocked-down units have only 3 to 10%. Garments and fabrics are imposed tariffs of 20 to 30%, while raw materials are imposed 3%. Petrochemicals have tariffs of 20%, while their raw materials have only 3%. The tariff reform program targets a uniform rate only by 2003. Does the Supreme Court decision on oil now mean that the tariff reform policy in all other sectors is also unconstitutional?

A tariff differential violates the concept of a pure open-market economy, but the court didn't recognise that it's a transition phase to that purity and that it's a prerogative of Congress and the Administration to decide that. A differential is maintained, at least for a reasonable time, to offset the risks of putting up and beginning to operate a plant. Importers don't face much of this risk, so, if there's no differential, few will invest in refining facilities and the country will increasingly be importing finished oil products. Even the three major oil companies can now be expected to just import finished products, resulting in a loss of job opportunities and higher dollar spending, plus lack of supply security in case of global oil shocks.

Petron, Shell and Caltex have cancelled, or at least put on indefinite hold, their expansion plans because it now becomes virtually impossible for them to convince their head offices to put more money in a market fraught with policy uncertainties and providing lower returns. For example, in China, which has lower costs and a larger market, there is fierce competition for capital among the subsidiaries of multinationals.

Corporate boards will allot their limited funds where the returns are likely to be the best. This means future demand in the Philippines won't be met and prices will go up as aging refineries are not modernised and upgraded. More than five billion pesos in investments and at least 200 million pesos in potential annual salaries and wages have been lost. The foregone expansion in capacity also means an increase in import payments by an incremental $400 to $500 million annually as the country eventually has to import finished products, which cost 25% more than crude oil. The rapid improvement in petrol stations that has occurred since deregulation will stop.

Worse, the new entrants are also unnerved by the Supreme Court decision and are now re-examining the impact on their rates of return and their status under the re-regulated environment. The question arises as to whether they are still legally entitled to operate in the country, as under the regulated environment an Energy Regulation Board licence was necessary. Others will be seriously reconsidering whether they should continue. None of them have yet reached the necessary 'critical mass' to justify continuing; it will be easier and cheaper to withdraw. Hence the decision, instead of removing barriers to entry, has actually erected them to the detriment of new players. And a new law won't fix it, the damage has been done. The uncertainties are now too high.

PRICES

The Supreme Court struck down the oil deregulation law because they thought it would lower the prices of domestic oil products, hence lowering inflation and easing the plight of the poor. It appears that the court didn't bother to look more closely into the oil-pricing structure, where prices of oil products used by mass transport (i.e., diesel) actually fell by 7% since the February deregulation, kerosene (used by the poor) fell by 8%, and LPG rose by only 3.5%. The more affluent car owners bore the brunt of the price increases; petrol prices rose by 6 to 11%. Therefore, a price roll-back to pre-deregulation levels will benefit the rich and make the poor worse off because petrol prices will have to be lowered while diesel and kerosene prices are raised.

Critics grossly exaggerate the impact of oil price increases on inflation. In broad terms, petroleum products, including the indirect oil cost from the use of electricity, are only 8% of the total cost of producing goods and delivering services. This means that for every 10% increase in oil prices, inflation goes up by only an additional 0.8%. Since deregulation, oil prices rose by an average of only about 5%, so they contributed only 0.4% to inflation. If petroleum product prices are rolled back, it would hardly create a dent on inflation. It's doubtful whether producers, manufacturers, wholesalers, distributors and retailers will also lower their prices, or that transport companies, who successfully lobbied for fare increases based on predicted diesel prices increases, will now roll back their fare increases.

The oil price increase has been only 5% since January, yet the exchange rate depreciated by 33% and crude oil prices rose by US$2 a barrel. Given that crude oil is about half of the total finished-product cost, a price increase at this time was more than justifiable. Other manufacturers have also recently raised their prices by 5 to 7%. As it was, the oil companies had planned to adjust their prices by an average of only about 5% in October, well below the increase in costs, preferring to absorb part of the cost increases instead of passing them on entirely to consumers. But the court said, no, it would only add to the burden of the poor. And by restraining oil-price increases, the justices actually exercised price control, a policy long abandoned almost everywhere else in the world because it never works.

The court also chose to support allegations that the three major oil companies are earning 'supra-normal' profits and hence are overpricing. But retail prices elsewhere in Asia, in a free-market environment, generally are higher, so this is not a defensible argument.

The Supreme Court also dismissed the prohibition on 'predatory pricing' as anti-competitive. Maybe they're right; under open competition, prices should be allowed to rise or fall and no regulation should block the operations of the market. But the reasoning is faulty. The court said that without the prohibition new players would be able to lower their prices to gain a foothold in the domestic market. Apparently, it didn't occur to the justices that the three established oil companies can also practice predatory pricing against new entrants, but they agreed that removing the prohibition would probably help consumers. However, it's uncertain whether it would help new entrants or not. This provision could/should be deleted, but that doesn't justify striking down the whole law with its consequent damage to the economy.

ANTI-BUSINESS ORIENTATION

The preceding discussion is not intended to argue the case of the three oil companies, but to establish how faulty the decision was and how such an erroneous ruling could occur on a simplistic model of nationalism. The Manila Hotel ruling, where the court declared a five-star hotel as part of the 'national economy and patrimony' and therefore could not be won by tender by a Malaysian firm, showed the court's own brand of nationalism.

In its latest ruling, the court asserted that the 'constitution mandates this Court to be the guardian not only of the people's political rights but their economic rights as well' and vowed to remain 'vigilant in upholding the economic rights of our people especially from the onslaught of the powerful'. Noting how our 'economy is in a dangerous tailspin', the court said that 'the perpetuation of Republic Act No 8180 threatens to multiply the number of our people with bent backs and begging bowls'. But it arrived at these conclusions without even consulting with those perhaps better equipped to understand the economy and economics.

Although it does not form part of the majority opinion, the statements of Associate Justice Artemio Panganiban in his separate concurring opinion underscores the court's populist tendency. We cannot help but quote extensively from Mr Panganiban's opinion in order to show why the decision has raised apprehensions in the business community, both foreign and local:

We are not unaware of the disruptive impact of the depreciating peso on the retail prices of refined petroleum products. But such price-escalating consequence adversely affects not merely these oil companies which occupy these hallowed places among the most profitable corporate behemoths in our country. In these critical times of widespread economic dislocations, abetted by currency fluctuations not entirely of domestic origin, all sectors of society agonise and suffer. Thus, everyone, rich or poor, must share in the burdens of such economic aberrations.

I can understand foreign investors who see these price adjustments as necessary consequences of the country [sic] adherence to the free market, for that, in the first place, is the magnet of their presence here.

Understandably, their concern is limited to bottom lines and market share. But in all these mega companies, there are also Filipino entrepreneurs and managers. I am sure there are patriots among them who realise that, in times of economic turmoil, the poor and the underprivileged proportionately suffer more than any other sector of society. There is a certain threshold of pain beyond which the disadvantaged cannot endure...Thus, to capitalists and people in power, it is only appropriate that we sympathise with those who are destitute and poor in times of need. Let us not complain about lack of profits or even temporary loss of income. And to greedy and heartless businessmen our people are already dirt poor. You should have some conscience.

It seems he didn't look at the SEC financial records of these companies, which certainly aren't among 'the most profitable corporate behemoths in the country'.

But most importantly, he didn't understand economics. He didn't understand that a controlled price is worse for the poor, not better. Either the cost of the fuel is paid for, or it is subsidised. If it is subsidised, it's the poor who suffer as government has insufficient funds to provide other, more necessary services. If prices are controlled, investment doesn't occur, so oil imports cost more. More dollars must be spent that could have created more pressure on the country's trade balance and the peso. And so on. It's a complex relationship that has been glossed over in the interest of a short-term palliative for the poor.

The impact of the decision on investments in other industries can't yet be fully quantified because we don't know who was planning to come in that will now put their plans on hold or shift elsewhere where the risks are lower and the returns higher. But potential investors have indicated that reversals by the Supreme Court have put a severe damper on their interest.

Past cases may be illustrative. In 1990, when the Supreme Court decided against a Taiwanese firm wanting to put up a petrochemical plant, not only did the country lose the $370 million investment for the plant but also some $1 to 2 billion in potential Taiwanese investments that could have flowed in over a five-year period. The Philippines' first petrochemical plant was also set back by at least eight years, when the rest of Asia already had theirs in the 1980s. JG Summit's plant won't be operational until 1998 at the earliest.

When the Supreme Court decided against the Malaysians in the Manila Hotel case, the government's privatisation program lost its momentum. No asset has been sold since then. It may be partly because the remaining assets were less financially attractive or the government decided to accord less priority to privatisation, but the fact that a losing bidder can potentially challenge in court and overturn a done deal puts a chill through investors looking for assets to buy and has certainly been a contributing factor.

Unless the legal framework is rid of ambiguities and policies become less volatile, investors are likely to hesitate because of the ever-present danger of losing their money on the grounds of a pure technicality. The privatisation of certain assets of the National Power Corporation and Build-Operate-Transfer projects in the pipeline would be the most vulnerable to the loss of investor interest. And with reduced interest, the government gets less for their assets and infrastructure projects suffer delay. Some may not take off at all.

Will potential investors in large-scale projects where investment runs into hundreds of millions of dollars and the return is 10, 20, or 30 years from now risk investment in the Philippines, particularly when there are many other countries competing for those funds?

During this period of regional economic turmoil, the only thing the country needed do to come out ahead of its neighbours was to sustain reforms and to assure investors that the reforms in place are permanent. The Supreme Court has undermined this one advantage the country had, as the policy environment has now become more uncertain.

Even if a new deregulation law is passed soon, it will be years before the confidence of investors can be revived. First the law will have to be 'approved' by the Supreme Court before it can be believed to be fixed. Then investors will wait to see whether the next administration and Congress will uphold that law or have a different policy. Then investors will still wait to be sure change still might not occur. It has set the industry back years.

GOVERNMENT FINANCES AND THE IMF PROGRAM

The reality is that costs have risen so prices must also rise. Restraining oil prices will only result in a short-term gain for the poor. Eventually, some-one has to pay up and the government will likely foot the bill, subsidising the price differential through the Oil Price Stabilisation Fund. This means either higher taxes, so the poor and the middle class end up paying for the fuel used by the rich for their luxury cars, or reallocation of the budget at the cost of reduced infrastructure spending so vital roads, ports and support facilities that could have spurred investments and created jobs in the countryside don't happen.

With oil prices frozen and the oil industry deregulated, the Oil Price Stabilisation Fund is restored and oil company claims grow by two billion pesos a month on present pricing. That's enough to wipe out the gains from the proposed Comprehensive Tax Reform Package (CTRP), funds that were intended to be used for infrastructure, in just three months.

The International Monetary Fund (IMF) imposed three final conditions for the Philippines to exit its three-year Extended Fund Facility program: an expanded value-added tax; deregulation of the oil industry; and passage of the CTRP. The first two had been done. It needed only the CTRP to pass for the Philippines to then stand on its own financial feet.

Now the oil deregulation has been reversed and exit from the program is in jeopardy. This makes attaining 'investment-grade' status for the Philippines even more remote and lowers the standing of the country in the financial markets. A downgrade is not now out of the question. This means higher interest rates for dollar loans and greater reluctance of businesses to invest.

Filipinos needing jobs will have fewer opportunities.

RISK TO POLICY CONTINUITY

Until now, the greatest threat to policy continuity, economic stability and continued growth of the country under a post-Ramos government lay in an ill-chosen president. Yet even this risk could be played down with the assurance that President Ramos had already nearly completed the most critical economic reforms that the Philippines needs for sustained growth. Although reform laws are not set in stone, our confidence stemmed from the fact that to change course, an ill-chosen president would have to contend with a Congress that will most likely be led and dominated by the same legislators who passed the reform laws. At worst, policy reversals would have to go through the same slow, painstaking process that attended the passage of the original reform laws.

Unfortunately, this positive outlook will now have to be tempered with a recognition of the judiciary's, particularly the Supreme Court's, potential to undo the basic elements of the government reform programs.

And even while taking stock of the ramifications of the court's decision on the oil deregulation law, a case to reverse another Ramos reform measure is now pending before the Supreme Court. The constitutionality of the

Mining Act of 1995, which liberalised the terms and conditions of the government's mining contracts for foreign and local mining firms, is being challenged by environmental groups. The measure has been responsible for the heightened interest of foreign mining firms in entering the local mining industry, which has been in decline since the 1980s. A total of 74 firms have applied for financial and technical assistance agreements.

Another reform measure that could be at risk if another losing bidder took its gripes to the Supreme Court is the Build-Operate-Transfer law. Indeed, it is in the infrastructure sector, where funding requirements run into hundreds of millions of dollars and gestation periods stretch into several years, where the Supreme Court's rulings on the Manila Hotel case and the oil industry deregulation law could have their most adverse impact.

Certainly, no one expects perfection in a developing country, especially a country that is striving to achieve the distinction of being the only Asian country to develop under a fully-functioning democracy. The risk of a change in government policy is not peculiar to the Philippines.

At the outset, a foreign investor is well aware of the risks of a change in investment rules arising from a judicial ruling. For an investor, the key is to be able to weigh the odds. An investor does this through assessing pertinent laws and established jurisprudence, that is, assuming that the courts would stick to strictly legal issues, an investor can reasonably assess the chances of being hit by an adverse court ruling later on.

For instance, if the Supreme Court had stuck to strictly legal questions and argued a strong case, the decision on Republic Act 8180 could be accepted. The problem is that the court relied more on its own appreciation of economic/business policy considerations rather than on established legal principles. An even bigger problem is that when the court starts to venture beyond its competence, as shown in the Manila Hotel case and the oil deregulation law, arbitrariness comes into play. This greatly increases the odds against stability of the operating environment.

The bottom line is that this was a hugely important issue with far wider implications than just the cost of oil products. The Supreme Court should have researched it far more thoroughly than it did and listened to independent expert advice and talked to new industry players before it decided. It should have been more cognisant of the immense harm a negative decision would create so it could better evaluate its responsibility to the people and the constitution it serves.

A new law now won't solve the problem. The damage has been done, and that can't simply be undone. It will take a long time to restore business confidence, unless the court reverses the decision. That might do it.

CHAPTER 9

BEYOND, BENEATH, BEHIND THE LABELS

By Baron L Buck

The enforcement of intellectual property rights (IPR) in the Philippines is a matter of great importance to trademark and copyright owners as well as the to consuming public. Counterfeiting in the Philippines is widespread and involves virtually every product from water-based typewriter correction fluid to computer software, pharmaceuticals and aircraft parts. Thus, when purchasing products in the Philippines one needs to be aware of the proliferation of counterfeits and mindful of the possible consequences of using a counterfeit product.

From both a business and a personal point of view, it is advisable to purchase products only from authorised sources even though similar, if not identical, looking items maybe available at reduced prices. When a price appears too good to be true, it usually is. The prices of some imported products in the Philippines are double or triple what one might pay in the country of origin, while other items are only slightly more expensive. The key to selecting a purchase is to be familiar with the item's approximate price at various other Philippine stores.

Counterfeiters seek to make money riding on the back of the advertising of well-known and popular brand names or trademarks. Few manufacturers will counterfeit an item that is not popular and selling well, so packaging and printing should be examined before purchasing any popular item. If these are of poor quality, the item is suspect and a decision to purchase should be based on the risks.

For example, in the case of a ladies' handbag that bears a designer name, the price will probably be an indicator that the item is not genuine. The general appearance and location of the store may indicate that it probably is not an authorised retailer of European designer handbags. If it looks similar or identical to the genuine item, what is the worst that can happen? The item would probably wear out sooner than the genuine article, there could be embarrassment if friends or associates recognise the item as counterfeit and, most serious, buying it would be contributing to the theft of someone's property, i.e. the trademark.

However, purchasing medicine from small drugstores and government hospitals should be avoided. Medications purchased from the major drugstores and the larger hospitals are estimated to be about 90% genuine. And the pharmaceutical companies in the Philippines have rarely investigated accusations that a particular medication is being counterfeited for fear that consumers will be scared away from purchasing the genuine item. Patients' reports to their doctors of adverse effects or ineffectiveness of a medication are rarely passed on to the distributors. In the case of antibiotics, the usual response to a complaint is to prescribe another type of antibiotic. In the case of maintenance medication, it is possible that the counterfeit could cause illness or death. Price becomes of little concern because only the genuine product is acceptable. Extreme caution should be taken regarding where the item is purchased, its cost, and the appearance of the packaging.

Automobile parts purchased from auto dealers are perhaps 85 to 90% genuine. It is best to frequent the same auto repair facility on a regular basis so there may be some recourse if a part does not perform as expected. Some repair shops are known to replace genuine working parts with counterfeit parts, then resell the genuine parts to other customers. This is especially common when it is expected that the customer may never return to that shop.

For the most part, petrol is adulterated by perhaps 10% at petrol stations. Motor oil is sold under the names of most popular brands and mixed with other oil products at all levels on a regular basis by legitimate distributors as well as by retailers and smaller shops doing auto repairs.

The most popular alcoholic beverages purchased from hotels, restaurants and liquor stores are counterfeit an estimated 10 to 20% of the time, except during the Christmas holidays when the most popular scotch whisky is counterfeit about 50% of the time. A number of years ago, as many as 15 people died allegedly as a result of drinking a counterfeit of the most popular imported brandy. Since there are no liability laws in the Philippines, there often appears to be little concern on the part of manufacturers except to claim that an alleged tainted beverage is counterfeit even though it is contained in genuine bottles. And that claim is acceptable to the public because it is a common practice for them to refill bottles from imported products with domestically manufactured products themselves.

The bottom line is that both individual consumers and business purchasers need to exercise caution when purchasing items from the Philippines.

IPR ENFORCEMENT

As a result of six years of pressure from the United States, the Philippines passed a new, more comprehensive intellectual property rights law in 1997. But the major problem with the enforcement of IPR in the Philippines under the former law was not the law itself; it was and still is the adjudication process. As a rule, it takes five to 10 or more years to resolve even the simplest criminal cases, including alleged trademark infringement complaints.

The process of making a trademark or copyright infringement complaint with the Department of Trade and Industry and/or the law enforcement authorities is complicated, time-consuming and frustrating. It is also costly. It is strongly advised that a specialist intellectual property rights firm be engaged to coordinate the desired anti-counterfeiting action. Taking an anti-counterfeiting or infringement action against a retailer is not particularly difficult, but taking action against a manufacturer is difficult in the extreme.

IPR enforcement consultants will do all of the investigation work and provide all of the samples of the counterfeits through controlled and documented evidence purchases. They also will prepare all of the legal documentation for the application for the search warrant, including the witnessed alleged offence affidavits. The law enforcement authorities do not have the expertise, interest or manpower to accomplish these tasks adequately.

Once the court has issued the search warrant, it is advisable for a representative of the trademark or copyright owner (usually the IPR consultant) to accompany the law enforcement raiding team during the service of the search warrant to answer technical and legal questions as well as to insure that no deals are entered into between the police and the offenders. The service of search warrants can be dangerous, as both the police and factory security personnel are heavily armed with assault rifles. The latter take their orders from the owners, who are not particularly intimidated by law enforcement authorities, who in turn are thought of as being corrupt and for sale to the highest bidder.

Once the search warrant has been serviced and the evidence confiscated, the complainant needs to arrange for secure storage of the evidence because neither the court nor the police have adequate evidence-storage capabilities. The complainant also needs to provide an attorney to prosecute the criminal case, much the same as in a civil case in the United States. One of the reasons for this is a lack of confidence in the state prosecutors. This practice is so widely followed as to have become normal.

However, despite the efforts of private prosecutors, there have been no known convictions for trademark or copyright infringement in the Philippines in at least 15 years. The most prudent advice to intellectual-property owners is to be diligent about taking action against infringers because there have been cases where Philippine courts have awarded rights to internationally famous trademarks in the Philippines to the infringers.

Once a case is filed with the prosecutor's office and an indictment secured, the most prudent thing to do is to work out a settlement of the complaint with the offender for minimal damages and a promise not to do it again. The main reason for this advice is that technically the offender cannot be charged again for the same offence because the court has not yet ruled that the intellectual trademark or copyright owner has the best legal rights to the use of the trademark in the Philippines. On occasion, counterfeiters have continued to produce and sell infringing items. In one case, TRIDENT Manufacturing was producing shoes bearing the SWATCH trademark for the three years the infringement case against it was being heard by the Department of Trade and Industry and also for the five years that a decision by the director of the Trademark office was pending. In the end, the director of the Trademark Office ruled that the shoes bearing the trademark SWATCH did not infringe on the internationally known SWATCH trademark.

ADJUDICATION PROCESS

The main problem with enforcing intellectual property rights laws in the Philippines is the adjudication process. Many think the reason for lack of IPR enforcement is corruption in the courts and the police force, but in fact the main problem is the judicial process in which up to 20 court hearings are scheduled per court per day. A judge actually hears only five to seven cases a day for 15 to 30 minutes each because the other 13 or so litigants request postponements that are almost always granted. The actual court presentations of 15 to 30 minutes once or twice a month often go on for five to ten years, and at some point the case is submitted to the judge for resolution.

In theory, the judge is expected to write an opinion on the merits of the case after reviewing five to ten years of transcripts pertaining to the case. No judge has sufficient time to devote to reading a case, much less to evaluate and write a coherent opinion. So, at times, the decisions defy logic.

For example, an infringement complaint was filed by the Yale Lock Company against a major Philippine manufacturer of padlocks for putting the Yale name on the padlocks he was manufacturing and selling throughout Metro Manila and the provinces. When the police officers served the warrant, they confiscated more than 40,000 padlocks bearing counterfeits of the Yale trademark in boxes also printed with the Yale name. During the trial, which lasted for six years, the offender's only defence was that the 40,000 locks were samples that he had produced to calculate manufacturing costs because he planned to make a proposal to seek a licensing agreement with Yale for the manufacture of padlocks in the Philippines.

The judge ruled against Yale on the grounds that the defendant's story was credible and that, since an official receipt was required by law as evidence of the sale of a counterfeit, there was no violation under the law. When the police officer, accompanied by four witnesses, had purchased a counterfeit Yale padlock from the manager of the factory, the judge noted, he was not issued an official receipt.

The judge totally ignored the portion of the law stating that it is a crime to affix another's trademark to an item produced. He also ignored the fact that it was not logical that the offender needed to produce 40,000 padlocks with packaging to calculate manufacturing costs, especially since he hadn't even obtained Yale's manufacturing specifications and tolerances. The locks were returned to the offender with no order from the court to destroy or remove the Yale name.

Even more interesting than the judge's decision, which many thought was corrupt, was the opinion of the chief of the Department of Justice Task Force on Counterfeiting. She stated before the presidential inter-agency committee on intellectual property that the judge was correct in his ruling because, without an official receipt, there is no sale. Carrying her logic one step further, the task force chief was saying that manufacturers in the Philippines cannot be successfully prosecuted for manufacturing counterfeit items because, not being retailers, they are not authorised by the government to issue official receipts. She agreed with that conclusion in front of the inter-agency committee without objection.

On average, Metro Manila criminal court judges carry more than 350 active cases on their dockets every single day and are expected to close 40 cases a month to stay even with the 30 to 50 new cases assigned to their courts each month. Under those circumstances, it is incredible that any cases are ever resolved. To close 40 cases a month requires reading five to 10 years' worth of transcripts and then writing opinions of five to 15 pages based on the evidence presented for two cases every day of the week. And that's after hearing five to seven cases a day. The situation is impossible, and the prospects for its getting better are not encouraging.

On the positive side, IPR consulting firms have been able to reduce the incidents of infringement for the trademarks they represent significantly through a variety of legal means designed to reduce the profit incentive of the counterfeiters. The enforcement of IPR in the Philippines is not hopeless. In fact, awareness is greater now than in past years and the open availability of the counterfeits is much reduced from what it was a few years ago when 95% of computer software used in the Philippines was pirated. There is still a long way to go, but almost every developing nation has gone through an IPR infringement phase. As Philippine products gain international acceptance, the incentive to enforce IPR will improve significantly.

CHAPTER 10

TARIFFS AND IMPORT TAXES

As of June 1997, the Philippines' nominal tariff averaged 13.43%, which was down from 15.58% the year before. Protective tariffs were established in May 1996, replacing import quota restrictions for sensitive agricultural commodities (except rice). Since then, four subsequent executive orders (EOs 328, 365, 388 and 390) have reduced rates for several products—namely, petroleum and information technology products—in preparation for future liberalisation. It is likely that the agriculture sector will always carry a much higher tariff than other sectors. Rates on some key products in 1997 were:

- Agriculture, 25.30%;
- Metals, 14.69%;
- Textiles, 14.41%;
- Machinery, 10.62%; and
- Chemicals, 6.64%.

Scheduled for yearly phase-downs to the year 2000, average nominal tariffs will be reduced to an overall 1998 level of 10.74%. In 1998, key sectoral averages will be:

- Agriculture, 20.69%;

- Textiles, 12.54%;
- Metals, 10.22%;
- Machinery, 8.33%; and
- Chemicals, 5.15%.

A value-added tax (VAT) of 10% is imposed on imports for resale or reuse. The VAT is based on the total value used by the Bureau of Customs in determining tariff and customs duties, plus import duties, excise taxes, and other charges. Other charges are those on imports prior to release from customs custody, including postage, insurance and commissions.

CUSTOMS VALUATION

Currently, customs valuation as a basis for determining the dutiable value of imports is based on export value. Export value is the selling price of the same or an identical product in the principal export markets of the source country. If the export value cannot be ascertained by this method, either the cost at the country of manufacturer/origin, the third-country selling price, or the domestic wholesale selling price may be used. This is an interim step until the final shift is made to using transaction value on 1 January 2000. (There is more information about valuation in the section titled 'Import documentation' under 'Globalised Comprehensive Import Supervision Scheme (CISS)'.

IMPORT LICENCES

The National Food Authority remains the sole importer of rice and continues to be involved in imports of corn. While trade and tariff reforms have greatly reduced import restrictions, other products are still subject to import regulation for such reasons as health, morals, national security, and industry development programs.

EXPORT CONTROLS

The Bureau of Export Trade Promotion of the Department of Trade and Industry lists 31 products that require clearance from various agencies prior to shipment. These products and their respective agencies are listed in Table 1.

Table 1. Products requiring export clearance and the clearing agencies

Product	Agency
Abaca and ramie seeds, seedlings, suckers and other planting materials*	Fibre Industry Development Authority
Aircraft	Department of Transportation and Communications
All plants, planting materials and plant products capable of harbouring pests; insect specimens, live and dead	Bureau of Plant Industry
Animals, animal products and effects	Bureau of Animal Industry
Antiques, cultural artifacts and historical relics	National Museum
Mangrove*	Forest Management Bureau, Department of Environment and Natural Resources
Milkfish fry, mother milkfish*	Bureau of Fisheries and Aquatic Resources
Buri seeds and seedlings*	Bureau of Plant Industry
Coffee	Department of Trade and Industry
Copper concentrates	Board of Investments
Firearms and ammunition	Firearms and Explosives Office, Philippine National Police, Department of Interior and Local Government
Garments and textiles, carpets, polyester stable fibre, filament yarns, fabrics, upholstered furniture and other natural and synthetic fibers and all products made up in whole or in part of these fibres for export to all countries with or without quota	Garments and Textile Export Board
Gold from small-scale mining or panned gold	Bangko Sentral ng Pilipinas
Grains and by-products	National Food Authority
Logs, poles and piles including log core and flitches/railroad ties	Forest Management Bureau, Department of Environment and Natural Resources
Lumber	Forest Management Bureau, Department of Environment and Natural Resources
Matured coconuts/seedlings*	Philippine Coconut Authority
Motion pictures/television films and related publicity materials	Movie and Television Review and Classification Board
Natural fibres	Fibre Industry Development Authority

Table 1. Products requiring export clearance and the clearing agencies, continued

Product	Agency
Legal tender, Philippine notes and coins, cheques, money orders and other bills of exchange drawn in pesos against banks operating in the Philippines greater than 5,000 pesos	Bangko Sentral ng Pilipinas
Prawn-spawner and fry*	Bureau of Fisheries and Aquatic Resources
Radioactive materials	Philippine Nuclear Research Institute
Raw materials for cottage industries*	Department of Trade and Industry
Shells*	Bureau of Fisheries and Aquatic Resources
Undersized raw shells	Bureau of Fisheries and Aquatic Resources
Stalactites and stalagmites*	Department of Environment and Natural Resources
Sugar and molasses	Sugar Regulatory Administration
Wildlife species: wild marine species, e.g. precious, semi-precious and all ordinary corals raw and by-products*	Bureau of Fisheries and Aquatic Resources
Wildlife species: wild and marine species, e.g. water snakes (Cerberus Rynchops); seasnakes; frogs: live, skin or products from the skin or meat	Bureau of Fisheries and Aquatic Resources
Wild terrestrial species whether live, stuffed or by-products*	Protected Areas and Wildlife Bureau
Other wild terrestrial species	Protected Areas and Wildlife Bureau

*Government prohibits export except for scientific or testing purposes

IMPORT/EXPORT DOCUMENTATION
Export documentation

The Department of Trade Industry, through its Export Assistance Network (EXPONET), assists exporters in setting up their business transactions. Export procedures involve the following steps:

- The exporter files an Export Declaration form with the Bureau of Customs (BOC) or with the One-Stop Export Documentation Centre for processing and approval.

- If a product requires clearance, the exporter secures this prior to filing the Export Declaration form. The exporter either obtains an export commodity clearance from the proper government commodity office if required by the buyer, or a certificate of exemption if the product is among the 31 items that require export clearance.

Once the required supporting documents are filed, the BOC grants Authority to Load.

The exporter provides the commercial bank or offshore banking unit with a copy of the duly accomplished Export Declaration form (for record purposes) if the export negotiation or payment of the pertinent export shipment is coursed through them.

Import documentation

An importer must check his product's commodity classification with the Bangko Sentral ng Pilipinas or any authorised agent bank. This commodity classification is the general basis for determining whether the item is freely importable, prohibited or regulated. Freely importable commodities do not need prior clearance from any government agency. Regulated commodities require clearances or permits from appropriate government agencies prior to importation. Prohibited commodities cannot be imported because of specific laws.

Because of sanitary and phytosanitary concerns, the Philippine government requires import permits for meat, fresh produce, planting seeds and plants. For meats, all imports must be accompanied by a Veterinary Quarantine Clearance certificate issued by the Bureau of Animal Industry. Any meat certified by the US Food Safety Inspection Service is now routinely issued a Veterinary Quarantine Clearance certificate.

For fresh produce, planting seeds, and plants, the Bureau of Plant Industry issues import permits. The Bureau of Plant Industry has established protocols for fresh grapes, apples and citrus fruits, allowing imports from the United States exclusive of those from Florida and Texas. There are also protocols in place for onions, potatoes and garlic, but importers report that gaining phytosanitary clearance is still difficult for these products. Protocols for other produce have not yet been developed, but are being written now for cherries and a variety of fresh green vegetables.

Despite the lack of protocols, many products still enter the country in small amounts for high-end hotels and restaurants. Currently, only the government's National Food Authority can import rice. In the past, the National Food Authority has typically only imported low-quality rice in bulk volume. Recently, however, they have started a program in which they will act as brokers for importers who want to import relatively small quantities of premium quality rice.

With the required health certificates, any properly registered Philippine entity can import any other agricultural products, although in some cases, particularly for domestically produced basic commodities, tariffs are prohibitive. With the health certificates, any product other than rice can also be brought into the country and sold at the country's extensive public and privately owned duty-free operations.

As a result of tariff-rate quota commitments made in the Uruguay Round, the government has also begun issuing minimum access volume certificates, which allow holders to import limited quantities of certain agricultural products at substantially reduced duties. The government issues minimum access volume certificates for imports of cattle, swine, sheep and goats, poultry, beef, pork, sheep and goat meat, poultry meat, fresh potatoes, coffee, corn and sugar. A committee of representatives from six cabinet-level agencies periodically accepts import requests from those with a 'demonstrated valid reason' to import these products. This means firms, associations, or individuals who have already traded in the product or are engaged in an activity that would allow them to import and sell this product.

Based on these requests, the committee awards minimum access volume certificates in volumes sufficient to satisfy the country's Uruguay Round commitments. Upon presentation to customs, these non-transferable certificates allow the holder to import the specified volumes and products at lower tariffs. The United States has recently challenged through the World Trade Organisation the Philippine process of awarding minimum access volume certificates for pork and poultry meat, as the Philippines has given most of these licences to producer groups that are unlikely to import. The Philippine Department of Agriculture can provide more detailed information on applying for certificates to import under the minimum access volume scheme.

Effective 1 April 1997, the Philippine Bureau of Food and Drug began enforcing regulations that require all packaged food products imported to the Philippines be registered. Any unregistered imported food products sold or offered for sale may be confiscated by the bureau. Product registration is aimed at preventing misbranding and adulteration. As of 1 April 1997, imported food products not also labelled with the name and address of the importer may be subject to confiscation. Stickering is currently permitted. Application for registration is made directly to the bureau. Registrations can be renewed for a minimal cost for either one or five years.

Generally, import documentation is routed through authorised agent banks. Several modes of payment can be used by importers:

- Letters of credit, documents against acceptance, open account, documents against payment and direct remittance are used for imports involving foreign-exchange remittances.
- Imports without foreign-exchange remittance are paid on a self-funded basis, whereby imports are funded from importer's own foreign-currency deposit accounts or from foreign exchange sourced outside of the Philippine banking system.
- Special import arrangements can be made on a consignment basis, open account arrangement and lease, lease-purchase, leverage lease, lease with the option to purchase or similar arrangements. These transactions do not require prior Bangko Sentral approval but will follow existing rules and regulations of the Bureau of Customs.

Customs Memorandum Order 149-88 requires the registration of all importers/consignees who regularly import or lease twice a year in commercial quantity. Application forms can be secured from the Customs Intelligence and Investigation Service or in the outports from the District of the Sub-Port Collector.

The Philippine Government has engaged the services of the Société Générale de Surveillance SA (SGS) to implement the Globalised Comprehensive Import Supervision Scheme (CISS) under which all importations into the Philippines valued at US$500 FOB and above are subject to pre-shipment inspection by SGS in the country of origin. Goods declared as off-quality under such descriptive terms as stock lots, side-rims, cull rolls, seconds, mill lots, scraps, off-grade, reconditioned, used, junk or similar terms conveying the article's condition as not being brand new or of first-rate quality will undergo pre-shipment inspections regardless of value. SGS issues a clean report of finding after inspection. Complete SGS guidelines are contained in a Bangko Sentral memorandum to all authorised agent banks and in Customs Memorandum Order 39-92 dated 31 March 1992.

Prior to or upon arrival of a shipment, an importer should file an import entry form, together with all supporting documents, with the Entry Processing Division of the BOC. When all documentation is completed and processed, the imported goods are released at the Pier and Inspection Division of BOC and/or, for warehousing entries, transferred to one of the following:

- The consignee's warehouse, customs-bonded warehouse or container yard-container freight station;
- The customs-common-bonded warehouse; or
- The firm's bonded manufacturing warehouse; or EPZA warehouse.

TEMPORARY ENTRY

All articles brought into the Philippines for repair, processing or reconditioning to be re-exported upon completion are exempted from the payment of import duties provided that a bond amounting to one-and-one-half times the ascertained duties and taxes and other charges is paid to the Bureau of Customs.

Labelling and marking requirements

Every imported or locally manufactured product must display the following information:

- Registered trade or brand name;
- Duly registered trademark;
- Duly registered business name;
- Address of the manufacturer, importer or repacker of the consumer product in the Philippines;
- General make or active ingredients;
- Net quantity of contents, in terms of weight, measure or numerical count in the metric system;
- Country of manufacture, if imported; and,
- If a consumer product is manufactured, refilled or repacked under licence from a principal, the label shall state such facts.

The following additional information may also be required by the responsible government agency:

- Whether the product is flammable or inflammable;
- Directions for use, if necessary;
- Warning of toxicity;
- Wattage, voltage or amperage; and,
- Process of manufacture used, if necessary.

Once a product has been certified to have passed the consumer product standard prescribed by the Bureau of Product Standards of the Department of Trade and Industry, its label must contain the product standard quality mark. Exemptions from specific Department of Trade and Industry marking requirements may include: articles that cannot be marked prior to shipment without injury or at prohibitive expense; crude substances, crude products, and products imported for use by the importer and not for resale in its imported form; or products produced 20 or more years prior to shipment. For these items, the container must indicate the country of origin and product name. Mislabelling, misrepresentation or misbranding may subject an entire shipment to seizure and disposal.

Agricultural items

Processed packaged food products are required to comply with the regulations of the Philippine Bureau of Food and Drugs. All labelling must be in English. For US products, compliance with US Food and Drug Administration requirements will virtually always assure compliance with Philippine regulations. It is the importer's responsibility to satisfy bureau requirements.

Textile and garment labelling

A reasonably legible label, with letters not less than 1.5 mm in size, on which the information is stamped, printed, woven or indicated in tags, is mandatory for the following:

- Finished textile fabrics in rolls or folds;
- Textile piece goods;
- Ready-made garments;
- Household and institutional linens such as bed sheets, towels, napkins, and place mats; and
- Textile products such as handkerchiefs, umbrellas, socks, hosiery, neckties and scarves.

Labels are not mandatory for special items made of textiles, such as narrow fabrics, artificial flowers, purses, doilies, bags, hats, belts, gloves, and other products not specified in the preceding list.

General label requirements for garments

For ready-made garments, the label must be durable enough to withstand normal laundering and shall include the manufacturer's name, trademark or both; the percentages of fibre content by mass, using the generic name of the fibre in the order of predominance; and the country of origin (the address of the manufacturer may also be indicated in the packaging). Labels for blouses, dresses, jackets, robes, nightgowns, shirts and sweaters must be affixed at the centre back neckline, or at any other appropriate place, such as side seam, facing of front placket, etc. Labels for pants, skirts, pyjamas, shorts, tights or half-slips must be affixed at any appropriate place, such as the inside of the waistband or inner facing of the fly.

Method of labelling for textile fabric

For finished textile fabrics in rolls or in folds, the label must be woven into the selvedge not more than two metres apart, regardless of the width of the fabric. The label must include the trademark, the percentage of fibre content by mass, using the generic name of the fibre in the order of predominance, and the country of origin. When it is not practical or possible to conform to this requirement, an alternative method is to print or stamp the required information on the outer-edge of the fabric roll or fold and, in addition, to attach tags at the beginning and end of the roll or folds. For textile piece goods, a tag must be attached to the goods when there is no label on the selvedge. In cases where tags are to be attached by the purchaser (retailer), the name of the store must be indicated.

PROHIBITED IMPORTS

The following commodities may not be imported into the Philippines:

- Dynamite, gunpowder, ammunition and other explosives, firearms and weapons of war, and parts thereof, except when authorised by law;
- Written or printed articles in any form containing any matter advocating or inciting treason, rebellion, insurrection, sedition or subversion against the government of the Philippines, or forcible resistance to any law of the Philippines, or containing any threat to take the life of, or inflict bodily harm upon any person in the Philippines;
- Written or printed articles, negatives or motion picture films, photographs, engravings, lithographs, objects, paintings, drawings or other representations of an obscene or immoral character;
- Articles, instruments, drugs and substances designed, intended or adapted for producing unlawful abortion, or any printed matter that advertises or describes or gives directly or indirectly information where, how or by whom unlawful abortion is produced;
- Roulette wheels, gambling outfits, loaded dice, marked cards, machines, apparatus or mechanical devices used in gambling or the distribution of money, cigars, cigarettes or other articles when such distribution is dependent on chance, including jackpot and pinball machines or similar contrivances, or parts thereof;
- Lottery and sweepstakes tickets except those authorised by the Philippine Government, advertisements thereof, and lists of drawings therein;
- Any article manufactured in whole or in part of gold, silver or other precious metals or alloys thereof, the stamps, brands or marks of which do not indicate the actual fineness of quality of said metals or alloys;
- Any adulterated or misbranded articles of food or any adulterated or misbranded drug in violation of the provisions of the Food and Drugs Act;

- Marijuana, opium, poppies, coca leaves, heroin or any other narcotics or synthetic drugs which are or may hereafter be declared habit-forming by the President of the Philippines, or any compound, manufactured salt, derivative, or preparation thereof, except when imported by the government of the Philippines or any person duly authorised by the Dangerous Drugs Board, for medicinal purposes only;
- Opium pipes and parts thereof, of whatever material;
- Used clothing and rags (RA 4653); and,
- Toy guns (Letter of Instruction 1264 dated 31 July 1982).

STANDARDS

The Bureau of Product Standards (BPS), a governmental body under the Department of Trade and Industry, develops, promotes and implements standards nationwide. It formulates Philippine national standards or adopts as Philippine national standards relevant international or foreign standards/guides for purposes of licensing local and foreign companies to use the product standard quality and/or safety certification mark. It accredits testing, inspection and/or certification bodies. The Philippines is a signatory to the GATT/WTO Agreement on Technical Barriers to Trade (Standards Code).

Together with Department of Trade and Industry's provincial and regional offices, BPS inspects over 60 specific products covered by mandatory standards. These products include lighting fixtures, electrical wires and cables, cement, steel bars, pneumatic tires, fire extinguishers, liquefied petroleum gas, sanitary wares, toys and household appliances. BPS affixes a product standard quality mark on products manufactured by companies that consistently conform to the quality and safety requirements of Philippine National Standards, or acceptable international or foreign standards, after rigid factory and product assessments. BPS released Department Administrative Order 1, series of 1997, on the national product quality certification scheme, which is designed to encourage Philippine enterprises to achieve and maintain world-class standards and to gain and continue access to international markets. A significant initiative of this scheme is the inclusion of a company's quality management system as well as the expansion of the product standard certification mark scheme to foreign companies.

BPS issues import commodity clearances to importers of commodities whose shipments comply with the quality and safety requirements of relevant national or acceptable international standards.

BPS has adopted the ISO 9000 standards as Philippine National Standards 1000 Series. The standards can be applied in the services sector as well as in manufacturing. It has concluded memoranda of understanding with TUV Product Service GmbH (Germany) and BVQI (UK) for joint quality system assessment work in specific fields.

Only the modern metric system (SI units) can be used for measurement of any product, commodity, material, utility, and in any commercial transaction, contract and other legal instrument, official record and document. The Philippine Government prohibits importation of non-metric measuring devices, instrumentation and apparatus without prior clearance from BPS.

CHAPTER 11

SPECIAL ECONOMIC ZONES

Industrial estates have been present in the Philippines since the 1970s. However, initial projects were unsuccessful in attaining the goal of dispersing industrialisation to the countryside because infrastructure facilities were not attractive enough to draw large manufacturing companies. In the early 1990s, the government renewed its call for industry dispersal by encouraging development of large private industrial estates in the Calabarzon (Cavite-Laguna-Batangas-Rizal-Quezon Provinces) growth zone. These estates were successful in drawing foreign investors and in no time became fully occupied. Apart from the facilities and amenities of Calabarzon estates, their success is due also to the presence of infrastructure and their proximity to Metro Manila. To date, there are 51 private and government-run industrial estates and export-processing zones throughout the country. Further, many industrial estate operators are undertaking expansion programs to take advantage of the strong demand that is expected in the coming years.

In 1992, encouraged by the success of Calabarzon, the government identified six other growth zones throughout the country as primary development sites due to their available infrastructure, abundant labour, and space for expansion. Other considerations included cost of land, proximity to air and sea ports, and raw-materials sources. The government enacted Republic Act 7916 in 1995 to encourage economic growth through development of special economic zones (SEZs, or ecozones). The phrases 'SEZ' and 'ecozone' were first coined in RA 7916, which is known also as the Special Economic Zones Act. It designates SEZs as sites for self-reliant or self-sustaining agro-industrial, tourist/recreational, commercial, banking, investment and financial centres. It is hoped that these sites will become catalysts in spreading industrialisation and development to the countryside.

Republic Act 7916 allows SEZ development through the initiative of the private sector, the Philippine Economic Zone Authority (PEZA), or local government with the assistance of PEZA. Local private companies developed most of the major industrial estates through joint venture arrangements with foreign companies. Republic Act 7916 has identified 91 potential SEZ sites within Calabarzon and the six growth zones identified in 1992. Developers may establish SEZs in these sites through such arrangements as the Build-Operate-Transfer (BOT) scheme and its variants. Identified growth zones have targeted areas of specialisation, so their location usually depends on the type of industry to which they cater. Development of an SEZ requires at least US$23 million worth of investments. The private sector will shoulder the bulk of this amount, alleviating the government's financial exposure; however, the government will facilitate access to loans from foreign commercial banks and multilateral lending agencies.

In addition, the Board of Investments (BOI) and PEZA provide incentives such as tax holidays and import-duty exemption to encourage the private sector to take the lead in developing SEZs. At present, SEZs are either industrial estates, PEZA-run export-processing zones (EPZs), free-trade zones, or other commercial/industrial developments. However, SEZs currently undergoing development are increasingly comprehensive in scope and often are self-contained communities. For instance, Tarlac's Hacienda Luisita, which houses Luisita Industrial Park, will feature such non-industrial developments as tourist and commercial facilities. Moreover, industrial estates are increasing their land holdings by acquiring contiguous areas for development into housing and recreational facilities.

Prospects for SEZs and auxiliary services generally are good. Demand for land within SEZs remains strong, as shown by high occupancy rates and expansion programs of existing SEZ developers. Further, with SEZs becoming more integrated by providing other community needs such as housing and schools, the range of required products and services is bound to widen and diversify. There are many opportunities for foreign companies that can either enter strategic alliances to develop industrial estates, probably with significant equity infusions, or provide equipment and supplies for infrastructure development of new or expanding industrial estates.

Japanese companies have dominated industrial estate development. These companies entered into strategic alliances with local partners and consequently brought in Japanese design and construction companies, generally under joint-venture arrangements with local companies. They also brought in Japanese equipment suppliers to provide infrastructure development requirements. The presence of many Japanese companies within industrial estates has boosted demand for Japanese infrastructure-development providers.

In contrast, US companies are involved mostly as consultants or contractors of specific services. Only one US company, Bechtel Investment Inc, has played a significant role as a strategic partner in developing Light Industry and Science Park of the Philippines. Foreign companies could boost performance in this sector by coming in as strategic partners in industrial estate development and, in the process, bringing in medium-sized companies to provide infrastructure-development requirements.

Considering the large investment requirements for industrial estate development, most medium-sized companies probably would not be able to enter as majority share-holders/equity providers. However, they might provide consulting services or supply such equipment or services for industrial estate facilities as communications, electric power, water (or provisions for connecting to the main Manila Waterworks Sewerage System water supply), sewerage and drainage, and pollution control. There also are opportunities for suppliers of construction equipment and materials. Given the trend toward developing mixed-use SEZs, there also are opportunities for foreign companies with expertise in providing such ancillary facilities such as housing and recreational, commercial and tourist facilities.

Foreign companies can penetrate the market by offering services directly to industrial estate developers or to identified or potential contractors or by entering joint-venture arrangements with Filipino companies.

The government has encouraged development of these industrial estates and EPZs to spread industrialisation to the countryside. Industrial estates and EPZs that mushroomed as a result of the PEZA program catered mostly to small and medium-sized province-based enterprises. Indeed, infrastructure facilities in these estates generally were not sufficient to attract large companies.

In the late 1980s, the government renewed its call to spur industrialisation in the countryside by promoting the Calabarzon growth area in South-

Table 1. Government-identified growth zones and their areas of specialisation

Growth zones	Area of specialisation
Cagayan-Iligan Corridor	Heavy industrial centre and major agro-industrial and trade centre
Northwestern Luzon Quadrangle	Financial centre and tourist haven
Cotabato-Davao-Zamboanga Crescent	Agro-business centre, major exporter of fresh and processed food and other products
Panay-Negros Pole	Light to medium manufacturing centre specialising in furniture, jewellery, toys, handicrafts, kitchen and housewares
Leyte-Samar Zone	Centre for heavy industries
West Central Luzon/Baselands	Ship and aircraft manufacturing and repair, regional warehousing and transhipment, defence industries and other light to medium industries

ern Luzon. To transform the region into a balanced agro-industrial centre, the Department of Trade and Industry initiated the Calabarzon project, a large multi-sectoral program designed to convert the traditional agro-based economies of the region into vigorous agro-industrial urban economies. Further, the Foreign Investments Act of 1991 liberalised investment regulations, and offered attractive incentives to foreign investors in Calabarzon. These incentives include tax holidays, as well as exemptions from import duties, export taxes and fees, local taxes, wharfage fees, and other forms of levy. Industrial estate developers responded to these incentives by establishing a number of industrial estates in Calabarzon, particularly in the provinces of Cavite and Laguna.

In 1992, following the success of the Calabarzon growth zone, the government identified six additional growth zones for development. Table 1 lists those growth zones and their respective areas of specialisation.

Aside from the growth of Calabarzon, development has also proceeded rapidly within the West Central Luzon/Baselands growth zone, the site of the former US military bases, Subic and Clark. As available infrastructure and proximity to Metro Manila spurred Calabarzon's development, anchor developments in Subic (the sea port) and Clark (the airport) have attracted investors.

Other growth zones have yet to enjoy the same success as Calabarzon and the former base lands. However, legislation has been passed to encourage development in other growth zones such as Cagayan-Iligan Corridor and the Cotabato-Davao-Zamboanga Crescent. Specifically, in 1995, the government approved legislation that identifies both Zamboanga City (Republic Act 7903) and the province of Cagayan (Republic Act 7922) as areas for SEZ development. The Zamboanga City SEZ will follow the free-port concept.

Due to its limited resources, the government encourages SEZ development through private initiative. The government also encourages SEZ development by providing incentives through PEZA or the Board of Investments (BOI).

SEZ developers may register with either PEZA or BOI to avail themselves of incentives that include exemption from national and local taxes and licences for new or expanding SEZ developers/operators and enterprises engaged in export, free trade, domestic market, utilities, facilities and tourism enterprises other than SEZ service enterprises. On the other hand, since 1989, BOI has come up with an annual Investments Priorities Plan (IPP) that identifies priority activities that are eligible for incentives. Incentives for BOI-registered firms include four-year income tax holidays, tax credits for locally purchased equipment, and 3% duty on imported capital equipment. Under its 1996 IPP, BOI will grant these incentives to developers of a 'technopolis' (a complete community of industrial zones, hospitals, training centres and educational facilities) for the first time.

GOVERNMENT PARTICIPANTS

The government agencies mainly involved in setting policy initiatives and performing administrative functions over SEZs are PEZA and over the Bases Conversion Development Authority (BCDA). Subic Bay Metropolitan Authority (SBMA) and the Clark Development Corporation (CDC) establish policies for the Subic and Clark free-trade zones respectively. BOI is also involved in determining policy direction for SEZs as it establishes and administers incentives for SEZ developers.

Republic Act 7916 provides PEZA with the mandate to set general policies for establishing and operating industrial estates, EPZs and free-trade zones. PEZA also reviews project proposals based on such legal criteria as the existence of required infrastructure and endorses approval of such projects. PEZA manages, registers, regulates and supervises the four government EPZs. It also oversees the operation and maintenance of utilities, infrastructure and other services in such zones. These include heat, light and power, water supply, telecommunications, transport, toll roads and bridges, and port services.

Republic Act 7227, also known as the Bases Conversion Act, mandates BCDA to turn over former US military lands in Metro Manila and around the country to the private sector for development. Private companies may be involved in developing former military lands through joint-venture agreements with BCDA or other arrangements. As a matter of policy, BCDA prefers joint ventures as opposed to outright sales to facilitate development since such arrangements enable BCDA to retain ownership of land.

SBMA and CDC formulate policies for their respective former US bases, Subic and Clark. SBMA, an affiliate agency of BCDA, was created by Republic Act 7227. CDC, on the other hand, is a subsidiary/implementing arm created by BCDA to manage a former military base; it is a private corporation duly registered with the Securities and Exchange Commission. CDC has authority to operate, administer, manage and develop the Clark Special Economic Zone. Subsidiaries such as CDC have their own officers and boards of directors, which are autonomous except for the oversight functions that BCDA performs.

The government requires developers of proposed SEZs to secure permits from the following agencies:

- Department of Agrarian Reform;
- Department of Agriculture;
- Housing and Land Use Regulatory Board;
- Department of Environment and Natural Resources; and
- National Water Resources Board.

MAJOR PLAYERS

SEZs may contain any one or a combination of industrial estates, government export-processing zones, free-trade zones or other commercial/industrial facilities.

The term 'industrial estate' refers to a privately owned tract of land subdivided and developed according to a comprehensive plan. Industrial estates typically provide basic infrastructure and utilities, with or without pre-built standard factory buildings and community facilities. An industrial estate usually features electricity supplied by such utilities firms as Manila Electric Company, telecommunications facilities, ground water wells and centralised water distribution system, a concrete road system, and a centralised sewerage or waste treatment facility.

A few industrial estates provide housing as well as educational and recreational facilities for employees at all levels. There are seven major private industrial estates, with six concentrated in the Calabarzon growth

Table 2. The seven major Philippine industrial estates

Industrial estates	*Location*
Carmelray Industrial Park	Calamba, Laguna
First Cavite Industrial Estate	Dasmarinas, Cavite
Gateway Business Park	General Trias, Cavite
Laguna International Industrial Park	Binan, Laguna
Laguna Technopark	Santa Rosa, Laguna
Light Industry and Science Park of the Philippines	Cabuyao, Laguna
Luisita Industrial Park	Tarlac, Tarlac

zone and one in Tarlac province. These estates contain two zones: a non-EPZ for firms engaged in domestic production and a special EPZ for those in export production. Firms located within the special EPZ may avail themselves of tax and other fiscal incentives administered by PEZA. Industrial estate developers usually sell land within the non-export zone to locators, although in some instances developers offer lease packages. EPZ land, on the other hand, is available for lease over a 50-year period and renewable for an additional 25 years. The lengthy allowable lease period provides locators permanence in occupying the land. The seven major industrial estates are listed in Table 2.

These estates are members of the Philippine Industrial Estates Association (Philea), a lobby group. With the exception of Luisita Industrial Park (Phase I), Philea industrial estates are the result of alliances between local companies and mostly Japanese companies under joint-venture arrangements. Typically, equity for these joint-venture companies is 40% foreign-held, with the balance coming from local companies. Through the formation of such joint-venture companies, foreign firms are able to participate in property development and comply with land ownership requirements. Besides providing financing, the foreign strategic partner also contributes technical expertise in estate planning and marketing.

Since the majority of the foreign strategic partners that developed Philea industrial estates are Japanese, most companies located within these industrial estates are also Japanese. For example, large Japanese trading and manufacturing firms such as Mitsubishi and Mitsui are strategic partners in developing Laguna Technopark and Light Industry and Science Park of the Philippines, respectively. Their marketing efforts succeeded in attracting such other large Japanese manufacturing companies as Honda Motors and Hitachi as locators. Since most major Japanese companies already have existing facilities in these industrial estates, Japanese industrial estate developers have adjusted their marketing efforts to focus on second-tier and small and medium-sized Japanese companies. Besides attracting most of the major Japanese manufacturing firms, private industrial estates also have been successful in attracting such large multinational companies as Procter and Gamble, Universal Motors Corporation, Tupperware and Intel.

A number of developers have announced plans to construct new industrial estates. With traditional sites such as Laguna and Cavite reaching saturation, developers are planning to locate their new estates in other Calabarzon provinces such as Batangas, Quezon and Rizal, Central Luzon provinces, and some areas in Northern Luzon such as Pangasinan. Acoland Inc, the real estate subsidiary of the Aboitiz Group and Company, is planning to develop a 300-hectare industrial estate in Balambanan, Cebu. Another company that has announced plans to develop SEZs is the Hong Kong-based Vancouver High Tech Development. This company joined with local firm Long River Developers Company to develop a two-phase industrial estate covering 160 hectares in San Simon, Pampanga. This consortium is also planning to put up several more industrial estates in other key cities, including Davao, Cebu, Iligan and Cagayan de Oro. Combined, the five projects will require some US$307.7 million in investments.

Aside from planned industrial estates, existing industrial estates have expansion plans. Laguna Technopark has started work to add 68 hectares. Light Industry and Science Park of the Philippines, Laguna International Industrial Park and Gateway Business Park recently announced plans to expand capacity by more than 120, 150 and 100 hectares, respectively. However, the largest planned expansion is that of Luisita Industrial Park. The 300-hectare expansion project, named Luisita Industrial Park 2, will be a joint venture between local partners and Itochu Corporation of Japan. Luisita Industrial Park 2 will be a self-contained community with residential and recreational facilities to support the industrial community.

GOVERNMENT EXPORT PROCESSING ZONES

EPZs are specialised industrial estates located, physically or administratively, outside the Philippines customs territory. There are presently four government-owned-and-operated EPZs located in Bataan, Cavite, Mactan and Baguio City. All are self-contained enclaves and cater primarily for various industries involved in the processing, assembly and manufacturing of goods for export. PEZA, as administrator of EPZs, allows locators to operate on a lease basis for up to 50 years and for another 25 years upon renewal of the lease agreement.

All EPZs except Cavite have standard factory buildings that are available for lease to locators. Facilities are similar to those in private industrial estates but generally are not as attractive because PEZA relies mainly on lease revenues to operate and maintain EPZs, while private industrial estates can generate larger cash flows through land sales to locators. In addition, lease rates of private industrial estates are significantly higher than those charged by EPZs.

Since the government intends to pass on responsibility for developing SEZs to the private sector, there are few planned EPZs or expansion programs of existing EPZs. One planned EPZ will cover 50 to 100 hectares in Ilocos Sur (Northern Luzon). Only the Mactan Export Processing Zone will expand. Acoland Inc is currently leading efforts to develop Mactan Export Processing Zone II (MEPZ II). When completed, MEPZ II will cover 62 hectares and will include commercial and industrial facilities.

FREE-TRADE ZONES

A free-trade zone is an isolated, policed area adjacent to a port of entry, such as a seaport or airport. Zone-based companies usually are involved in such activities as unpacking for immediate trans-shipment, repacking, sorting, mixing or storage of imported goods.

The expiration of the 1947 Military Bases Agreement in 1991 brought about the total withdrawal of American forces by the end of 1992. The US Government turned over two vacated facilities to the Philippine government for conversion to civilian use. Two major free-trade zones are the Subic Bay Special Economic and Freeport Zone and Clark Special Economic Zone. SBMA and CDC manage their respective facilities. Development plans envision the conversion of Subic and Clark lands, which have a combined area of about 34,000 hectares, into strategic sea and air ports, respectively. Once these crucial infrastructure developments are in place, Subic and Clark will serve as catalysts for industrialisation of the Luzon region and the northern Philippines. (Chapter 12 includes detailed analysis of the Subic and Clark zones.)

OTHER COMMERCIAL/INDUSTRIAL DEVELOPMENTS

Other major commercial/industrial developments include former military compounds. Specifically, the government plans to convert more than 10 former military camps within Metro Manila and parts of Luzon for civilian use. The most prominent project is Fort Bonifacio, of which the Metro Pacific Corporation-led consortium, Bonifacio Land Corporation (BLC) bought 214 of the total 440 hectares for US$1.508 billion in 1995. BLC formed the Fort Bonifacio Development Corporation (FBDC) as a joint venture with BCDA (BLC with 55% and BCDA with 45% equity share). FBDC will convert the zone into a premier central business district surrounded by mixed-use and high-end residential segments.

The remaining 226 hectares within Fort Bonifacio will contain an institutional zone with schools and a hospital of international standards, a vast existing memorial park and socialised housing projects for relocated residents of the former military camp. Because of the extent of planned developments for Fort Bonifacio, FBDC has tapped mainly large foreign companies as planning consultants. But while broad concepts originate from the foreign companies, local companies will undertake detailed engineering.

The sheer magnitude of development that will take place in Fort Bonifacio opens up many opportunities for companies offering various products and services. Participants in the Fort Bonifacio development need not be large companies but must possess a solid track record to prove that they can meet FBDC's standards.

Apart from the Fort Bonifacio project, there are six smaller former military compounds in Metro Manila under BCDA jurisdiction. Victory Liner, a local transport company, will develop the Joint United States Military Advisory Group's 1,391-square metre property in Quezon City. BCDA is conducting a study to identify possible uses for the soon-to-close Villamor Air Base. It is also currently studying possible uses for the four other camps: Bago Bantay, Melchor, Atienza and Claudio. Development of these camps will likely be through joint-venture arrangements. BCDA favours undertaking joint ventures rather than implementing these projects under the BOT scheme or selling outright to third parties. This preference for joint ventures enables BCDA to preserve some ownership and allows it to participate in project development. Developers have yet to finalise the master plan for the former John Hay Poro Point in La Union province, pending resolution of the area's land-use problems.

ROLE OF US COMPANIES

Industry observers note that US companies have not been active in property development in general and industrial estate development in particular. In developing SEZs, US companies have participated mainly as consultants and contractors of specific requirements. For instance, the US-based ROMA Design Group took the lead in urban planning efforts for developing Carmelray Industrial Park. Similarly, the US firm, The SWA Group, formulated the master plan of Hacienda Luisita, site of Luisita Industrial

Park. Participation of these companies as consultants in these projects did not entail equity infusions.

Japanese firms have dominated this field because of the pressing need to find a less expensive place to do business than inside Japan. In the late 1980s and early 1990s, large Japanese companies saw the Philippines as a viable site for relocating their manufacturing activities. Japanese companies formed strategic alliances with local partners to develop industrial estates. These developers were able to bring in Japanese design and construction companies as well as equipment suppliers to fill infrastructure development requirements of industrial estates. As strategic partners, Japanese companies also performed marketing functions and thus brought in Japanese manufacturers as industrial estate locators. Because of these marketing efforts, Japanese companies represent the majority in most of the larger industrial estates. The locators in turn comprise a captive market that relies on Japanese contractors and suppliers to put up factories and other facilities.

Japanese companies also have gained prominence in providing the infrastructure development requirements as well as expansion programs of existing government EPZs. For example, the Japan-based Overseas Economic Cooperation Fund financed development of the Mactan EPZ and will also finance the planned MEPZ II.

RECOMMENDATIONS

Industry players agree that prospects for SEZ developers and providers of auxiliary services are excellent, at least over the next five to 10 years. Demand for land within SEZs has been strong, shown by full occupancy rates in existing SEZs and high take-up rates of planned expansion programs. Requirements of SEZ developers are increasingly more varied since the trend is towards SEZs that are self-contained communities rather than strictly industrial complexes. Philippine SEZs continue to have an edge over those in neighbouring countries. According to a study prepared by the University of Asia and the Pacific (formerly the Centre for Research and Communication), the Philippines' major competitors within the region suffer from the following setbacks:

- Thailand is clogged by infrastructure bottlenecks due to over-expansion of its economy. Thus, even Thais are looking at other countries as possible new sites for their plants.
- Malaysia is suffering from a labour shortage. With demand for manpower going up, salaries and wages will also rise, making the country unattractive as an investment site for foreign investors.

- Vietnam, the new investment attraction of the region, does not yet pose a threat since it lacks the adequate infrastructure to sustain industrial development.
- China, concerned that its economy is overheating, has started to reduce incentives to foreign investors.

There are numerous opportunities for companies that can form strategic alliances to take the lead in developing and operating private SEZs, probably with significant equity infusions. Companies that do not meet the intensive capital requirements for this can assist in developing SEZs as planning and design consultants. Since US firms are acknowledged leaders in this field, local developers will be more receptive to contracting services of those companies. Foreign firms can also provide construction and technical consulting services.

Small and medium-sized foreign companies can provide equipment and supplies or join with local companies undertaking SEZ development to clear and level the site, provide road networks, install sewerage and drainage systems and construct power and telecommunications facilities. There is also demand for developers of facilities for cargo-handling, food distribution/warehousing, and transport as well as for providers of construction equipment and materials and pollution control devices and control systems. Further, with the trend towards developing mixed-use SEZs, there are opportunities for companies with expertise in design and construction of housing and recreational, commercial and tourist facilities.

In addition, foreign companies also can sell small power-generation facilities, waste-water treatment facilities, electro-mechanical works such as street lights and wiring, and telecommunications facilities.

Opportunities for foreign firms, and for the private sector in general, to provide services for EPZs are limited. This is due to the fact that, aside from the planned EPZ in Ilocos Sur, the government does not plan to put up additional EPZs. Further, limited funds and sources of financing place constraints on plans for expansion and improvement of existing EPZs and, since loans are typically from Japanese lending institutions, contractors likely will be Japanese companies.

Developers of industrial estates and other SEZs generally are receptive to sourcing consulting services and infrastructure developers from foreign companies. However, they stress that, because foreign companies have maintained a low profile in the market, they must develop a more pro-active stance in marketing their products and services. Even experienced Philippine developers may not be aware of the full range of products and services foreign firms can offer. Foreign companies may penetrate the market using the following strategies:

- offering services directly to developers of implementing agencies such as BCDA, or implementing arms such as CDC;
- offering services to identified or potential contractors that are willing to subcontract certain services for the larger property-development projects; and
- entering joint venture arrangements with Filipino companies (recommended for companies that possess technology with practical applications in SEZ development).

CHAPTER 12

THE FREE PORTS: CLARK AND SUBIC

By Eric Moltzau Anderson

Two former US military installations in the Philippines now operate as self-sustaining industrial, commercial and investment centers. These are the Subic Bay Freeport in Subic Bay and the Clark Special Economic Zone in Angeles City. Subic is now a bustling community of more than 200 enterprises, mostly exporters. Firms within Subic are exempt from import duties and national taxes on imports of capital equipment and raw materials needed for operations within the zone. These establishments are required to pay only a 5% tax based on their gross income. The approximately 100 companies registered at Clark enjoy the same incentives as those at Subic. Both zones boast their own international airports with 3000-metre strips originally built by the Americans for US Navy and Air Force planes. The eruption of Mount Pinatubo in June 1991 drove the Americans from Clark, and the Philippine Senate in September 1991 rejected US pleas to renew the military bases agreement under which the United States wanted to cling to Subic. This forced the US Navy to hoist anchor in November 1992. Both Clark and Subic have power plants, telecommunications facilities, housing complexes and tourist facilities—some entirely new and others converted from US military operations.

MANUFACTURING AND TOURISM

At a time when the world trend in trade policy is to move toward an open economy by establishing trade blocs, competitive advantage is a key factor. In an effort to enhance competitive advantage in the Philippines, industrial estates and export processing zones (EPZs) have been established, but the results to date of some of these efforts have been mixed. However, the two most recent EPZs, Clark and Subic, are expected to have a clearly beneficial effect on the Philippine economy. With lessons learned from previous experience and a virtually paid-up infrastructure, Clark and Subic are favourably positioned to play a positive role in the Philippine economy.

Today, with the exception of the Philippine military areas within Clark and Subic, the rest of the two bases are administratively under the management of the Bases Conversion Development Authority (BCDA). Clark Development Corporation (CDC) and the Subic Bay Metropolitan Authority (SBMA) are the two arms of BCDA responsible for the management of the bases.

Since Clark and Subic became the property of the Philippine Government, the main thrust has been towards establishing small to medium-sized manufacturing companies for exports and to develop tourism. Duty-free shopping and various services also have been instituted. These, combined with the existing airport and harbour facilities, military installations and the general infrastructure, provide a strong basis for economic development. The tourist facilities and industrial estates also generate a continuous inflow of foreign currency. As foreign investment is attracted, employment opportunities generated and taxes collected, it is doubtless that Clark and Subic have been instrumental in improving the competitiveness rating of the Philippines to 33 out of 41 in a recent evaluation by the World Competitiveness Report of the World Economic Forum headquartered in Switzerland.

Economically, manufacturing is the primary activity at Clark and Subic. The overall concept is that of an industrial estate. Of Clark's total land area of 4,440 hectares, approximately 900 have been set aside for the industrial estates, with 400 hectares zoned for export-oriented manufacturing and the rest mainly for airport services. In the case of Subic, of a total land area of 6,600 hectares, 210 have been set aside for industrial estates, all of which are for export-oriented manufacturing.

The two greatest benefits for manufacturing at Clark and Subic are their respective infrastructures and their free-trade zone status. The combined infrastructure was estimated to be worth US$9.2 billion at the time of the handover from United States to Philippine control in 1991 and 1992, with $1.2 billion at Clark and $8 billion at Subic. This means that CDC and SBMA are distinguished from the rest of the Philippines by the quality of their infrastructure. Duty-free import status has been extended as a result of the declaration of Clark and Subic as EPZs. Duty-free status is preferable to duty-drawback, which requires the exporter to apply for a duty refund after the end of the year rather than receiving an exemption up-front.

The greatly perceived drawback for manufacturing companies at Clark and Subic is a regulation that restricts sales domestically outside the EPZs to 30% of total production. (The imported contents of EPZ-manufactured goods sold domestically outside the EPZs are not exempt from duty.) This regulation is imposed to bias investment in manufacturing toward exporters, a fact that is known to applicants from the start. As a result, most companies do not sell on the local market and are not affected by this regulation.

Tourism is not yet an important feature at Clark and Subic. To begin with, the Philippines has a relatively underdeveloped tourist industry. Nationwide receipts from international tourism are roughly one-fourth of total merchandise export earnings. Clark and Subic alone are hardly in a position to tempt a significant number of foreign visitors. This is because the two zones lack tourist attractions of enough importance to interest the international traveller. It is difficult to envision tourists visiting areas that are hosts to industrial estates, and only a very small ratio of foreign visitors include Clark and Subic in their itineraries unless they have business there. Gambling is presently the only aspect of tourism with immediate potential.

At Clark, 170 hectares are devoted to tourism and recreation. At Subic, the figure is 2,245 hectares, 2,000 of which are a nature reserve.

In other Philippine EPZs, pitfalls such as poor location, overvalued exchange rates, large investment capital, substitution of foreign investment with subsidised domestic loans and foreign exchange barriers are present. Some of these pitfalls have been avoided at Clark and Subic. Investment for infrastructure is minimal, and financing is obtained from the World Bank and the private sector through privatised operation of certain services such as the harbour operation. Subsidised loans to foreign investors are no longer available. Political instability is not perceived as a serious threat at this time, and technology transfer is not even included in the present mission statement. The fact that minimum wages and labour regulations are rigorously enforced at Clark and Subic guarantees workers there a substantial improvement in income and reduces the risk of labour unrest. Lastly, foreign exchange controls have been liberalised.

Companies are listed at Clark and Subic on a project-approval basis. While manufacturing is the main thrust, retailing is also strong. Taiwan is the main foreign investor followed by the United States, but Japan is coming on strong at Subic in particular. At Clark, the potential employment from existing projects is more than 49,000 people by the year 2000, while at Subic this number is more than 40,000. Cumulative downstream employment effects on the local economy are considered to be five additional jobs for every new job created within the zones, thus the total economic effect on Clark and Subic may approach 500,000 by the millennium.

The jobs generated at Clark and Subic differ in nature from those during the US military presence. There was substantial migration and some job retraining initially following the exodus of the Americans, but this migratory pattern is of little consequence now. Most employees at Clark and Subic are local hires, as encouraged by CDC and SBMA policy.

By far, most of the firms rely on foreign markets, showing that the zone's export bias is a success. Furthermore, perhaps most of the products produced at Clark and Subic are too high-end for the Philippine market. Light and medium industries, as directed in the mission statements of Clark and Subic, are indeed the main areas of manufacturing.

Besides taxes and profit-sharing, CDC and SBMA rely largely on income from services—basically real estate—to finance their operating expenses. The portion of services that serve foreign clients is of economic interest because it affects the national balance of payments. Foreign clients servicing Clark are mainly connected with tourism. At Subic, Federal Express and Coastal Petroleum are the major foreign clients doing so.

Clark offers tourism activities such as golf, trekking and climbing, skydiving, ballooning, auto-racing, ultralight flying, flight excursions, four-wheel-drive excursions and shopping. Subic offers such activities as gambling, swimming, jet-skiing, windsurfing, sailing, scuba-diving, bungee jumping, horseback riding, ball games, jungle trekking, car racing, rock concerts and shopping. Charter flights bring tourists in mainly for gambling.

MILITARY BASE VERSUS FREE PORT

It is only natural to compare CDC and SBMA performance with Clark and Subic as military bases. US government expenditures on operating, developing and maintaining Clark and Subic at the end of the lease period were US$90 million per year. A total of 30,000 Philippine nationals were employed at Clark under US administration and 42,000 at Subic. American security assistance to the Philippines would at best have contributed sporadic bursts of economic assistance had the military bases agreement been renegotiated. For this reason it is best to disregard security assistance as a factor for opportunity cost.

In summary, the opportunity cost of Clark and Subic from termination of the bases agreement is mainly attributed to the loss of approximately US$100 million in foreign influx from operating costs and US$300 million in foreign influx for aid. This influx of foreign money simultaneously indirectly funded about 72,000 jobs at Clark and Subic alone. Clark and Subic created about 350,000 downstream jobs, and others were created as a result of the aid expenditures.

Nearly all the present employment at Clark and Subic can be attributed to employment opportunities generated directly by Clark and Subic. There are a few exceptions, such as domestic companies that transferred their existing operations from other parts of the Philippines to Clark and Subic, thus not adding new jobs. This accounts for about 700 of the jobs at Clark and Subic now.

Regarding the influx of foreign money, this is now derived from foreign direct investment, domestic content exports, services with foreign clients and domestic-content import substitution. It should be noted that some of the new companies that decided to locate at Clark or Subic could have chosen another spot in the Philippines if Clark and Subic did not exist. There is a fair amount of uncertainty attached to the opportunity cost, both from the standpoint of how speculative the forecast is, how long the American military presence would have been sustained had the bases agreement been extended, and in what condition the facilities would have been left had the handover occurred much later.

The timing of the handover of the bases is important when considering the cumulative impact of the financial results. Would the income from the American military presence have increased or decreased if the handover had occurred later? Would the success of the CDC and SBMA have been greater or less? When considering the increased pressure the US Government has been under to decrease military spending since the break-up of the Soviet Union, the upbeat attitude toward South-East Asian markets and the present level of income generated under CDC and SBMA administration, it seems likely that delaying the handover would have resulted in a lower cumulative financial result.

THE MINDANAO COMPARISON

To obtain a general idea of how Clark and Subic compare with other industrial estates in the region, information has been collected from the Philippine Veterans' Investment Development Corporation (PHIVIDEC) in the large southern Philippine island of Mindanao. The PHIVIDEC Industrial Authority (PIA) was created on 13 August 1974. Located in Misamis Oriental Province, Mindanao, PHIVIDEC Industrial Estate has been given the task of dispersing industries to rural areas.

PIA encourages domestic and foreign investment in order to create employment, increase the volume of exports and accelerate regional development. Land is leased for 15 years, with leases renewable for up to a total of 30 years. The rental rate is 15 pesos per square metre per year with 10% annual escalation. At 3,000 hectares, PIE is one of the largest industrial estates. PIE is 20 kilometres from Cagayan de Oro City, the nearest urban centre with regional administrative functions. The estate has harbours that can accommodate vessels up to 305,000 tons deadweight. A tax incentive of exemption from local taxes is offered; however, this exemption does not include property tax. Duty drawback can be applied for goods exported. The PHIVIDEC Industrial Estate aims to attract medium to heavy industries that are power-intensive, non-polluting and with sizeable land area requirements.

One of the most important features of Clark and Subic is their duty-free status, which allows material costs to be closer to international levels. Other industrial estates, such as PHIVIDEC, which operate on a duty-drawback basis, are not as competitive because duty drawback imposes a financial burden on the manufacturer without easing the burden of red tape.

At Clark, land rental is five pesos per square metre per month, with leases running 25 to 50 years, renewable for another 25 years. Building rentals range from 40 to 60 pesos per square metre per month, depending on whether the building is constructed of wood or concrete. These rates are increasing by 10% a year. At Subic, leases are confidential, but reports indicate that developed land ranges from 13 to 26 pesos per square metre per month, with leases for 50 years, renewable for 25 additional years. Building rentals start at about 78 pesos per square metre per month and are relatively short-term, some as short as five years.

Except for the domestic telephone system, the infrastructures at Clark and Subic are good. The telecommunications problem is shared with some of the other countries in the region, but as these other countries inevitably develop their systems, Clark and Subic will lag behind. Electrical power supply at Clark and Subic is satisfactory. The tax burden at Clark and Subic is not excessive; effectively, most companies pay between 2% and 8% tax.

Another consideration is long-term viability. There is an ever present threat from Mount Pinatubo, which could cripple Clark in an instant. However, as time passes without eruptions similar to the one in June 1991 that inundated Clark and much of Subic with ash and devastated much of the countryside, the threat tends to be ignored. It is now generally thought that the worst-case scenario would be moderate amounts of airborne ash landing on the area. Political instability is not expected to affect Clark and Subic since it would not be in the interest of any government administration to effect changes in the organisation of Clark and Subic that would detract from their special status. Trade relations are not a problem for the Philippines and, so far, quotas have been unrestrictive. Except with Singapore, the Philippines has not suffered the kinds of problems that have alienated China, Myanmar, Vietnam and Indonesia, where political tensions threaten to reduce trade through various repercussions.

Foreign investment by weighted average accounts for 79% of the production at Clark and Subic—97% at Subic and 22%% at Clark. These percentages are good indicators of the extent to which Clark and Subic are perceived to be competitive compared with other foreign industrial estates in the region as only Philippine-based investors would have any reason to invest if they could not compete with other regional estates. But it is important to keep in mind that Clark is in a very early stage of operation and has not yet had time to become well known abroad.

HOW THEY DECIDE

The factors that motivate firms when deciding where to locate vary depending on the products they manufacture, but whatever their specific requirements, all investors have to base their decision on the following overall considerations:

- Price competitiveness—cost of labour, material transport, etc.;
- Quality—qualified labour, climate, suitable building/land;
- Logistics—infrastructure, market location, material availability, transport availability, etc.; and
- Long-term viability—political stability, government cooperation, security, expansion space.

Within the Philippines, seven factors are most important: proximity to markets, road access, reliable electric power, telephone infrastructure, suitable land, suitable building and space for expansion. For locally owned firms, a suitable plot of land is the most important factor; for foreign-owned firms, reliable electric power and telephones are most important. This is as expected since local firms have less basis for comparison than foreign firms when considering availability of electric power and telephone service. They also are more willing to cope with problems associated with these factors because they do not have an alternative.

The manufacturing sectors on Clark and Subic are composed largely of small to medium-sized firms that focus on exports. Strategies for large firms differ somewhat from those of small and medium-sized firms. Because they don't have the resources to create brand recognition on an international scale, small export firms compete first and foremost on price. Thus factors that affect price would be of greater importance to small and medium-sized export manufacturers. For this reason, the following factors have been added to a survey of Clark and Subic firms that is described in the next section: available materials, price of labour, price of land, building rent and taxes. Suitable labour has been included as well because it is one of the selling points of Clark and Subic. Security is another: Clark and Subic are well secured areas, which is an important factor in long-term viability.

Because Clark and Subic are particularly export-oriented, being close to port is another consideration. Then, too, political stability is important in view of events in recent years, including the downfall of Ferdinand Marcos in the People Power revolution of 1986, a series of coup attempts during the presidency of Corazon Aquino and the question of whether the relative stability during the term of Fidel Ramos, president from 1992 to 1998, will endure.

SURVEY OF FIRMS

The following are the results of a survey conducted in1996 in which all but one of the export firms at each of the two free ports participated. The firms were asked to rate the factors that influenced their decision to locate in Clark or Subic, or which ones they viewed as most important to their business.

Cheap labour

Cheap labour was rated important by 85% of those surveyed. At Clark and Subic workers generally are paid the minimum wage for the region. Apprentice wages are permitted for a period not exceeding six months. A one-week paid vacation and one week's paid sick leave, as well as a legally required one-month paid maternity absence. A Christmas bonus of one month's extra pay generally is given also. Social security and medicare taxes are shared between the employer and the employee.

Although labour productivity is rated low in the Philippines, this is mostly a reflection of the low level of capital investment.

Suitable labour

Availability of suitable labour was also rated important by 85% of the companies. The rating for skilled labour is very high for the Philippines in general, but each year many skilled workers join the ranks of the estimated 4.5 million who are working overseas. Furthermore, the educational standard of the Philippines was drastically reduced during the Marcos administration, and it will be some time before that damage will be undone. Curiously, UNESCO statistics for the 1991–92 school year indicated a marked difference between the sexes for those in higher education: 681,565 males and 975,250 females. One aspect of education that has had a strong beneficial effect for the Philippines is the emphasis on English as a second language.

Proximity to market

Proximity to market is not rated as important by most of the companies. This is a reflection of the fact that distant markets such as North America and Europe make up a large share of the customer base and that the competitive advantage often is great enough to overcome the additional freight costs incurred with long-distance transport. It also signifies that Clark and Subic are competing with industrial estates worldwide.

Good roads

Good roads are rated as important by 75% of the companies. This is because on-time delivery has become one of the strong selling points for products manufactured in the Philippines and it lowers the cost of some supplies as well as the cost of shipping out of Manila.

The road network accommodates approximately 60% of freight and 80% of passenger traffic in the Philippines. Roads inside Clark and Subic are good; roads between Clark and Subic are not good, and it takes at least two hours to drive the 80 kilometres from one to the other. Roads from Clark to Manila are good except for from Manila to Valenzuela and from San Fernando to Clark. It takes slightly more than an hour to drive the distance, 80 kilometres, when traffic conditions are good. The road from Subic to San Fernando, the junction point on the road from Angeles to Manila, is not good and is further complicated because of ash flows from Mount Pinatubo. It takes two-and-a-half hours at the very least to cover the 125 kilometres from Subic to Manila by car. Traffic in Manila is heavy. Truck bans and curfews have been implemented and, as in Mexico City, a plate-number scheme has been imposed that prohibits private cars from driving one day per week.

In addition to bad roads, slow vehicles are a cause of traffic congestion. There are also complaints of a shortage of traffic police. However, it would be more accurate to say that there is a prevailing inability to enforce traffic regulations. Flooding is common during heavy rain.

The traffic situation is expected to worsen in the short run since construction of new public transportation facilities and overpasses will partially block existing roads. Outside Manila, roads generally are routed through villages rather than around them, causing delays in travel time. Bad weather conditions cause landslides and rapid erosion. When strategic bridges are out of use, whole regions are cut off to ground transport for long periods of time. Slow vehicles such as tricycles are difficult for other vehicles to pass on the narrow roads, resulting in hazardous situations.

Electric power

Electric power is rated as one of the most important factors by the companies. But, since manufacturers at Clark and Subic are relatively low-intensity consumers of electrical power, it is dependability rather than price that is important.

In 1973, at the time of the first major increase in international petroleum prices, the Philippines was dependent on imported oil for 95% of its energy supply. By 1985, that dependence had been reduced to 51%, reflecting the development of various domestic sources of energy, notably coal, hydroelectric power, geothermal steam and non-conventional sources (mainly bagasse, agro-waste and dendrothermal). By 1990, the rate had increased again to 60% as a result of prevailing drought.

By the mid-1980s, the Philippines had an installed capacity of 894 megawatts from geothermal energy, propelling the country to second place, exceeded only by the United States. Further development of geothermal energy is being carried out by the Magma Power Company in Leyte. Some estimates suggest that the total potential for this source of energy could exceed 35,000 megawatts. Geothermal resources now meet 5% of the country's energy requirements.

A nuclear energy plant was started up in Bataan, the peninsular province between Subic and Manila, in 1986-1987, and this would have provided a generating capacity of 620 megawatts. But the project was beset with political controversy and, in May 1993, it was announced that the Bataan nuclear plant would be converted to a non-nuclear facility.

The abandonment of the Bataan nuclear plant resulted in undercapacity and, by 1984–85, the grid for Luzon, the largest Philippine island that includes Subic and Clark as well as Metro Manila, could not meet peak demand. Blackouts and brownouts of up to half a day were frequent during the dry season. In Mindanao, drought and the destruction of watersheds resulted in severe power shortages in 1991–93 on the usually energy-abundant island.

Because the energy shortage represented a major obstacle to economic growth, the government commenced a fast-track program designed to end the power shortage. This program gave priority to the construction of gas turbine power plants since the lead time for this type of technology is the shortest. By the end of 1993, the blackout situation was improving and it is now largely resolved.

At Clark, internal power generation consists of eight generators with a combined capacity of 50 megawatts. External power is provided from the National Power Company's substation in Mexico, a town near Angeles City, which can deliver 200 megawatts. Subic has one exclusive power plant with a capacity of seven megawatts and another belonging to the National Power Company, which supplies116 megawatts to the national grid. It is planned that the National Power Company power plant will supply Subic directly at some time in the very near future. There have been occasional brownouts in Clark and Subic as a result of typhoons and technical malfunctions rather than insufficient capacity.

Telecommunications

Good telephone service was also rated as one of the most important factors by the companies. The telephone infrastructure in the Philippines is severely underdeveloped. Out of 41 countries rated by the National Competitiveness Survey in 1994, the Philippines rated only 39th. International access is relatively good, but domestic access is inadequate. One company at Subic remarked that it sometimes sets up a conference call through a foreign city in order to reach a domestic destination.

Naturally, the direct effect of this problem is that foreign investors shy away because they find it too difficult to operate without adequate telecommunications. But the indirect effect is also important: foreign investors cannot understand how a government can allow something as important as the telecommunication infrastructure to lag so far behind. Since the telephone system is operated by the private sector in the Philippines, lack of funding is not the limiting factor. However, regulation is. If the government is unable to properly regulate the telephone system, which is among the foremost priorities in any economy, then how does it regulate everything else? In other words, the shortcomings of the telephone system underline the structural weakness of the national government itself.

Although there is no lack of telephone lines within Clark and Subic, the national shortfall affects the efficiency there by isolating them from their domestic outside contacts who have not been able to obtain telephone lines. As a last resort, cellular telephones are being used, but this is not an acceptable solution. Cellular telephones are expensive, and they are not convenient because of the poor audibility, limited range and difficulty in connections.

Until the telecommunications infrastructure problem is solved, firms must rely on the assistance of groups such as the Department of Trade and Industry, which sends regional agents out as intermediaries for the firms with messages and replies to the more remotely situated of their outside contacts. In spite of the admirable contribution made by these public servants, this system has no place in today's competitive environment.

How serious is the problem of the telephone backlog? In 1993, the Philippine Long Distance Telephone Company embarked on a zero-backlog program under which it hoped to fulfil outstanding orders for 1.6 million lines. By 1996 it had reached nearly 2 million lines, still with a backlog of well over a million amid ever rising demand. The number of telephones per 100 inhabitants for August 1995 was 2.3 for the Philippines, 41.7 for Taiwan, 1.2 for Indonesia, 0.4 for Vietnam and 2.2 for China. Of the 1599 municipalities in the Philippines, only 329 had local exchange service. The National Telecommunications Department set a target for telephone penetration of 10 telephones per 100 inhabitants by 2010 and 100% penetration of local exchanges by the same year.

How are these targets going to be met? The National Telecommunications Commission (NTC) has divided the country into 11 service areas, some of which are profitable, others not. In addition, the NTC has regulatory control over the profitable operations of both Cellular Mobile Telephone Systems and International Gateway Facilities. By making the licensing of profitable services conditional upon the servicing of non-profitable areas, the NTC ensures that disadvantaged regions will eventually obtain more telephone lines.

Does this point to a prompt solution to the telephone shortage? Unfortunately, the answer is 'no'. The present situation is that licensed telecommunications companies are conspiring to bar new entrants, pointing to a future fraught with collusion and unlawful transactions. The group of companies jointly known as Club 109 fought to block the entry of Bell Telecom, which had pledged to install 2,603,000 local service lines within a decade. Although the Philippine Congress voted to grant a franchise, which was duly approved by the president, NTC prevented the franchise from going into effect on the grounds that it would spawn a climate of 'ruinous competition'. Thus, the office of the president was seen to be approving the competition, while the government's administrative arm blockaded it. The Department of Transportation and Communication (DOTC) had to step in to pressure the NTC into disciplining several telephone companies for lagging behind their installation schedules.

Cheap land and cheap building

Cheap land was rated very important by the firms at Clark and almost as important at Subic. Cheap building was rated was less important by the manufacturing firms than cheap land, and at Subic it was only rated important by 37% of the manufacturing firms. This reflects the long-term commitment, particularly at Subic. It also reflects that land and building are cheaper at Clark than at Subic. However, firms at Clark have lower real estate costs due to the perceived risk of volcanic activity from Mount Pinatubo. Real estate prices at Clark and Subic appear to be market-driven rather than regulated for economic development.

Suitable land and suitable building

Suitability of land and building is rated very important by the manufacturing firms, and again the ratings also indicate the preference at Clark for rental of building space rather than lease of land relative to Subic. The high rating of this category reflects concern for quality.

Expansion space

Space for expansion is rated extremely important at Subic and important at Clark. Again, this underlines long-term commitment. Expansion space is not yet a problem at Clark and Subic, and future shortages can be avoided by rezoning land.

Availability of materials

Availability of materials is only rated as being important to about half of the manufacturing firms at Clark and Subic. This rating is somewhat biased by the fact that many foreign companies source their materials from abroad at competitive prices, so local sourcing is unimportant.

However, availability of materials should not be underrated because material cost is clearly the largest cost component for the products manufactured at Clark and Subic. At Clark the products assembled for export are furniture, garments, gas cylinders, air conditioners, electrical panel boards, motorcycles, electronics, valves, investment castings, machine parts, building products, accessories and small leather goods, industrial filters, crystal glass articles, camping tents, hot air balloons, chemicals, adhesive tape, ice cream, toys and golf carts. At Subic the products assembled for export are electronics, armoured vehicles, machine parts, luxury gift items, plastic products, textiles, garments, light bulbs, accessories and small leather goods, leather garments, industrial cranes, computer cards, luggage carts, camping tents, fishing rods, car seats, brochures, boats, ships, ink, electrical cable, wetsuits, microphones, loudspeakers, shoes and display furniture.

The low percentage of domestic content at both Clark and Subic firmly reflects the low quality and high production cost in the Philippines. In reality, the level of domestic content is even lower since the figures include the cost of labour and services as well as material.

Port facilities

Closeness to port is rated important by most of the manufacturing firms. For Subic the rating is somewhat higher than for Clark, reflecting the fact that Subic has its own port. The seaport network in the Philippines handles about 40% of national freight and about 10% of passenger traffic. The two most important ports are Manila and Cebu. The capacity of the two international ports in Manila is adequate to handle the present load. Port access for Clark is via Manila or Subic. Although Manila is not very distant, traffic conditions in Manila and processing slows down transit time considerably.

Subic has its own port, but so far the four regular shipping lines servicing this port are not direct, but call via Manila. So far Kaohsiung and Singapore are the only destinations without trans-shipment requirements, but it is hoped that Clark will eventually be better able to take advantage of the port at Subic when roads improve. This will contribute to increasing the volume of freight, enabling direct shipments to many destinations.

Good security

Good security is rated important by almost all the manufacturing firms at Subic and most of those at Clark. This reflects the fact that security at Clark is rigid compared with the much more user-friendly system at Clark. On a national level, there is a severe problem with security. According to the newspapers, crime syndicates, supposedly formed by former law enforcement and military personnel, regularly kidnap prominent members of the business community. This is causing foreign investors, particularly Chinese and Japanese, to shun the country. The inability of the government to deal with the problem does nothing to instill potential investors with confidence.

So far there have not been any cases of kidnapping at Clark or Subic, and security seems to be under control. However, prior to establishment of CDC, Clark's reputation became somewhat tarnished during the Pinatubo evacuation when looting was prevalent. In all fairness, it should be noted that the looting was somewhat exaggerated in order to capitalise on insurance claims.

Taxes

Low taxes were rated important by nearly all the manufacturing companies at Clark and Subic. Taxation within Clark and Subic is very moderate. Essentially, as long as businesses earn more than 70% of their income from foreign sources, they pay only 5% tax on a so-called 'gross income earned', which deducts labour, production costs, materials, debt servicing, rent and depreciation. Depreciation is calculated over a period of five to 10 years. Three-fifths of the tax is paid to the national government, one-fifth to local government units and one-fifth to a special development fund.

However, it is not obvious that the taxes within Clark and Subic are competitive with national taxation for all firms. This depends upon the amount they are able to deduct according to the rules of gross income earned and the extent to which they would be able to evade tax if they operated outside Clark and Subic. It appears that the net effective tax inside Clark and Subic would be around 1%. But some firms claim that they are unable to deduct many of their raw materials and that, because of hidden costs, they pay as much as 8%.

Political stability

Political stability is rated important by nearly all manufacturing firms at Subic and most at Clark. After some tumultuous years, socio-political instability seems to have settled down somewhat. Coup attempts have ceased and military insurgency has decreased and is not expected to affect Clark and Subic. International trade relations are friendly and union activity has not taken hold at the two former bases.

Hidden costs

Many firms mentioned that hidden costs were also an important factor. This was particularly evident among American, European and Oceania investors and among smaller companies that generally are harder hit by bureaucratic demands.

CONCLUSION

The impact of Clark and Subic on the balance of payments of the Philippines has reached more or less the same level as during the US military administration. Employment is likely to exceed the 72,000-job level that existed before termination of the military bases agreement between the United States and the Philippines. Direct foreign investment is very strong, particularly at Subic. However, domestic-content exports will eventually have to replace this investment influx as a steady state is approached. Because the domestic content of exports is low, an effective way to benefit from exports is to support an increase in the proportion of domestic content.

The infrastructure at Clark and Subic—combined with duty-free status, good security and favourable taxes—has propelled their competitive advantage beyond that of the country in general and is helping to improve the image of the Philippines abroad. But the poor national infrastructure, particularly the insufficient domestic telephone system, is holding back the two export processing zones.

The product base at Clark and Subic is diverse and economies of scale have not yet occurred. For this to happen, competitive factors must be developed further, which requires a commitment from the government to back up such selected industries as rattan furniture and handicrafts with aggressive upstream programs.

Attractions of both domestic and foreign investment for manufacturing at Clark and Subic is clearly a positive factor for the Philippine economy, and manufacturing should by far be the main focus of attention for both CDC and SBMA. Clark and Subic do not lend themselves well to tourism in a major way, and some of the entertainment and shopping facilities at Clark and Subic could be located equally well outside the former base areas. Clark and Subic can be viewed as a testing ground for an open economy, and it will be very important to monitor their progress.

CHAPTER 13

EASING THE BURDEN

In recent years, the Philippines has introduced a range of special induce-
ments to persuade foreign companies to invest. The following summary of
some of the ways the government is trying to make life easier for those who
want to put their money in the Philippines was prepared by the American
embassy in Manila.

Incentives for firms engaged in government-preferred activities and
registered with the Board of Investment (BOI) under Book I, 'Investment
with Incentives', of the Omnibus Investments Code include:

- Income tax holiday—An income tax holiday of six years and four years,
  respectively, is available to registered new pioneer and non-pioneer
  firms. For registered expanding firms, the holiday is three years and
  proportionate to the firm's expansion.
- Additional deduction for labour expense—For the first five years from
  registration, there is an additional deduction from taxable income of
  50% of the wages corresponding to the incremental number of direct
  labours, provided the project meets the prescribed capital equipment-
  to-workers ratio set by the BOI.
- Tax and duty exemption on imported capital equipment and accompanying spare parts—Projects registered for incentives on or before
  31 December 1994 that are located outside the National Capital

Region may be exempted from internal revenue taxes and duties on imported capital equipment and accompanying spare parts for the period provided in their registration document or until 31 December 1999, whichever comes first. On the internal revenue tax portion, capital-equipment imports by companies that register with the BOI after 1994 are subject to the value-added tax as provided under an expanded value-added tax law that took effect in January 1996.

- Tax credit on domestic capital equipment—Firms outside the National Capital Region and registered with the BOI on or before 31 December 1994 that purchase local capital equipment before the end of 1999 may claim tax credits equivalent to the taxes and duties that would have been waived had the machinery been imported. Post-1994 BOI registrants, like other enterprises covered by the value-added tax system, can claim a tax credit or refund on machinery purchased equal to the actual value-added tax paid and passed on to it by the supplier.
- Tax and duty exemption on imported breeding stocks and genetic materials and/or tax credits on local purchases thereof (equivalent to the taxes and duties that would have been waived if imported)—These incentives apply to purchases made within 10 years from a company's registration with the BOI.
- There is unrestricted use of consigned equipment, machinery and spare parts.
- Employment of foreign nationals—For a period not exceeding five years from registration the employment of foreign nationals is allowed in supervisory, technical or advisory positions. This period is extendable for limited periods at the discretion of the BOI. The positions of president, treasurer and general manager (or their equivalents) may be retained by foreign nationals beyond the stipulated period when the majority of capital stock is owned by foreign investors.

Incentives to projects in less developed areas

To encourage the regional dispersal of industries, BOI-registered enterprises that locate in less developed areas are automatically entitled to pioneer incentives, which, among others, would allow up to 100% foreign ownership. In addition, they are entitled to deduct from taxable income an amount equivalent to 100% of outlays for infrastructure works. They may also deduct 100% of incremental labour expenses from taxable income for the first five years from registration (double the rate allowed for BOI-registered projects not located in less developed areas).

Incentives for exporters

In addition to the general incentives available to BOI-registered companies, a number of incentives provided under the Omnibus Investment Code apply specifically to registered export-oriented firms. These include: tax credit for taxes and duties paid on raw materials used in processing export products; exemption from taxes and duties on imported spare parts for firms exporting at least 70% of production; and access to bonded manufacturing warehouses.

Time-bound incentives under EDA

Firms earning at least 50% of their revenues from exports may also register for incentives under the Export Development Act (EDA) enacted in December 1994. Subject to certain conditions, firms registered for incentives with BOI or other government agencies (including the Philippine Economic Zone Authority) that meet the minimum export requirement may also register under the EDA to avail themselves of any additional incentives available under that law. Time-bound incentives under the EDA include:

- A tax credit until 1999 for imported inputs and raw materials not readily available locally that are used for export production/packaging; and
- A tax credit on incremental annual export revenue ranging from 1.5 to 10%, depending on export growth rate and local content/value added. Among other conditions, exporters who already enjoy an income tax holiday under other incentive laws and/or have a local value-added of 10% or less are excluded from this incentive.

Incentives for multinational regional headquarters/warehouses

Subject to certain conditions, Book III of the Omnibus Investment Code grants incentives for the establishment of regional or area headquarters in the Philippines. Incentives to the regional or area headquarters include exemption from income tax and from local licences/fees/dues and tax- and duty-free importation of training and conference materials. Privileges extended to foreign executives include tax- and duty-free importation of household effects and multiple entry visas for themselves and their families, as well as exemption from various types of government-required clearances and from fees under immigration and alien-registration laws. Under Book

IV of the Omnibus Investment Code, multinationals establishing regional warehouses for the supply of spare parts, manufactured components or raw materials for their foreign markets also enjoy fiscal incentives on imports that are re-exported. Imported merchandise intended for the Philippine market is subject to duties and taxes.

PERFORMANCE REQUIREMENTS

Performance requirements are established for individual investors at the time incentives are granted and vary from project to project. Performance benchmarks usually are based on the proponent's approved project proposal. In general, the BOI and proponent agree on yearly production schedules and, for export-oriented firms, export-performance targets. The BOI requires registered projects to maintain at least a 25% equity component. The BOI is not overly strict in enforcing individual export targets, provided that performance does not fall below the minimum requirement (50% of production for local firms and 70% for foreign firms) needed to qualify for BOI incentives. The BOI also exercises flexibility in enforcing production targets, for justified reasons.

The BOI generally sets a 20% local value-added benchmark when screening applications. The BOI is not strict in enforcing local value-added ratios committed in the registrant's approved project proposal, provided that actual performance does not deviate significantly from other participants in the same activity. Currently, the BOI strictly specifies industry-wide local content requirements only for participants under the government's automotive manufacturing program. Current guidelines also specify that participants in this program generate, via exports, a certain ratio of the foreign exchange needed for import requirements. Pursuant to its Uruguay Round/World Trade Organisation commitments, the government has issued guidelines to phase out these trade-related investment measures by the year 2000.

TRANSPARENCY OF THE REGULATORY SYSTEM

The Philippines has taken several significant steps to reduce bureaucratic regulations and to foster competition. Still, the perception remains that one must overcome substantial bureaucratic red tape to do business in the Philippines. The government is trying to address the issue, although continued reform and streamlining remains to be done. Some agencies, such as the Securities and Exchange Commission (SEC) and Board of Investment, have one-stop shops to minimise bureaucratic delay. The government is also increasing inter-agency cooperation to minimise red tape.

The Philippines has tax, labour, health, safety, environmental and other laws and policies with the aim of regulating industry and investment efficiently. However, the impact of these laws is sometimes skewed by difficulties enforcing them effectively and uniformly. Selective enforcement reduces the intended benefits of policies to the country and sometimes adds to the risk of doing business.

CORRUPTION

There are laws and regulations intended to combat corruption under the revised penal code, the Anti-Graft and Corrupt Practices Act, and a code of ethical conduct for public officials. The Office of the Ombudsman investigates graft and corruption cases involving public officers. The *Sandiganbayan*—anti-graft court—prosecutes and adjudicates cases filed by the ombudsman. There is also a presidential commission against graft and corruption, created to serve as a watchdog at the highest level. Corruption is punishable with imprisonment, fines, suspension and/or public censure.

Although there are government mechanisms directed at combating corruption, a large body of anecdotal evidence suggests that corruption remains a problem at almost all levels in all branches of the Philippine government. Stories and rumours abound about corrupt officials managing government procurement or bureaucrats demanding 'facilitation money' to expedite paperwork, issue permits or other documents or to skirt or reduce taxes or fees, even for basic traffic penalties.

The US Corrupt Practices Act strongly discourages US business representatives from engaging in bribery, but some members of the US community feel that third-country businesses operating in the Philippines do not operate under the same constraints. The US embassy and the American Chamber of Commerce in Manila have in the past successfully represented US business interests in cases where US firms seemed disadvantaged because of reportedly questionable tender/award proceedings.

CAPITAL MARKETS AND PORTFOLIO INVESTMENT

Foreign portfolio capital is welcome in the Philippines. Foreigners may purchase public or privately issued domestic securities, invest in money market instruments and open peso savings and time-deposit accounts. Like direct equity investments, however, portfolio investments in publicly listed firms should conform with applicable foreign ownership ceilings stipulated under the Foreign Investment Act and other laws. Hostile takeovers are virtually unknown, partly because many company shares are not publicly listed and controlling interest tends to remain with a small group of parties. While the securities market is growing, it remains small and relatively underdeveloped, not yet able to offer investors a wide range of choices. Except for a number of major firms and conglomerates, long-term bonds/commercial papers are not yet major sources of long-term capital.

Credit generally is granted on market terms, with the exception of policies that require financial institutions to set aside stipulated percentages of loanable funds for agricultural and agrarian purposes and for small enterprise borrowers. Effective January 1997, liberalised regulations have allowed foreign firms to obtain peso credits without having to comply with stipulated debt-to-equity ratios.

The banking system generally is sound. Liberalisation and intensifying competition are exerting pressure on the Bangko Sentral to refine and heighten supervision and monitoring efforts. The ratio of past-due loans to total loans stood at less than 5% of total loans at the end of 1996. As of March 1997, the largest five commercial banks had estimated total assets of 791 billion pesos (about US$30 billion), equivalent to over 40% of total commercial banking system assets.

Philippines 2000, the annual publication of the SEC, offers this overview of the rise of the commercial paper market:

> The development of the Philippine capital market in the past few years has been a vital engine in the country's economic growth, which has been observed to parallel its business growth. During this period of growth, companies, in order to stay competitive in the business environment, expand their operations, increase their working capital requirements and initiate structural changes in the organisation.

The capital market is made up of three pillars, namely banks, the equity market and the public-issued debt-security (PIDS) market. The PIDS market is mainly comprised of commercial papers and bonds.

Briefly, a commercial paper (CP) is an evidence of indebtedness of any corporation to any person or entity with either short- or long-term maturities. Short-term CPs have a maturity of 365 days or less, while long-term CPs have a maturity of more than 365 days. CPs are sold to investors through financial intermediaries for the accounts of the individual or institutional investors. Aside from those that are publicly issued, which normally are registered with SEC, there are also CPs in private placements.

The commercial-paper market plays a major role in the growth of various companies, particularly in supporting activities that require additional funds that would otherwise be unavailable or have higher interest rates. It provides an alternative avenue for reaching additional capital resources and for raising cash as it enables the issuer to source funds from non-bank intermediaries, especially during times when bank facilities are not readily accessible due to limited capital and less attractive loan packages. Thus the commercial-paper market allows issuers flexibility in designing their financing schemes to take advantage of better interest rates and to broaden their pool of fund sources.

The boom in initial public offerings (IPOs) of the past few years has not really affected the growth of the commercial-paper market. This experience shows that CPs continue to be a viable and attractive source of capital. The largest and most frequent issuers of commercial papers are non-financial corporations that need huge amounts of capital to meet the increasing demand for manufacturing services, infrastructure development and housing investments. CP investors are corporations with surplus funds, institutional investors like trust and pension funds such as the social security system and the armed forces of the Philippines, and individual investors.

Why issue commercial papers?

For companies, including blue chip corporations, CPs have been a reliable source of funding. There are several advantages of raising capital through issuing commercial papers.

Interest rates on CPs generally are lower than those for bank loans, running at about 0.5% below prime. These interest rates generally are based on treasury bill rates of a similar maturity plus a small margin that varies according to the credit standing of the issuing corporations. CPs enhance the leverage of an issuer with its bankers and they diversify an issuers' source of funds. CPs have flexible repayment terms and collateral is not normally a requirement. Larger amounts can be borrowed. CPs can be used as a prelude to the public offering of an issuer's capital stock.

Bonds and long-term commercial papers are essentially the same. Bonds, as defined by the SEC, are 'denominated units of indebtedness issued by a corporation to raise money or capital obliging the issuer to pay the maturity value at the end of a specific period which should not be less than 360 days, and, where applicable, payment of interest on stipulated dates'.

Corporations have resorted to the issuance of long-term commercial papers instead of bonds in order to bypass some of the stringent requirements imposed for the latter. The law requires that bond issues be approved by a two-thirds vote of the shareholders, while the issuance of commercial papers requires only the approval of the board of directors. In addition, the registration fee for bonds is higher than that for long-term CPs. CPs have thus become a more attractive and less cumbersome option for raising funds. Moreover, the issuance of long-term CPs is seen by several corporations to be more advantageous than going on an IPO, as this does not dilute the ownership or equity of the existing shareholders.

To protect investors, the SEC promulgated certain rules and regulations concerning the issuance of short- and long-term commercial papers in 1981 and 1984, respectively. Prospective commercial paper issuers must submit to the SEC such basic requirements as a sworn registration statement, board resolution, latest audited financial statements, accomplished schedules specified by the SEC, selling agreement for the CP issues and the preliminary prospectus. Every applicant for a CP issuance pays the SEC a filing fee upon registration and upon renewal of the CP line. For short-term commercial papers, the issuer pays 1/50th of 1% of the total commercial paper line being applied for, while this amounts to 1/20th of 1% of the total CP line for long-term CP lines.

In addition, the SEC has set the floor for the maturity value of each registered CP line at 300,000 pesos for short-term CPs; for long-term CPs, the floor is 100,000 pesos for lines extending to two years, 50,000 pesos for those between two and four years and 20,000 pesos for lines with a term of more than four years.

However, the Commission may impose other requirements besides those mentioned. Normally, a registrant has to approach the Credit Information Bureau Inc (CIBI) for a credit rating. CIBI provides a third-party opinion on the company's capability to pay both the principal and interest on the CPs upon maturity.

The credit rating process usually takes 30 to 45 days and is composed of several steps designed to obtain adequate and accurate information on and from a particular issuer. A rating is given only when there is sufficient information to come up with an objective opinion and after extensive quantitative and qualitative analyses have been undertaken. Among the factors considered in rating credit are: the issuer's market position, management, competition and the structure of the industry where the company operates, profitability, liquidity and cash flow, capital adequacy and financial flexibility.

CIBI's credit-rating report is forwarded to the SEC and forms part of the materials for the commission meeting in which the SEC decides if it will grant the licence to issue the CP line. Once the applicant has been granted a licence to issue CPs, periodic reports, such as monthly reports on CP availments as of the end of each month and quarterly unaudited financial statements, have to be filed with the SEC for monitoring purposes.

Advantages of rated CPs

The 1970s can be considered as the first boom years of the unregulated Philippine debt-securities market. However, in the early 1980s, the commercial paper market suddenly slowed down as a result of what is known as the Dewey Dee fiasco. Mr. Dee, a textile magnate, absconded the Philippines with a large amount of funds obtained through commercial paper issuances by his various companies. This led to the downfall of then respected and aggressive investment houses. Understandably, confidence in CPs plummeted.

It was after this incident that the Central Bank of the Philippines (now the Bangko Sentral ng Pilipinas) and the SEC established CIBI, paving the way for renewed confidence in commercial papers. The creation of CIBI was purposely geared toward preventing the recurrence of such an incident.

In 1985, Shell Chemical Co. (Philippine) was the first to have a credit-rated commercial paper in the Philippines. As of April 1996, there were about 40 firms with outstanding commercial papers. To date, CIBI figures show outstanding credit-rated commercial-paper lines to amount to 63.2 billion pesos, up from 46 billion pesos in 1995. Of the total amount of credit-rated CPs during the first four months of 1996, 52.1 billion pesos was accounted for by long-term CP issues, overshadowing short-term issues, which account for only 11.1 billion pesos.

Generally, it is more prudent for the public to invest in rated issues. One of the persistent problems investors have faced has been transparency and the disclosure of relevant information; this is what credit ratings purposely intend to address. Credit ratings can provide some degree of security and comfort since they give an independent assessment of the level of risk associated with a particular investment. Ratings can provide the investing public with a measure of creditworthiness and an unbiased independent opinion of the strengths, weaknesses, advantages and external events that may affect the operations of the issuer to the detriment of investors.

To instil confidence in the market and to protect the interest of investors, credit rating involves an in-depth and comprehensive analysis of the debt-paying ability of the issuer. It assists in capital mobilisation as ratings can act as quick comparative indicators to measure the relative risk that the issuers will miss payments over the life of the rated CP. Thus a rating helps provide a reasonable ranking of the credit risks associated with credit-rated companies.

Credit ratings can objectively provide a standard to price CPs in relation to other rated debt in the market and in accordance with their level of risk as implied by the ratings. There is no similar standard to rank debts that are not rated. Ratings also level the playing field for all market players. It is a summation of what could possibly be a time-consuming and complicated analysis. Many investors do not have the resources to conduct their own credit checking.

Finally, the monitoring system, a standard feature of the credit-rating process, is another key benefit in investing in rated debts. This system is based on an evaluation of current industry and company developments. With monitoring, the credit quality of an issuer is reviewed regularly, and investors are updated regarding their purchase decisions through an upgrade or a downgrade of a rating. With the public's attention to investments in commercial papers, a company can attain financial flexibility and gain access to alternative sources of funds through CP issuances, which may be more appealing if they are credit-rated.

OTHER FACTORS AND CONSIDERATIONS

Subject to certain registration and/or other requirements, imposed mainly to enable access to foreign exchange from the banking system, there are no restrictions on the full and immediate transfer of funds associated with foreign investments (i.e., repatriation and remittances), foreign debt servicing and the payment of royalties, lease payments and similar fees. There is no difficulty in obtaining foreign exchange, and in general foreign exchange may now also be freely bought and sold outside the banking system. There are no mandatory foreign-exchange surrender requirements imposed on export earners. The exchange rate is not fixed and varies daily in relation to market forces.

EXPROPRIATION AND COMPENSATION

Philippine law guarantees investors freedom from expropriation except for public use in the interest of national welfare or defence. In such cases, the government offers compensation for the affected property. In the case of expropriation, foreign investors have the right under Philippine law to remit sums received as compensation in the currency in which the investment was originally made and at the exchange rate at the time of remittance. There have been no major reports of expropriatory actions involving foreign parties in the recent past. Nor are there known pending expropriation cases involving foreign investors.

Expropriation cases filed with the courts can be complicated and long-drawn. To avoid legal delays, the government generally strives to reach a compromise agreement for the acquisition of affected property. Claimants have complained that the government's proffered compensation falls significantly below prevailing market prices. Actual payment can face considerable delay depending on budgetary resources. Most expropriation cases involve right-of-way and acquisition problems for implementing major public-sector infrastructure projects.

SETTLEMENT OF INVESTMENT DISPUTES

The Philippines is a member of the International Centre for the Settlement of Investment Disputes (ICSID) and of the Convention on the Recognition and Enforcement of Foreign Arbitral Awards. There are currently two significant unresolved issues involving foreign investors in the Philippines. These are Telecom interconnections and national patrimony.

Telecom interconnections

The Philippine Long Distance Telephone Company (PLDT) has been slow to honour its legal requirement to interconnect with other competing telephone companies, most of which have foreign equity. The National Telecommunications Commission (NTC) has failed to intervene, claiming it is expected to do so only during a deadlock. PLDT claims that the delays in providing interconnection are due to shortages of fibre-optic cable. According to industry sources, carriers have requested that NTC prohibit PLDT from making new telephone connections in areas where PLDT has not adequately interconnected competing carriers.

National patrimony

On 3 February 1997, the Philippine Supreme Court overturned the government's 1995 award of 51% ownership of the Manila Hotel to a Malaysian firm. The court based its decision on a constitutional mandate that 'qualified Filipinos' be given preference in cases involving the 'national economy or patrimony'. The decision, following the 1996 presidential overruling of a contract for upgrading the Subic Container Port, has raised some questions about Philippine openness to foreign investors.

The country has an insolvency law and jurisdiction over such matters is divided between the SEC and the local courts. However, the bankruptcy law has some shortcomings, such as lack of detailed guidelines and standards for reorganisation and liquidation, and does not clearly specify how interests of debtors and creditors should be balanced.

Reflective of the country's history, the Philippine legal system has been heavily influenced by both American and Spanish statutes. The 1987 constitution is the basis of the legal system and is supported by the Civil Code, Labour Code, National Internal Revenue Code, Tariff and Customs Code, Corporation Code, Investment Code, Environmental Code, Revised Penal

Code and other codes and statutes. The judicial system can be accessed easily, and the courts are known to intervene in commercial and regulatory issues. The judiciary is independent from the executive and legislative bodies and, for the most part, avoids interference from these branches. While this attribute is commendable, the courts have been criticised for over involvement in technical issues, corruption, and slowness in decision-making.

POLITICAL VIOLENCE

Politically motivated attacks against businesses or foreign-government facilities have declined markedly in recent years, and it is unclear if political motives were behind three minor incidents directed at an American embassy facility in April 1997. United States and Philippine authorities have cooperated on international counter-terrorism cases and an extradition treaty between the two countries is in effect. In a late 1995 kidnapping incident in the southern Philippines, American citizens apparently were seized in a case of mistaken identity. They were quickly released.

Overall political stability has improved significantly in recent years, thanks largely to the government's focus on national reconciliation coupled with economic liberalisation. President Ramos' efforts to negotiate peace settlements with Muslim, Communist and military rebels all have borne fruit, leading to dramatically reduced political violence and a more stable political environment. Crime remains a national problem, especially the kidnapping of wealthy Chinese-Filipinos for ransom. Statistically, however, crime seems to be on a downturn.

The Philippines faces no serious external threat, although overlapping claims to the Spratly Islands in the South China Sea are a source of concern. (China, Taiwan, Vietnam, Brunei and Malaysia also claim all or some of the islands, and China has built a facility on Mischief Reef.) The United States and the Philippines remain treaty allies despite the rejection of the renewal of the lease on the American bases in 1991, with security cooperation based on a mutual defence treaty.

BILATERAL INVESTMENT AGREEMENTS

The Philippines has bilateral investment agreements with Chile, Canada, Iran, Thailand, Czechoslovakia, Australia, France, South Korea, Romania, Spain, China, Vietnam, Italy, the Netherlands, the United Kingdom and Switzerland. As of May 1977, agreements were under negotiation with Papua New Guinea, Turkey, India, Austria, Hungary, Russia, Egypt, Belarus and Qatar. The general provisions of the bilateral agreements include reciprocal protection and non-discrimination; the free transfer of capital, payments and earnings; freedom from expropriation and nationalisation; and recognition of the principle of subrogation.

OPIC AND OTHER INVESTMENT INSURANCE PROGRAMS

The Philippines currently does not provide guarantees against losses due to inconvertibility of currency or damage caused by war. However, a full Overseas Private Investment Corporation (OPIC) agreement is in effect and US investors may contract for coverage under this arrangement. The Philippines is a member of the Multilateral Investment Guaranty Agency (MIGA), which also provides coverage against non-commercial risks such as currency inconvertibility and transfers restrictions, expropriation, war and civil disturbances, and contract repudiation by host countries.

The estimated annual dollar equivalent of expenditures in Philippine pesos by US government agencies is US$50 million. Local currency purchases are made as needed by soliciting competing quotes from US and Philippine banks, including the Bangko Sentral. The exchange rate was approximately 26 pesos to one dollar in early 1997, but increased to the mid-30s following drops in the value of other South-East Asian currencies, notably the Thai baht and the Malaysian ringgit.

CAPITAL OUTFLOW POLICY

There are no restrictions on the repatriation of capital and remittance of profits for registered foreign investments. Outward capital investments from the Philippines do not require prior Bangko Sentral approval if:

- The outward investments are funded by withdrawals from foreign currency deposit accounts;
- The funds to be invested are not purchased from the banking system; or
- The funds to be invested, if sourced from the banking system, are less than US$6 million per investor per year.

MAJOR FOREIGN INVESTORS

Among the Philippines' top 2,000 corporations in terms of gross revenue in 1995, according to *Philippines 2000*, about one-quarter reflected investments/operations by foreign multinational firms. The United States is the Philippines largest investor, with an estimated 32% share of the Philippines' foreign direct investment stock as of the end of 1996. The following is a ranking of the larger companies in terms of total equity in millions of US dollars. The figures represent total book value of foreign and local equity as of 1995. Original values expressed in pesos have been converted to US dollar equivalents using the 1995 closing rate of 26.23 pesos to one US dollar.

1. Pilipinas Shell Petroleum, British, 593.5 million
   Philippine Petroleum, British, 84.1
   Shell Gas Eastern, Dutch, 49.9
   First Philippine Industrial, British, 42.4
   (The above companies are members of the Shell group)
2. Petron, Dutch (Aramco through a Dutch subsidiary), 564.6
3. Philippine American Life Insurance, American, 425.4
   Philam Insurance, American, 52.2
   Philippine American General Insurers, American, 53.6
   (These companies are members of the American Insurance Group)
4. Coca Cola Bottlers Philippines, Inc., American, 340
   Coca Cola Export, American, 40.7
5. Caltex Philippines, American 228.7
6. Digital Telecom (Philippine), British, 215.8
7. Nestle Philippines, Swiss, 180.1
   Magnolia Nestle, American (Nestle SA through US subsidiary), 29.2
8. Globe Telecom (GMCR), Singaporean (Singapore Telecom), 164.3
9. Enron Power Philippines, American, 55.2
   Batangas Power, American (Enron Power), 55.2
   Subic Power, American (Enron Power), 30.9
10. Toyota Motor Philippines, Japanese, 81.5
    Toyota Autoparts Philippines, Japanese, 44.3
11. Citibank NA, American, 132.3
12. Procter and Gamble Philippines, American 93.9
13. Sun Life Assurance of Canada, Canadian, 21.5
14. Eastern Telecom Philippines, British (Cable & Wireless World), 88.2
15. Phil. Automotive Manufacturing, Japanese (Mitsubishi Motors and Nisshio Iwai), 87.3
16. Matsushita Electric Philippines, Japanese, 83.6
17. Republic-Asahi Glass, Japanese, 81.5
18. Banque Indosuez, French, 79.7
19. Wyeth Philippines, American, 76.6
20. Mico Equities, Bahamas/Swiss/German, 73.6
21. Kepphil Shipyard, Singaporean, 69.6
22. Makati Shangri-la Hotel & Resort, Hong Kong-British (Jellico/Sligo Holdings), 68.7
23. Dole Philippines, 67.4
24. Texas Instruments Philippines, American, 67.3
25. Uniden Philippines, Japanese, 65.2

26. Amkor/Anam Pilipinas, British (TL Ltd.), 58.7
27. Del Monte Philippines, American (Filipino, British and other nationalities since April 1996), 57.9
28. Motorola Philippines, American, 56.5
29. East Asia Power, American (East Asia Power Resources), 55.9
30. Rohm Electronics Philippines, Japanese, 54.4

CHAPTER 14

BANKING AND FINANCING

More than 50 commercial banks currently operate in the Philippines. Of these, 17 are foreign-controlled, with 14 foreign branch banks and three majority foreign-owned domestically incorporated subsidiaries. Of the 17 foreign-controlled banks, 13 entered the Philippine market under May 1994 amendments to the country's General Banking Act, which provided the first major opening for foreign banks since 1948. This market opening is beginning to improve overall banking services by increasing competition and efficiency and by encouraging the introduction of new products and technology. There are also 35 or so offshore banking units (OBUs) and foreign bank representatives in the Philippines.

Statistics as of March 1997 place the commercial banking system's assets at about two trillion pesos (US$72 billion), 40% of which represents the combined shares of the five largest banks. Intensifying competition and the accelerating pace of globalisation has prompted banks to expand capitalisation and branch networks aggressively. The system's net-worth-to-risk asset ratio was estimated at nearly 18% at the end of 1996, significantly higher than the statutory floor of 10%.

Banks are able to provide foreign exchange for import payments under various arrangements provided that the commodities imported are not prohibited or regulated, in which case the importer must show that import clearance has been obtained from the appropriate government agencies.

GENERAL FINANCING AVAILABILITY

Domestic capital

Most corporate clients raise capital by borrowing directly from banks or trust funds. However, long-term loans at relatively more attractive rates are accessible to more established borrowers with proven track records. Venture-capital corporations and government banks cater more readily to small and medium-sized enterprises, but their resources are limited. Current laws require banks to set aside a certain percentage of loanable funds for agricultural purposes and for small and medium-sized enterprises. Keener competition posed by the liberalisation of the banking sector is beginning to improve access to banking services and many local banks aggressively target the middle-income market.

The Philippines securities market is growing but remains relatively small and underdeveloped. The equities market has been increasing in importance as an alternative source of capital. Market capitalisation of publicly listed companies has grown dramatically since 1992 and stood at the equivalent of US$72billion at the end of April 1997. Partly because of the large volume of short-term government securities, the longer term commercial paper and bond markets currently are not major sources of capital. However, a regime of lower and more stable interest rates has allowed the government to float longer term issues with increasing success over recent years. The ongoing Capital Market Development Program aims to rationalise and strengthen securities regulation and to develop a longer term securities market in the Philippines.

Foreign loans

The Bangko Sentral ng Pilipinas continues to regulate foreign borrowings to ensure that they can be serviced with due regard for the economy's overall debt-servicing capacity. Certain loans in the private sector must be approved by the Bangko Sentral regardless of maturity, the source of foreign exchange for debt service and/or any other consideration. These are:

- Private-sector debt guaranteed by the government corporations/financial institutions or covered by foreign-exchange guarantees issued by local banks;
- Loans granted by foreign currency deposit units funded from or collateralised by offshore loans or deposits; and

- Loans with maturities of more than one year obtained by private banks and financial institutions for re-lending.

Private-sector foreign loans outside these categories that will not be serviced with foreign exchange purchased from the banking system do not require prior Bangko Sentral approval.

Subject to certain conditions, which include disposition of the loan proceeds, type of borrower and/or source of credit, some categories of foreign loans that will be serviced using foreign exchange purchased from the banking system also need not be approved by the Bangko Sentral, but should be registered for access to debt service-related foreign exchange. Examples of these are most short-term loans and private-sector loans extended by foreign companies to their local subsidiaries.

In approving foreign-currency borrowings, the Bangko Sentral gives priority to such government-promoted sectors as export-oriented projects and to projects under the government's Investment Priorities Plan and Medium-Term Public Investment Program.

EXPORT FINANCING AND INSURANCE

Obtaining attractive, competitive financing very frequently is the key to concluding business deals in the Philippines. Government and private importers of goods and services often buy a financing package rather than the best quality or most appropriate items.

Limited financing is available from foreign currency deposit units in local commercial banks, but generally long-term dollar financing is not easy to find in the Philippines. Companies rely on Eximbank to purchase the foreign equipment they need. In May 1996, Metrobank and Standard Chartered introduced Eximbank's bundling facility to Philippine importers. Eximbank also offers matching credit to help foreign exporters compete against other countries' mixed credit packages. Eximbank's current exposure in the Philippines is about US$2.3 billion. Therefore, foreign exporters are urged to take advantage of various Eximbank loan, loan guarantee and export credit insurance programs. As in other countries, the US Embassy's Economic and Commercial sections serve as Eximbank's liaison for Americans in the Philippines.

In addition to the Eximbank, the Asian Development Bank (ADB), US Trade & Development Agency and Overseas Private Investment Corporation (OPIC) all are active in the Philippines and provide funding for a wide range of projects. The ADB, headquartered in Metro Manila, provides loans to the Philippines for energy, social infrastructure, finance, industry, agriculture and agricultural industry, and non-fuel minerals.

The World Bank is also active in the Philippines, providing an assistance level of US$300 to $400 million over the near term. Foreign firms are eligible under certain other-country grant and financing programs, such as the Japanese Overseas Economic Cooperation Fund.

OPIC is financing and insuring projects for a significant number of clients in the Philippines. The US Embassy represents OPIC's interests and provides comments and concurrence on the various OPIC projects. Companies seeking medium- or long-term project financing, political risk insurance, or both should contact OPIC for further information on eligibility and registration procedures.

PROJECT FINANCING AVAILABLE

In addition to commercial sources of project finance, possible bilateral and multilateral sources of funding include the ADB, the World Bank, the United States Agency for International Development (USAID) and the Eximbank. All of these institutions have active portfolios in the Philippines, usually disbursed through accredited government agencies and financial institutions. The Eximbank is placing new emphasis and resources on project financing for major infrastructure investments in countries such as the Philippines. Notably, Eximbank has completed six project finance deals in the Philippines, more than in any other country. The ADB lent $5.8 billion in 1996 to promote economic and social progress in its developing member countries. The transport and communications sector received the largest share of lending, followed by energy, agriculture and natural resources, and social infrastructure. The ADB's medium-term strategy focuses on poverty reduction, improving the status of women, population planning and environmental protection. Going into the next century, the ADB has also assumed the role of catalyst for development. In implementing this policy, the ADB leverages its own financial resources through co-financing and other modalities to attract additional private capital to fund the development needs of its member countries.

Both the ADB and the International Finance Corporation, which is part of the World Bank group, also make financing available to private enterprises without government guarantee.

The Philippines has a particularly good record of successful project financing, especially in the power sector. The Philippines is considered well suited for project financing because of this good track record; its relatively sound policy and legal framework, which is essential for contract enforcement; investor confidence and capital flows; and the existence of potential institutional investor resources. It is relatively easy to acquire information necessary to set project finance machinery in motion. Future project financing could address Philippine infrastructure needs in the water, transportation and telecommunications areas, as well as in power.

The US Trade and Development Agency is able to provide funding to support the necessary feasibility studies for large infrastructure projects in both the public and private sectors. Their funds, which are in the form of grants, are often used by private investors to assist in preparing studies required by the various project financing institutions. The Trade and Development Agency supports studies for projects in the energy, telecommunications, transportation, water, and environmental sectors.

CORRESPONDENT BANKING

A number of Philippine commercial banks have branches in the United States, Europe and other Asian countries. Reflecting a long history of economic and political ties, all commercial banks in the Philippines have correspondent banking relationships too numerous to list, particularly with banks in the United States.

PHILIPPINE BANKING TODAY

By Leo Gonzaga

After Bangko Sentral ng Pilipinas raised the required minimum bank paid-up capital at the start of 1997, Chief Operating Officer Octavio Espiritu of the Far East Bank & Trust Company said it was 'the beginning of the end' for the formation of new banks. He believed the regulatory climate 'has become more hospitable now' for bank mergers. The increase was from 2.5 billion to 4.5 billion pesos for universal or expanded commercial banks, from 1.2 billion to 2 billion for commercial banks and from 150 million to 250 million pesos for thrift banks.

At that time, Asian Bank and PDCP Bank were already holding talks on a possible merger, while Philippine Commercial International Bank and

Prudential Bank & Trust Company were courting Philippine Banking Corporation and Pilipinas Bank, respectively. A number of other banks were also looking for partners.

Subsequently, Asian Bank and PDCP Bank abandoned their negotiations owing mainly to differences between their stockholders on assets' valuation. None of the other banks took the plunge. Two of them, Solid Bank and Urban Bank, declared that they would hike capital purely on their own. But another two, Bank of the Philippine Islands and CityTrust Banking Corporation, did make a trip to the altar. The former merged with and absorbed the latter before the central monetary authority required more equity infusion in banks by stockholders.

The higher capitalisation requirement did not stop the formation of new commercial banks and/or the elevation of thrift banks to commercial banks. Growth of banking was at such a rate that Federico Pascual, president of Allied Banking Corporation, complained of overcrowding. He cited a study by Merrill Lynch showing that Metro Manila has 50% more bank head/ branch offices than does Bangkok, Thailand.

At the end of 1996 there were 44 commercial banks with 2,009 branches and 1,101 thrift banks with 995 branches, mostly in metropolitan centres. There were also 14,456 rural banks with 658 branches in the provinces. Based on the latest count, the number of commercial banks has increased by eight to 52. Among the newcomers are Access Banking Corporation, Asia Pacific Banking Corporation, Bank of Southeast Asia, Global Business Bank, Pan Asia Banking Corporation, Philippine Exchange Bank and TA Bank. Banco de Oro and Orient Development Bank are among thrift banks which have gone into commercial banking.

For all the new banks, banking density of one bank for every 11,892 people in 1996—while up from 12,961 the previous year—is still far below the average of one to 1,000 in Europe. This is because banks have to service a rapidly expanding population. The number of Filipinos swelled to about 71 million in 1996 from 68 million in 1995.

FIRST TEN

To those from overseas who are looking at banking opportunities in the Philippines, the focus is on the second batch of foreign banks that will be allowed to come under the Bank Liberalisation Law of 1994. The ten in the first batch include: ANZ Bank (Australia–New Zealand), Bangkok Bank, Bank of Tokyo, Chemical Bank (USA), Development Bank of Singapore, Fuji Bank, Internationale Nederlanden Group, International Commercial Bank of China (Taiwan) and Korea Exchange Bank (South Korea). Bank of

Tokyo has added Mitsubishi to its name while Chemical Bank has been renamed Chase Bank.

To open banking to a second batch of a still unspecified number of foreign banks, the 1994 law will have to be amended. Bangko Sentral Governor Gabriel Singson wants to wait until a full assessment of the impact of the first ten has been completed. The governor has provided a partial assessment showing that, in the first year of operations of their wholly owned full-service branches in the Philippines, they brought in 37.55 billion pesos (US$1.25 billion) of investments and also extended loans to and infused equity in domestic entities totalling 42 billion pesos (US$1.41 billion.

Moreover, their Philippine operations served as a challenge to local banks, which responded not only by recapitalising and expanding their branch networks but also by going hi-tech in the new era of automated teller machines and of money changing hands by mere taps on computer keyboards. The position taken by the Department of Finance was that the Philippines should keep pace with other South-East Asian countries rather than take the lead over them in further liberalising the financial sector.

ACQUISITION ROUTE

Instead of waiting for amendment of the liberalisation law, some foreign banks have been coming in via the acquisition route. For instance, Malayan Bank Bho of Malaysia bought 60% of PNB Republic Bank and renamed it Maybank of the Philippines. Malaysian MBF Holdings Bhd purchased Unitrust Development Bank and made a bid for Premier Bank. Malaysia's diversified Westmont conglomerate invested in Westmont Bank.

Taking the same route, Indonesia's Dharmala group and Lippa Bank bought stakes in Ambes Development Bank and Premier Bank, respectively. Kepphel Bank of Singapore is now the majority owner of Monte de Piedad Savings Bank, which it has renamed Kepphel Monte Bank and plans to upgrade into a commercial bank. Though already in the first batch of ten foreign banks, Development Bank of Singapore purchased 60% of the Bank of Southeast Asia. Japan's Tokai Bank has 30% equity in Global Business Bank.

In contrast, American Express Banking Corporation withdrew from Bancom Development Corporation and International Corporate Bank; Bank of Boston from the Philippine Commerce Bank, Grindlays Bank of the United Kingdom from General Bank, and Royal Bank of Canada from Traders Bank. All came under the General Banking Act of 1949, which limits foreign equity in local banks to 30% in general and 40% on a case-by-case basis. Not covered by the cap because it came before 1949 are Bank of America and Citibank NA as well as British-owned Hongkong & Shanghai Banking Corporation and Standard Chartered Bank. Bank of America got out of BA Finance; Citibank out of CityTrust Banking.

The entry of Asian banks and exit of those from the West took place while government policy was in continuous flux. In the 1960s, the central monetary authority imposed a higher minimum capital requirement to force banks into mergers, the bias then favouring fewer but bigger banks. Now, the government position seems to be 'the more, the better', or that the market should decide winners and losers in banking competition.

Policy change has often taken other forms, principally the lifting of most of the restrictions on transactions involving dollars and other foreign currencies. Still in place, on the other hand, is the so-called DOSRI rule, which limits how much a bank can lend to its directors, officers, stockholders and related interests (DOSRI). Also in place is another rule called 'agri-agra', stipulating that a bank must set aside a certain portion of total loanable funds for borrowers in the agriculture and agrarian reform sectors at preferential interest rates.

What banks can lend out of deposits has been reduced by the requirements that they should maintain separate reserves against deposit and deposit-substitute liabilities and to cover liquidity. But apart from agri-agra loans, they can charge market rates on others. Despite recent lowering, the average lending rate is still above 20% per annum—it was once as high as 35%—and this is only for prime borrowers. Those with lower credit ratings must pay 5% or so more. On the other hand, interest banks pay to sever is at average rates of only 6% on savings and 10% on time deposits. So, banks are well ahead of the game in the resulting interest spread of 10 to 14%.

GROWING UP

The banking system itself has been undergoing change after change over the years. For one, it has shed conservatism. Gone are the days of no advertising. Banks now are very visible in print and broadcast commercials in billboard and movie sales pitches. One of them, Rizal Commercial Banking, helps in sending poor students to college. Another, Hongkong & Shanghai Banking, has been underwriting essay-writing contests among high school students for several years.

In another change, there are no more purely family-owned and managed banks; families have broadened the base of bank ownership by listing shares in the stock market. On any given day, shares of as many as 21 banks are being traded in that market, while earlier there were so few of them that they were listed under Commercials–Industrials. Now, banks form a separate list. Families have also hired professionals, preferably Ivy-League types, to manage their banks for them.

Banks at present are no longer satisfied with doing just the core business of generating, landing and investing pesos deposits and holding, buying and selling dollars and other foreign currencies. They have ventured into such unfamiliar financial territories as mutual funds and derivatives, as well as familiar ones like trust funds. Many have set up subsidiaries in various areas of economic activity ranging from thrift banking to securities trading and from insurance to real estate development.

CHEAPER PESO

Devaluation of the peso in July 1998 and its continuing losses since then are believed to be both a plus and minus for banks, with no clear indications yet of how the cross-current effects will eventually balance out. On one hand, dollar and foreign currency deposits in banks have appreciated considerably in peso terms; on the other, the quality of loans has eroded considerably.

For borrowers of foreign currencies, the heavier debt-service load is aggravated by higher interest rates. The double whammy has already forced at least one group of companies to seek Securities and Exchange Commission help to prevent bank creditors from running after its assets. Almost two dozen troubled entities or groups are known to be experiencing severe cash-flow problems. Long before the peso became cheaper and interest rates higher, one sugar refining company and its distributor-affiliate sought and got protection from the securities regulator after defaulting on payments of loan principal and interest.

PROPERTY MARKET

Operational misfortune has been known to begin after diversification into real estate development. There has been deep concern over overbuilding by property-market-based entities and, accordingly, over their capability to pay bank loans upon maturity. Bangko Sentral has limited lending to some developers to 20% of the total loan portfolio of banks.

According to Bangko Sentral, the loan exposures of banks in real estate development was less than 10% of the total loan portfolio last year. However, the International Monetary Fund thinks the percentage is much higher than that considering the usual use of property as loan collateral and investments by banks in property-market-based entities. Under the law, universal and commercial banks are allowed to invest in non-related activities.

CROSS-OWNERSHIP

One concern of the financial community stems from the so-called cross-ownership factor, or the equity presence in banks of individuals or entities with stakes in real estate development. With ownership crossing corporate borders, the central monetary authority imposed a cap on bank loans to their own directors, officers, stockholders and related interests as far back as two decades ago.

Before the DOSRI rule was imposed, there were several forced bank closures. In each of them, the troubled banks were placed under receivership. Among them were Bangko Filipino, a thrift bank owned by the Aguirre family, and Overseas Bank of Manila, a commercial bank whose biggest stockholder was businessman Emerito Ramos. The Aguirres and Ramos had large investments in real estate.

Cross-ownership also existed then, as now, in several other cases. Ayala Land is with the Bank of the Philippine Islands and BPI Family Bank of the Ayala group. Filinvest Development and Filinvest Land is with the East West Bank of *taipan* (a Chinese term meaning the head of a foreign business) Andrew Gotianum. Robinson Land is with the Gokongwei group, which has investments in Far East Bank and Philippine Commercial International Bank. SM Development is with Banco de Oro of Henry Sy, another *taipan*. PMMIC Property is with BASavings Bank and Rizal Commercial Banking of a third *taipan*, Alfonso Yuchengco.

BANK FAILURES

There have been some notable bank failures, usually as a result of over-aggressiveness in expanding and diversifying or of panic withdrawals. By and large, however, the banking system appears sound and depositors are keeping their money in banks despite talk of loan-payment defaults by more and more borrowers.

Nonetheless, not everyone is optimistic. In warning against what it calls 'present dangers' to the local economy and the banking system in particular, Deutsche Morgan Grenfell says non-performing loan accounts are on the rise, whereas there has been a slowdown in earnings growth. Dollar loans of banks are also said to exceed the country's international reserves. About 20% of the loans are unhedged, and loan principal represents 50 times the average daily trading volume of dollar buying and selling.

Bangko Sentral disagrees with the assessment of Deutsche Morgan Grenfell. The central monetary authority points out that there has been a decelerating trend in foreign currency lending by banks. Up to 60% of total loans have been extended to exporters and are all hedged since the borrowings are against export letters of credit, purchase orders and/or sales invoices. Another 14% have been extended to public utilities, which have few currency risks and whose rate billings incorporate exchange-rate fluctuations.

Sharing the official assessment, Moody's Investor Service says the Philippine banking system is 'strong enough' to withstand pressures resulting from devaluation of the peso and the rise in interest rates. While acknowledging that there could be a reduction in bank earnings and erosion of the quality of credit risks, the US rating agency is of the view that the banking system is 'sound and stable'.

That the banks still feel comfortable about some of their loan exposures is perhaps best indicated by their agreement to provide temporary relief to some of their clients through debt-service moratoriums pending restructuring of liabilities. In the case of one group, creditors formed a committee to study ways of giving it a chance to sort out its financial troubles. There were no moves to call in loans or seize assets.

CLOSE WATCH

At the same time, banks are closely watching unhedged foreign currency borrowers for signs of debt-service difficulties. Most borrowers have been borrowing in foreign currency because interest charges averaged less than the peso interest rates and exchange-rate fluctuations were not only within a narrow band but also not always against local currency. Defaults have risen as the value of the peso decreased and credit became more expensive.

By sector, the closest watch is on real estate development. Some developers themselves have opted for caution. Ayala Land, for instance, put off plans to build more office space. The greatest backlog is in low-cost housing. Condominiums and commercial buildings have been in oversupply.

Even before Bangko Sentral imposed a cap on bank lending to property-market-based borrowers, banks themselves were already observing voluntary restrictions. At that time, a financial disturbance in Thailand whipped up by real estate overbuilding was already spreading to banking. With both the regulator and the regulated aware of the risks and doing something about them, the ripple effect in the Philippines of Thai turbulence has not turned into a cripple effect when it comes to banking, the property sector or the entire economy.

AN HISTORICAL PERSPECTIVE

By the Bankers' Association of the Philippines

The history of Philippine banking dates to the 18th century when funds invested in loans secured by real estate helped to finance the Spanish galleon trade between Manila and Acapulco. The first bank, formally established in 1851, was the Banco Espanol Pilipino de Isabel II. Forerunner of the Bank of the Philippine Islands, it was the largest private commercial bank in the country and the first institution to issue currency prior to establishment of the Philippine Central Bank, which assumed operations in 1949.

In its charter, the Central Bank—since renamed the Bangko Sentral ng Pilipinas—adopted the macroeconomic role of promoting economic growth while maintaining internal and external monetary stability. Consonant with these objectives was the responsibility to supervise banks and to control and manage the level and direction of bank lending with a view to obtaining price and exchange stability and equilibrium.

The growth and financial performance of the banking industry since the postwar years have been dictated largely by the regulatory framework instituted by the Bangko Sentral as well as by the economic environment. One of the first policy measures initiated by the bank was to control the rapid decline of the country's international reserves. This was due to building pressure on the foreign exchange with growing import requirements for rehabilitation and reconstruction as well as the pent-up demand for consumer goods following the end of World War II. Commercial banking activities expanded rapidly in the late 1950s and 1960s to meet the country's demands for postwar rehabilitation and development. Banks relentlessly pursued deposits and import-financing activities associated with rehabilitation programs.

A sizeable portion of new deposits went to banks abroad to cover commitments in dollars for large import orders. The bank's rediscount window became a major source of financial-system requirements as a system of priorities provided varying degrees of subsidies to different industries seen as essential for economic development.

178

The mid-1960s ushered in a new phase of banking with the introduction of money-market instruments, including T-bills, and deposit-substitute instruments such as promissory notes, banker acceptances and repurchase agreements. The instruments issued in the unregulated money market compared with traditional deposits as forms of investment, given the prevailing ceilings on interest rates on savings and time deposits. The volume of money-market instruments subsequently grew rapidly toward the late 1960s and1970s, accompanied by a flow of funds away from traditional deposits. However, the growth of the savings-deposit base of banks was not substantially eroded given the larger minimum placements required for investors in money-market instruments.

Moreover, the branch expansion strategies of banks were directed mainly toward the less sophisticated and retail markets in the provincial areas where the demand for financial assets were predominantly in the form of traditional deposit accounts. The efforts of the national government to promote savings via the Savings for Progress campaigns initiated in 1973 and the favourable growth of incomes during the early stages of martial law, declared in September 1972 by then President Ferdinand Marcos, cushioned the impact of the competition from money-market instruments on the savings-deposit market. Imposition of interest-rate ceilings and a transactions tax on short-term deposit substitutes in 1977 dramatically reduced the demand for deposit substitutes, resulting in a marked slowdown in the volume of money-market placements.

Since then, savings and time deposits have grown remarkably at more than 30% per year, stimulated to a large extent by financial reforms. It is also noteworthy that, from 1974 to 1980, the initial phase of financial liberalisation was initiated by the government, including reforms that encouraged capital expansion by commercial banks, liberalised the entry of foreign equity into the system, reduced the number of bank categories and authorised the Bangko Sentral to set interest rates.

On the lending side, the portfolio of commercial banks has been highly skewed in favour of short-term maturities because of the absence of a well-functioning market for long-term funds. This discouraged the commercial banks from transforming their deposits into long-term credits. Furthermore, the industrial development during the 1950s and up to the 1970s was largely dependent on short-term credit, primarily to finance the requirements for raw materials and supplies.

Commercial banks derived a significant portion of their income from short-term and roll-over credits extended to large triple-A names in the industrial, trading and service sectors, where default risk and transactions costs are relatively small. Consequently, high-risk ventures such as those in agriculture and small-scale business were kept to the minimum. Furthermore, government policy encouraged loans to flow to the import-substituting, capital-intensive and manufacturing industries. The high import dependence of domestic companies belonging to both export- and domestically oriented industries became a major financing outlet for banks in the industrial credit market.

Realising the paucity of agricultural credit, the government initiated policies aimed at directing loans to this preferred sector of the economy. A presidential decree mandating banks to channel 25% of their loanable funds to agriculture was issued in 1975. Government maintained low interest rates for agriculture through special credit programs including supervised and non-supervised credits depending on the priority projects for which funds were used.

The 1980s were marked by a growing restiveness of the population, which in terms of the financial system was reflected in the increasing anxiety and mistrust of financial institutions. The flight of a Chinese businessman who was heavily indebted to a number of institutions triggered a crisis of confidence that shook the foundation of the financial system. The Bangko Sentral took immediate steps, which included the granting of emergency loans to financial institutions performing quasi-banking functions that were hit by the financial panic and provision of financial assistance to highly distressed industries.

The inflationary impact of these advances was minimised by the issuance of Central Bank Certificates of Indebtedness. Furthermore, regulations on commercial papers were introduced and a rating agency for issuers, namely the Credit Information Bureau, was established. The government launched the second phase of the financial liberalisation effort, which included landmark reforms, particularly the full deregulation of interest rates and the implementation of universal banking. The financial reforms of the 1980s reduced specialisation among banks as they allowed commercial banks with universal banking-function licences a broader scope of financial services. These include investment-banking functions such as underwriting and securities dealership and equity investment in non-allied undertakings.

On the premise that size fosters economies of scale, greater stability and a larger potential for long-term lending, minimum capitalisation was also increased as part of the package of financial reform. To complement these institutional reforms, the Bangko Sentral generally pursued a policy aimed at raising domestic savings, encouraged by long-term financing and enhancing the efficiency of financial intermediation. By the end of 1982, the deregulation of interest rates was fully completed with the removal of the ceilings on short-term loans. This final step was needed to give financial institutions greater flexibility in mobilising funds on a competitive basis. Furthermore, in step with the strengthening of the banking system, the minimum capitalisation of commercial banks was raised to 300 million pesos, as compared to 100 million pesos in 1973.

The 1980s will be remembered as a period marked by the greatest number of closures of financial institutions in the system. Some of the big bank closures resulted in the filing of court cases against the Bangko Sentral. The authorities had to intervene in private banks and government financial institutions. The government banks were liquidated in 1986 and their largest bad assets, approximately 30% of the banking-system assets, were transferred to the national government.

A few private banks were bought into by foreign financial institutions to the extent allowed by the Monetary Board. The Bangko Sentral policy of encouraging mergers and acquisitions was supplemented by measures aimed at strengthening the capitalisation of the banking system. By the end of 1989, the minimum paid-in capital of commercial and expanded commercial banks was raised to 750 million pesos and 1.5 billion pesos, respectively. Likewise, the general policy governing the extension of lender of last resort to weak banks was also laid down in that same year for the reason that the Bangko Sentral does not wish to unduly sustain the operation of weak banks for long periods in order to foster monetary and financial stability in the system.

The policies geared toward strengthening and enhancing the stability of the banking system at the end of the 1980s were followed by measures that sought to raise competition, enhance efficiency of financial intermediation and raise access to foreign-bank capital and technology. These included the lifting of the moratorium on the establishment of new branches in 1985, followed by the liberalisation of bank branching and entry. An auction system was instituted that enabled banks to compete in awarding franchises to operate branches located in seven areas of the country. The definition of restricted-branching areas was liberalised and locations formerly prohibited as over-banked were liberalised.

Furthermore, branching incentives were provided to encourage banks to set up branches in formerly over-branched areas in relation to economic activities and population. In 1991, a bill seeking to liberalise the entry of foreign commercial banks was passed on second reading at the House of Representatives. To improve the efficiency of financial intermediation and delivery of services to a bigger volume of clientele in a broader geographical area, the establishment of on-branch and off-branch automatic teller machines was allowed by the Bangko Sentral. This paved the way for the accelerated growth in consumer banking and electronic-funds-transfer services. To reduce intermediation costs and raise financial efficiency, the gradual unification of reserve requirements across deposit and bank types was implemented in 1989 and 1990.

As 1991 drew to a close, the liberalisation rules governing foreign-exchange transactions were announced. These include the increase in the foreign-exchange retention limits of exporters, relaxation of the surrender requirement to various types of service exporters and the expansion of allowable foreign-currency-denominated financial products and services. By the third quarter of 1992, all foreign-exchange controls except those governing external borrowings and foreign investments by residents were ended completely and the electronic trading of foreign exchange on the inter-bank market, otherwise known as the Philippine Dealing System, became operational.

The 1980s and the early 1990s also marked the substantial growth of government securities, off-balance-sheet intermediation and increased use of direct equities by the corporate sector. Banks experienced a rapid growth in their trust- and portfolio-management accounts as they looked for various ways of alleviating the heavy interest and intermediation cost burdens. Furthermore, the rising volume of short-term government borrowings in the domestic financial markets provided impetus for them to expand their government securities-trading activities. Non-bank financial market players, likewise intimidated by high and volatile interest rates, reduced or avoided debt altogether, replacing debt with equity or simply contracting the balance sheets.

The recovery of the economy from 1986 through 1989 from the 1984–85 recession spurred the development of the securities markets. There were several new public listings in the country's stock markets, and the commercial banks played a principal role in underwriting several major equity issues. The banks were also involved in loan syndications, financial packaging and loan origination, thus allowing them to provide investment-banking services to a growing corporate-finance client base.

The universal banking licences of several commercial banks permitted the diversification of their investments towards such non-allied undertakings as airlines, real estate development, manufacturing and other ventures. The banking sector likewise introduced new mechanisms and products such as floating-rate instruments, asset-backed securities, financial futures and convertible debt securities as a way of managing liquidity and interest-rate exposures. The dominance of the commercial banks in the financial system is evident from the balance sheet accounts and branch network.

In the future, the banks will continue to provide the catalyst role in the savings mobilisation and financial intermediation process, provide multi-currency lending capabilities to a wide spectrum of commercial and industrial enterprises and support the government's monetary and fiscal objectives, as well as small-scale and agricultural development programs. However, the volume, price and quality with which banking services are delivered to the public will be influenced substantially by the ongoing deregulation of the banking system and the recent wave of investments in banking technology. Increased automation will bring forth a substantial increase in the transaction-processing capability of banks, thereby enabling them to offer a greater volume and variety of services to their clientele at lower cost. In turn, deregulation will engender keener competition for market share through financial innovations, strategic locationing and pricing.

THRIFT BANKING SYSTEM

Thrift banks—savings and mortgage banks, private development banks and savings and loan associations—have been organised primarily to generate long-term loans for the economy. As a whole, thrift banks comprise about 15.4% of the total number of branches and offices of the system. After the commercial banks, thrift banks capture the second largest share in terms of the nationwide office network.

Savings and mortgage banks are organised primarily to accumulate small savings of depositors and invest them together with the capital forces in bonds, unsecured loans, loans secured by bonds, real estate mortgages and other such forms of security of loans for personal finance as automobiles and appliances and mortgage credits for home-building and development. Loans extended such as equipment loans, mortgage loans and real estate and mortgage loans may have maximum maturities from five years for equipment loans to 10 years for mortgage loans and 20 years for real estate mortgage loans.

Private development banks are organised principally to help finance development undertakings in agriculture and industry through the extension of medium- to long-term loans. Of the private development banks' loanable funds, 75% is invested in medium- to long-term loans for miscellaneous purposes. Despite the role that these institutions can potentially play in capital formation, they are constrained by the small size of their resource base.

Savings and loan associations are corporations engaged in the business of accumulating the savings of members or stockholders and transforming these funds into government and private securities. Like the private development banks, the savings and loan associations are also very limited in terms of resources.

Since 1978, thrift banks have been allowed to accept cheque accounts, thus forming part of the deposit-money banking system that is authorised by law to issue current deposits. In the 1980s, the thrift banks also were authorised to accept foreign currency savings and time deposits, particularly in US dollars.

In coming years, the ongoing liberalisation of the banking system will enable the savings banks to offer a wider array of products and services in local and foreign currencies such as remittances, funds transfers and foreign-currency deposits, thereby going deeper into the competition in the retail and personal banking markets.

RURAL BANKS

Under the Rural Bank Act, the Philippine Government authorised the creation of rural banks to promote and expand the rural economy by increasing the availability of credit to agriculture and rural enterprises. Through cooperatives, self-help groups and non-governmental organisations, the rural banks can provide small farmers and entrepreneurs access to financial resources. However, the strategy of the 1970s and the early 1980s of the Bangko Sentral actively supporting the rural banks by extending subsidised re-discounting credits impaired rural savings mobilisation and subsequently undermined the viability of the rural banking system.

This was aggravated by the high past dues and arrearages arising from government credit programs and preferential lending schemes. Links between weak rural banks and the bigger commercial banks were encouraged. In the coming years, the strengthened rural banking system will play an increasingly important role in financing the countryside, as the government focuses its development efforts on empowering the poorer sectors of the community.

OFFSHORE BANKING SYSTEM

To enhance the access of the country to foreign capital, offshore banking units were allowed to operate in the Philippines in 1977. Since then, these institutions also augmented the trade financing available to the Philippines, having been major providers of the short-term revolving trade facility. As an attraction to foreign banks, the Philippine offshore banking system imposed a more concessional income tax rate and exemption from local dues and licensing fees. In the future the liberalisation of bank entry and branching policies and the trend toward increased globalisation of banking services will enable these banks to play a stronger role in the banking system in terms of increasing foreign investments and international trade opportunities.

CHAPTER 15

THE WORK FORCE

Benildo G Hernandez

The Philippine Government wishes to attract investment by foreign firms seeking a foothold in the rapidly expanding markets of South-East Asia.

The government's economic strategy has focused on making Philippine industry more competitive in world markets, rapidly deregulating industries and liberalising market entry. As part of this strategy, the government puts a high priority on improving worker productivity through programs for staff-management cooperation and expanded training opportunities.

There is a large manpower pool of over 26 million Filipinos from age 15. Filipinos are among the most productive, creative, and easily trainable people in Asia. They are also among the most educated, with a literacy rate of 85%. Investors can reasonably expect a productive and cooperative work force that rivals any in South-East Asia.

There has been a major turnaround in the labour-management climate since the politically tumultuous period of the mid-1980s when the People Power revolution overthrew the Marcos regime. In 1996, there were fewer than 100 strikes nationwide, reflecting changes in trade union goals and a robust economy with 5 to 7% GNP growth rate in the last few years.

Foreign managers in the Philippines are likely to find a highly motivated work force. According to studies and surveys since 1996, the Filipino worker generally ranks higher than his counterparts in other Asian countries, including China, Indonesia, Thailand and Vietnam. Based on points for quality, cost, availability and turnover among workers in East Asia, a leading Hong Kong consultancy firm gave Filipino workers the best overall score. Skilled and managerial employees are considered the best in terms of wages and quality of any country in Asia. According to the September 1996 *Economist*, although India may provide the cheapest and most available labour, only the Philippines scored reasonably well in all categories.

Discussions with many foreign managers in the Philippines confirm these survey results. Recently located plant managers generally are pleased with their initial experience in recruiting and training Filipino workers, and they often point to the high level of motivation and ease of training of the work force.

Highly motivated

Locally hired workers have close family and other ties to their communities that motivate them to put forward their best efforts. Younger workers make essential contributions to their families' budgets. And as many recent school graduates have had to seek employment overseas over the last decade because the local job market could not absorb their skills, they appreciate the chance to work near their families. Turnover among Filipino workers generally is very low.

Easy to train

Literacy is high and employers give good marks to the quality of Filipino secondary education, including schools in areas distant from Manila. As a result, most young Filipino workers can read and speak English to a degree that permits managers to use English-language training materials and English-speaking trainers from the first phases of new production. Managers say that Filipino workers readily ask questions and offer suggestions for improvement that help facilitate the training process.

Experienced foreign managers in the Philippines emphasise the importance of establishing a personal relationship of mutual respect as a key ingredient for good labour relations in the Philippines. It is useful for top management to be perceived as involved in personnel issues and talking directly to staff about their concerns. A policy of remembering birthdays and sponsoring occasional social events will yield major benefits. Employees will reciprocate managers' personal gestures by enhanced commitment to the company's goals.

Employers find that Filipino workers usually respond well to productivity goals and wage incentives for increasing their output. Foreign firms find that their Filipino employees take considerable pride in their firms' performance, which helps management maintain a commitment to quality control as well as to total output. Supervisors frequently point out that their workers are able to adapt quickly to new production systems and use the adjective 'flexible' to describe the key trait that makes their staffs responsive and adaptable to rapid changes in production-line processes and management objectives. Department of Labour and Employment surveys show a clear upward trend in productivity; in 1996, the average worker's output was up by 2.3% over the previous year.

TRADE UNIONS

Many employers indicate they have a productive working relationship with local trade-union leaders. In general, the trade-union movement recognises that its members' welfare is tied to the productivity of the economy and, more specifically, to the competitiveness of the firms for which they work. Globalisation pressures motivate unions to factor new concerns into their bargaining and organising approach. The example of frequent plant closures in industries affected by trade and increased imports makes unions across the board more willing to consider productivity issues as part of an employment package.

A leader of the major mainstream labour confederation, the Trade Union Congress of the Philippines (TUCP), told a seminar for investors in March 1997 that his members are committed to addressing productivity and quality-control issues and welcome globalisation as creating opportunities for Filipino workers.

However, the trade-union movement is fragmented. Although the unions often are unified on single issues, no one organisation speaks for them generally. Much often depends on the personal leadership style of local union leaders. There are seven current national labour centres and 159 labour federations that serve about three million organised workers. There are also numerous independent unions that are unaffiliated with any federation. Most federation member unions come from several industrial sectors. Few follow industry lines.

Traditionally, only a minority—currently about 16%—of the Philippine industrial work force has been organised. And if the large numbers employed in the informal home-based sector were included, the percentage would be lower. Most unionised workers traditionally have been in large industrial sectors, leaving other major sectors, particularly services, largely unorganised. There currently are only about 430,000 workers with collective bargaining agreements (CBAs) among a total work force of over 28 million.

However, union representation is higher in multinational firms. Union leaders have often favoured organising in foreign firms. They believe that expatriate managers generally are prepared to offer attractive pay and working conditions in any case, making it easier for the union to attain an acceptable CBA for its members. Collective bargaining is enterprise-based, with little pattern bargaining and no master agreements. Otherwise, the CBA's usual provisions are similar in nature to those found in US contracts. However, there are labour-code-mandated benefits, including maternity/paternity leave and the payment of an annual bonus equal to a month's extra pay.

The splintered national union leadership has fostered an environment in which unions often raid each other for members. Reportedly, employers can seek to pre-empt an organising drive by an undesirable union by quietly encouraging a more moderate union to seek their workers' support.

Mainstream unions intent on traditional collective-bargaining issues account for more than 75% of those with CBAs in the Philippines. The TUCP has long taken part in a dialogue with the government and employers through a tripartite council for periodic meetings on workers concerns at a national level. In addition, the TUCP has been affiliated with the mainstream International Confederation of Free Trade Unions in Brussels and worked closely with representatives of the American AFL-CIO, who have promoted a free trade-union movement in the Philippines.

Meanwhile, radical leftist unions, including the communist-affiliated Kilusang Mayo Uno (KMU), remain active, although their membership has steadily declined in recent years. According to its leaders, KMU members put ever higher priority on bread and butter issues over political goals. Some employers report that their local union leaders, although affiliated with the radical KMU, take a cooperative and pragmatic approach to labour issues, reflecting their concern over the profitability of the company and job security for its members. Nevertheless, radical labour groups are on the watch for unresolved labour grievances that can serve as an opening to involve workers in supporting confrontational tactics. For instance, local leaders affiliated with a conservative Christian Democratic federation (Federation of Free Workers) allied themselves with a radical labour group as a tactic to pressure the management side in a protracted 1996–97 strike at a German-owned electronics plant.

190

In the Philippine context, managers should review closely whether it is prudent for their company to pursue a non-union environment. Mainstream TUCP leaders point out that, instead of engaging with responsible union leadership, a non-union company is simply leaving itself open for radical unions to take advantage of the labour issues that eventually will arise. However, many foreign firms do seek to avoid the entry of traditional unions. Some locate in areas outside Manila in the belief that smaller cities and rural areas are more difficult settings for union organisers to work in.

National trade-union centres and confederations

The following are the major trade-union centres and confederations:
- Trade Union Congress of the Philippines (TUCP)
- Federation of Free Workers (FFW)
- Lakas Manggagawa Labour Centre (LMLC)
- National Confederation of Labour (NCL)
- Pambansang Diwa Ng Manggagawang Pilipino (PDMP)
- Kilusang Mayo Uno (KMU)Alliance of Progressive Labour (APL)
- Kapisanan Ng Mga Pangulo Ng Unyon Ng Pilipinas (KPUP)

GOVERNMENT POLICIES

In January 1997, President Ramos announced an action agenda for productivity. In light of the Philippines' new commitments to open its markets within the World Trade Organisation (WTO), APEC (Asia Pacific Economic Cooperation forum) and regionally within ASEAN, the government is redoubling its focus on training and workplace cooperation. Ramos is concerned to find ways to ensure that the Philippines is globally competitive in order to create the jobs needed for a young and growing population. The government has put a high priority on improved worker training and on mechanisms to secure harmonious employee–management relations in the workplace.

An employer identifying training needs among new staff in the first phase of plant production can draw on government subsidies in the form of reduced wage costs. Philippine law permits employers to pay new staff at only 75% of their basic rate, which in many cases is only the minimum wage, during an initial six-month training period. This can be extended by six more months upon application. Even before opening its doors, a firm can draw on this opportunity for reduced trainee-wage costs by enrolling them in programs of up to six months at other training sites. There is an extensive network of private technical schools in the Philippines that coordinate with the government for guidance on the programs most useful to employers.

Under Ramos' productivity agenda, the government is committed to regular consultations with company CEOs at regional levels to exchange views on best practices for productivity and to establish benchmarks for progress. In addition, the government is shepherding a key amendment to labour law through the Philippine Congress that will give employers a tax exemption for the cost of paying incentive bonuses to their staffs. Another goal is to help establish internationally recognised management-system standards in companies. Several government agencies are coordinating an effort to raise public awareness of the importance of a productive workforce that is aimed at creating a culture of productivity.

The Philippine Department of Labour and Employment (DOLE) seeks a balance between a hands-off approach and government intervention to resolve labour disputes. Recent labour secretaries have successfully pursued a goal of avoiding contentious strikes. A key goal of DOLE is to keep the annual number of strikes below 100 in order to demonstrate to potential foreign investors that they can expect a productive work force. In the last decade, DOLE has offered an increasingly effective service for mediating labour disputes through its National Mediation and Conciliation Board.

The Department of Trade and Industry (DTI) has pursued its own program for promoting industrial harmony for the last decade. Initiated under former President Corazon Aquino, the program was designed at a time of numerous and often politically inspired labour disputes. Some foreign companies were then leaving the Philippines, reflecting their concern over the frequent strike threats and general political instability.

Since then, DTI has succeeded in promoting the widespread use of labour-management councils in larger firms to facilitate communication and to defuse potential tensions over workplace issues. Often established through on-site training administered by DTI teams, the labour-management councils are designed to address the entire range of questions affecting workers, including both basic wage and benefit questions and the issues of increasing productivity. More recently, the DTI has launched pilot programs for sending teams to conduct factory-floor seminars for workers and line supervisors on methods for improving productivity.

SPECIAL ECONOMIC ZONES

A central role in attracting new investors in the Philippines has been played by the Special Economic Zones (SEZs), which are industrial enclaves where investors obtain tax benefits for new plant investment as well as expedited access to government administrative services. The government has greatly expanded the number of SEZs, from 19 to more than 40 in 1996–97. They have helped produce the fastest growth in new jobs, as both Filipino and foreign firms seek the advantages of operating in areas devoted to fostering export industries. In 1996, foreign investors spent $1.6 billion on new plant facilities in SEZs, where total employment climbed to over 150,000 from less than half that three years earlier. In addition, there are large areas within the former US military bases at Subic Bay and Clark that are administered as investor-friendly economic growth areas.

The SEZs normally include their own labour centres for providing investors with assistance in recruiting staff, mediating labour disputes and coordinating with DOLE and social security agencies. Generally, foreign firms entering an SEZ sign a covenant that commits them to using the SEZ services, including labour, in return for the SEZ's serving as their advocate in coordinating with government offices. In general, the SEZ labour-centre administrations have kept a major part of their bargain with investors by providing a pool of job candidates who are young, educated and flexible enough to train easily.

Both Philippine and foreign trade-union leaders claim that local SEZ administrators often foster a non-union environment. In fact, there are few unions in the SEZ areas. It appears that a combination of local political pressures and restricted access to the SEZs has hampered trade unions from making organised inroads. In addition, a close screening of applicants through a system of recommendations from local community officials has apparently also made SEZ employees reluctant to support union organising. Young, newly hired workers are unprepared to resist strong community pressures.

UNEMPLOYMENT

Philippine labour statistics help explain why skilled and well-motivated people are available in the job market.

The Philippines suffers from chronic unemployment. The widespread poverty that is especially prevalent in rural areas is a spur to many to seek work in the Philippine metropolitan areas, in the SEZs or overseas. Manila's growing housing problem reflects this migration of aspiring workers from rural regions. A major motive for establishing the SEZs is to create jobs outside of Metro Manila. The government faces a major test in its effort to create enough jobs to keep pace with a rapid 2.2% growth rate for its young population (over 70 million). The labour force grew to 29.6 million in 1996 from 28.9 million a year earlier. The DOLE has set a goal of creating 1.5 million jobs in 1997 alone. In the last two decades, the number of overseas workers (more than half of them female) fleeing unemployment or under-employment has risen dramatically to about 4.5 million.

There has been recent optimism that the job outlook has improved as unemployment figures edge downwards. But an analysis of the Philippines' declining unemployment rate indicates that the numbers may disguise major shortcomings in the labour market. In March 1997, the government announced its unemployment rate had improved to 7.7% from 8.3% a year earlier. However, the figure represents a national average; in the predominantly industrial region of Manila, the rate stands at12.1%. And while the low 2.6% rate for the Autonomous Region for Muslim Mindanao (ARMM) brings the overall rate down, the majority of those counted as employed are self-employed or unpaid family members in a predominantly rural, low-wage setting. In fact, the ARMM is the most impoverished region in the country.

Incomes in each region can vary dramatically. In the Manila area, the annual average income is more than $6,000, while in the ARMM it is only about $1,900, reflecting a poverty incidence of over 60%.

COLLECTIVE BARGAINING AND DISPUTE RESOLUTION

The Department of Labour and Employment uses a tightly defined set of legal steps to deal with labour disputes to encourage both sides to use the proper grievance procedures and other avenues for conciliation. Although the DOLE secretary has considerable authority to step into a dispute to help arrange a settlement, top DOLE officials seek at the outset to allow the collective bargaining agreement (CBA) process to work.

Disputes over terms of a current CBA

DOLE requires that CBAs prescribe a set of grievance procedures to be used in case of a dispute arising in the normal five-year term of a CBA. If a dispute persists after the grievance steps are exhausted, DOLE requires that, as a final step, both parties submit to voluntary arbitration to help resolve the issue. DOLE has expanded the corps of voluntary arbitrators since the early 1990s and even subsidises their fees for mid-size firms that might otherwise hesitate to use their services.

There are two options if an impasse remains:

- The union may file a notice of a strike, which requires a subsequent 15-day cooling-off period; or
- The union may file the case with the National Labour Relations Commission for binding resolution.

In the event of a strike notice, the National Conciliation and Mediation Board re-enters the dispute, sending its expert mediators who convene a mandatory meeting to seek common ground and possibly find a resolution during the 15-day cooling-off period. The increasing effectiveness of the board's process has been one factor in the marked reduction of strikes in the Philippines in recent years.

If the board's efforts fail, there are two further steps before the union can legally begin a strike:

- The union must win a simple majority strike vote among its members conducted seven days before a strike can begin; and
- The DOLE secretary reviews the case and determines that it is not necessary to enter the dispute.

The second option is available to the DOLE secretary if he/she finds the industry is considered 'indispensable to the national interest'. This definition is interpreted broadly. Since the early 1990s, DOLE secretaries have intervened in strikes at insurance and credit card companies, consumer electronic and garment factories, and hotels, often blocking strikes. They order workers back to their jobs and management to cease any lockout measures. In 1996, DOLE even intervened in a strike threat at Manila's International School.

When the DOLE secretary assumes jurisdiction, the order is legally binding over both parties. However, there is a right to appeal to the Supreme Court. Two prominent cases currently before the Supreme Court involve the Philippine Air Lines (PAL) and a German electronics firm.

Disputes involving deadlocked CBA talks

The process for resolving a dispute over deadlocked CBA talks involves the same steps as for those over terms of a current CBA with one exception: the cooling-off period after a strike vote is a longer 30-day period to allow for negotiating a new CBA. If the DOLE secretary intervenes, the back-to-work order assumes an extension of the terms of the current CBA until a new one can be negotiated.

Although this description abbreviates much in the dispute process, it is clear that labour disputes can easily become litigious. There usually are attorneys on the staff or in the leadership of trade unions who are prepared to match legal wits with the lawyers on the management side. Many expatriate managers advise that it is best to take a direct role in labour talks, maintaining a pragmatic approach and avoiding a trend toward legal battles.

WAGES

Multinational managers generally report that their total compensation package in the Philippines is low enough to be a very good value—especially for their mid-level management and skilled staff. For semi-skilled and line workers, they report that their comparative wage costs are somewhat higher than they might find in certain other countries in the region.

Minimum-wage costs are determined on a regional basis through the determination of wage and productivity boards that meet periodically in each of the Philippine government's 14 administrative districts. In recent years, the regional boards have adjusted the minimum wage rate about once annually.

The Manila regional board normally sets the national trend. As of 1997, the daily minimum was 185 pesos, less than US$6 after the peso began losing value in the middle of the year. The minimum in other regions is about 20 to 40 pesos less than Manila's. Exceptions are granted by wage boards, including separate rates depending on the type of industry. For example, Manila exempts certain garment export industries from adhering to the new minimum.

Wage boards consist of government, business and labour members in a ratio of three members for government and two each for business and labour. The government is represented by officials from DOLE, DTI and the National Economic Development Agency. A rise in oil prices has often been the trigger for rising worker concern over wage levels, creating pressure on the government to convene a wage board.

The boards usually pay close attention to a major government concern, that is, whether Philippine wage gains may make its industries uncompetitive in the region, so wage restraint appears to be a common guideline for the boards' decisions. Real wages adjusted for inflation have not changed since 1989, even though the economy's total productivity has risen. The minimum wage in the Manila area is below the officially defined poverty line for a family with a single wage earner. More than one-third of the population has income below the poverty line.

A minimum-wage rise frequently has a ripple effect throughout a company's wage structure. Workers at wages above minimum level expect corresponding wage adjustments when the minimum wage rises.

Many company managers criticise the intervention of the wage boards, preferring to keep decisions on wages within their CBA negotiations if they are unionised. However, there is considerable political interest within the government in retaining the process. Philippine congressmen are especially attracted to the election-campaign benefits that can result from retaining a hand in the wage process. Unions focus many media and union mobilisation campaigns on exerting influence on wage board decisions. However, this may be a flawed strategy for the unions. Observers agree that, as workers rely on nominal annual increases through wage board mandates, their reliance on unions and commitment to the CBA process appears to weaken.

CHAPTER 16

MARKETING AND INVESTING

The pace of market-based reforms in the Philippines has accelerated since 1992 under the administration of President Fidel Ramos. Significant strides have been made in liberalising trade, foreign investment, and foreign-exchange regimes; privatising state companies; lowering entry barriers into such important industries as banking, insurance, aviation, telecommunications, and oil; and enlisting the private sector in addressing urgent infrastructure needs under a Build-Operate-Transfer (BOT) program. The Philippines became a founding member of the World Trade Organisation (WTO) in December 1994.

Combined with widespread evidence of restored political and macro-economic stability, economic reforms since 1992 have stimulated growing interest from potential foreign investors and renewed confidence domestically. Following the macroeconomic instabilities and severe electricity shortage of the early 1990s, the economy began to recover in 1992. Since then, growth has accelerated (6.9% in 1996), spurred by exports, investments and expanding consumer incomes.

Prices have been influenced by monetary policy swings and occasional weather-related food-supply bottlenecks, but average annual inflation (8.4% in 1996) has been at single-digits since 1992. Successive national government fiscal surpluses since 1994, together with staggered reductions in reserve requirements on peso deposits, have resulted in generally lower and more stable domestic interest rates. Foreign-debt servicing, estimated in 1996 at 12% of export receipts of goods and services, is no longer a severe burden, and the Philippines re-entered the voluntary international capital markets in 1993 after a decade's absence. The government continues to work to wean the country from exceptional financing.

The consensus is that the Philippines is closer now than in previous growth periods to its goal of breaking away from the boom-and-bust growth pattern of the past. Nevertheless, more work remains for the Philippines to solidify the economic gains of recent years. Long-term fiscal stability is a particularly urgent concern as non-recurring privatisation receipts decline. A widening merchandise-trade deficit and reliance on unpredictable sources of balance-of-payments (BOP) financing, such as portfolio capital and workers' remittances, indicate possible vulnerabilities in the external accounts. A low national savings rate (estimated at 23% of GNP in 1996), pressing infrastructure requirements, and a relatively underdeveloped capital market also pose important challenges for sustained long-term economic growth.

GROWTH SECTORS

A series of six-year development plans prepared by the National Economic and Development Authority guide Philippine development. The current Medium-Term Development Plan for 1993–98 is anchored on the twin strategies of people empowerment and international competitiveness within the framework of sustainable development. It calls for:

- Broad-based growth through agri-industrialisation to disperse industries to regions outside the Metro Manila area;
- Comprehensive agrarian reform;
- Rehabilitation and sustainable use of the country's resources;
- Technological upgrading of production sectors; and
- Greater contribution of tourism to economic growth and regional development.

The structural reforms and policies that will bring about this economic transformation are based on short-run macroeconomic policies for stability, long-run policies for sustainable growth, poverty alleviation and human/social development to attain an improved quality of life for all Filipinos by the year 2000. In line with this strategy, the government identified several regional agri-industrial centres. They are designed to: spread economic activity widely throughout the country by intensifying the links between the agriculture and industry sectors, provide a boost to the manufacture of export goods and improve job generation.

Over the six-year period, agriculture's share of the GDP is planned to decline from 22.8% to 19.5%, shifting industry's share of the GDP from 34.2 to 38.7%. Construction (9.8% average annual growth) will set the essential infrastructure support necessary to implement critical macroeconomic policies and reforms. Along with construction, manufacturing (6.9% average annual growth) is seen to keep pace with the growth in industry, benefiting mostly from the increased demand for energy generated by the growing economy. Services, on the other hand, will continue to provide robust growth to the economy, propelled by the programmed liberalisation and deregulation in its sub-sectors.

GOVERNMENT ROLE

With the exception of such basic public utilities as transport, water and electricity, prices of goods and services generally are determined by free-market forces. Although nationalist blocs and vested interests can some-times pose obstacles to the pace of reforms, deregulation and liberalisation policies have accelerated under President Ramos' leadership. Reforms in trade, investment and foreign-exchange policies are important examples. The Ramos administration continues to re-privatise a once large portfolio of public-sector-controlled firms. Furthermore, the original scope of privatisation has been expanded from mere divestment to broadening private-sector participation in such activities as providing public utilities and infrastructure that once were the government's sole domain. Because of limited financial resources, the government is relying increasingly on the private sector to undertake vital infrastructure construction, main-tenance and rehabilitation work under its BOT scheme and similar arrangements.

BALANCE OF PAYMENTS

The Philippines' increasingly open economy and improving macroeconomic fundamentals have encouraged the rapid growth of overseas workers' remittances through formal bank channels, peso conversions of foreign currency deposits, and increasing levels of both debt and non-debt capital flows. These have financed the country's widening merchandise-trade deficit. During 1996, import growth of 20.3%—reflecting mainly investments in capital equipment and export-related raw-material requirements—outpaced export expansion of 17.7%. Nevertheless, the Philippines' balance-of-payments ended that year with a record US$4.1 billion surplus. Although still outpaced by imports, exports have grown more strongly since 1993 than in the preceding decade, an initial indication that market-based reforms may already have begun to correct the anti-export bias of a long history of import-substitution policies. About 60% of export receipts are generated by the sale of electronic/electrical equipment and garments. Coconut and mineral products are also important foreign-exchange earners.

Diversification, differentiation, and productivity are important challenges, as Philippine exports face intensifying competition from lower wages in emerging economies—a pressure that is already being felt in the garments industry. Although the Philippines' balance of payments situation has improved significantly with continuous structural reforms, vulnerability to external shocks arising from unexpected reversals in unpredictable sources of BOP financing—such as workers' remittances and portfolio capital—indicate the importance of further increasing exports and attracting higher levels of long-term investments.

In early 1995, the government decided not to conclude a fifth debt-rescheduling agreement with official (Paris Club) creditors, a determined step towards weaning the country from exceptional financing and improving the country's credit rating in the voluntary capital markets. Completion of a comprehensive tax reform program to address concerns over sustainable revenue flows is all that currently stands in the way of the country's exit from over three decades of conditional International Monetary Fund lending programs.

INFRASTRUCTURE

The legal framework the Philippines created for its BOT and BOT-type projects in 1996 has set the country apart from other countries that are also actively pursuing private financing alternatives for their infrastructure development program. BOT (and its many variants) as a development technique applies not only to power, telecommunications, airports, ports and roads, but also to education/health, information technology, and even tourism. Earlier amendments to the BOT law provided incentives for private-sector participation in infrastructure projects. Under the new law the government can, for example, accept unsolicited proposals for BOT if it involves a new technology.

Despite its limitations, the BOT law and its implementing guidelines created a more confident and optimistic environment that is conducive to private-sector investment and participation. As of 31 March 1997, there are 82 active BOT projects, of which 26 are completed, 34 are ongoing and 22 are in the pipeline. Given the enormous pressure to create additional power generation capacity during the early 1990s, the energy sector accounted for all the completed BOT projects.

In addition to the active and ongoing BOT projects, several projects have been implemented through other modes of private participation. These are joint-venture agreements with the Philippine National Construction Corporation and the Public Estates Authority to develop all roads in Metro Manila and with the Philippine National Railways and the Bases Conversion and Development Corporation to construct a rapid-rail transit system from Metro Manila to Clark. There are also various ongoing studies to increase private-sector participation: the Philippine National Railways' privatisation and light rail transit integration is financed by the United States Trade and Development Agency (USTDA); the Philippine Transport Strategy Study and Civil Aviation Master Plan are assisted by the Asian Development Bank; the Metro Manila Urban Transport Integration Study is assisted by the Japan International Cooperation Agency (JIPA) and the Light Rail Transit Authority (LRTA) financial restructuring study is financed by the Overseas Economic Cooperation Fund.

New tax measures are also aimed at relieving problems in revenue collection that continue to complicate infrastructure development. Today, line agencies are better able to find matching funds so that foreign development-aid funds can be put to better use. The Philippine Government also is striving to improve internal government coordination of infrastructure-development management, which has been a hindrance in the past.

POLITICS

Philippine domestic political stability has elicited increased foreign investment in the country, and the United States and Japan remain the Philippines' largest trading partners. Despite the closure of the former US military bases in 1991 and 1992, The Philippines remains an American ally under the a mutual defence treaty. US aid to the Philippines has declined sharply since the withdrawal of American forces. The last great US aid project was a major airport and harbour constructed in General Santos City in south-eastern Mindanao with funding from the US Agency for International Development (AID). The AID-sponsored Growth with Equity in Mindanao program promotes development through private enterprise.

After taking office in June 1992, Ramos restored political stability while pressing successfully for economic liberalisation. With national reconciliation a major priority, Ramos initiated a domestic peace process aimed to negotiate peace settlements with Muslim, Communist and military rebels. The government signed a peace agreement with the military rebels and is negotiating with the Communists, who have weakened substantially due to internal conflicts, the world communist movement's demise and the restoration of Philippine democracy. In September 1996, the government signed a historic peace accord with the Moro National Liberation Front, the largest Muslim insurgent group. The pact fosters enormous investment opportunities in Mindanao.

DISTRIBUTION AND SALES CHANNELS

Metropolitan Manila is the country's nerve centre for industrial and financial activity, transportation and communications, trade, and educational services. Approximately 85% of Philippine foreign trade passes through the Port of Manila and 90% of imports enter the port to be distributed to the other principal cities via trucks and inter-island vessels. Most of the Philippine's national importers and distributors are located in Manila.

About 90% of all Philippine industries are located in three major locations in the greater Manila area. The first, an area of heavy industry, is situated along the banks of Pasig River, which flows through the city and into the port area in Manila Bay. Cargo discharged from vessels in the bay is often loaded on barges and lighters for transport via the Pasig River to the industrial area. The second industrial district, containing medium-sized plants, is located about 15 miles outside of Manila at Antipolo in the Marikina Valley. Supplies and raw materials generally are carried there from the port area by truck. The third major industrial area is in Makati, the central business area in the country and the most prosperous of the Manila suburbs. In addition to small manufacturing plants, a considerable number of distribution centres, trading firms, and commercial banks are located there. Makati is also a shopping area for higher income residents.

Interregional centres

In addition to Manila, the other major interregional centres are Cebu City, Iloilo, Davao, and Zamboanga. Cebu City, the third largest city in the Philippines, is the prime trading centre in the southern part of the archipelago. Its hinterland is accessible mainly by boat. Iloilo shares with Cebu the servicing of the country's central area. Davao, the second largest city in the Philippines, enjoys a trade monopoly in Southern Mindanao, due mainly to the presence of land and water connections with nearby provinces. Zamboanga functions partly as an interregional centre. Transportation to the hinterland is almost entirely by water since there are only a few roads along the peninsula.

Major and secondary centres

Furnishing the archipelago with basic economic, political, and social services are about 40 major and 35 secondary centres situated throughout the Philippines. These are comparatively small, with populations of up to 60,000. Their importance lies in the fact that they render essential urban services to their respective territories. Most of these centres are on the coasts and a number of them are medium-sized ports.

Use of agents/distributors: finding a partner

Agent/distributor arrangements are common in the Philippines. Given the Filipino affinity for American products, Filipino companies generally are eager to pursue discussions once they have examined a firm's product literature and have determined that there is a market for the product. Manufacturers and their Filipino agents/distributors are bound by a contract that should contain the following key elements:

- General provisions
    - –identification of parties to the contract,
    - –duration of the contract, conditions of cancellation,
    - –definition of covered goods,
    - –definition of territory or territories, and
    - –sole and exclusive rights;
- Rights and obligations of manufacturer
    - –conditions of termination,
    - –protection of sole and exclusive rights,
    - –sales and technical support, tax liabilities,
    - –conditions of sale,
    - –delivery of goods,
    - –prices, order refusal,
    - –inspection of distributor's books,
    - –trademark/patent protection,
    - –information to be supplied by the distributor,
    - –advertising and sales promotion,
    - –responsibility for claims/warranties, and
    - –inventory requirements; and
- Rights and obligations of distributor
    - –safeguarding manufacturer's interest,
    - –payment arrangements,
    - –contract assignment,
    - –customs clearance,
    - –observance of conditions of sale,

–after-sales service, and
–information to be supplied to the manufacturer.

There are no Filipino laws that impede termination of an agent/ distributor contract should either party wish to do so. Contracts usually specify that 30 days' notice must be given in the event of cancellation. The standard agent's commission is 5%, but this can vary.

There is no typical profile of a Filipino agent or distributor. Firms can range in size from those with fewer than 25 employees handling only a few specialised products on behalf of a limited number of manufacturers to large trading companies handling a wide range of products and suppliers. Some Filipino firms focus only on the Metro Manila area, while others also service provincial commercial centres such as Cebu, Davao, Iloilo, and Baguio. Any Filipino agent/distributor should be registered with the Philippine Securities and Exchange Commission. Foreign firms selecting a Philippine representative should consider, along with the usual factors, the following:

- Whether the distributor has sufficient financial strength to maintain appropriate stock, provide effective after-sales service, and allow competitive payment terms; and
- Whether the geographic sales area includes the increasing rich markets in central and southern islands of Cebu and Mindanao.

Firms seeking agents or distributors in the Philippines are encouraged to use such services of the US and Foreign Commercial Service, Manila, as the Agent/Distributor Service (ADS) or the Gold Key Service.

FRANCHISING

The Philippine Franchise Association lists 94 foreign franchises operating in the country as of 1996. The list includes garment companies such as Esprit, Guess, JC Penney, Marks &Spencer, and Oshkosh B'Gosh. In addition, in the growing food sector are Jack-in-the-Box, Hard Rock Cafe, Domino's Pizza, Au Bon Pain, and Donut Magic. Some of the foreign companies in non-food enterprises are FedEx, Makro, and Days Inn. There also are several local franchises that are mostly food-related. Jollibee continues to be the most successful and has expanded internationally.

Foreign franchise success rate is high at 94.6%. Only five have discontinued operations: Pizza Inn, Arby's, Yoshinaya, Fosters Freeze, and Yummy Korean Barbecue. In 1996, 70% of all franchises were in the food category. However, by mid-1997, the 11 food franchises comprised only 23% of 47 new franchises. Because Philippine retail laws prohibit foreign ownership, most foreign franchises operate under a master-licence agreement in which a single entrepreneur controls a geographic territory and, in turn, licences other business owners to operate individual franchise locations. Some franchises, including McDonald's, retain a majority of their own outlets and use employees as managers.

DIRECT MARKETING

Direct, or multi-level, marketing is a popular mode of selling products in the Philippines. Such firms as Tupperware, Avon, SaraLee, High Desert, Forever Living, Encyclopedia Britannica, Herbal Life and Amway have established distributorship networks in the country. The legalities of direct marketing are covered by the Consumer Code of the Philippines. Direct marketing, like franchising, is restricted to 100% Filipino-owned corporations. However, foreign firms can engage in wholesale activities and sell to Philippine distributors. The Direct Sellers Association of the Philippines has 26 members.

JOINT VENTURES/LICENSING

An increasingly common method for enterprises embarking on business operations in the Philippines is joint ventures with local enterprises. Philippine law on joint-venture corporations states that where activity to be undertaken is partially nationalised, the foreign entity is limited to 40% equity participation. 'Nationalised' means reserved for ownership by Filipino citizens only. The Bureau of Patents, Trademarks, and Technology Transfer under the Department of Trade and Industry is the government body that approves and supervises all licensing/technology transfer agreements.

In the Philippine context, technology-transfer arrangements refer to contracts or agreements entered into by and between domestic companies and foreign/foreign-owned companies involving the: transfer of systematic knowledge for the manufacture of a product or the application of a process; rendering of a service, including management contracts; licensing of computer software except software developed for mass market; and the transfer, assignment, or licensing of all forms of industrial property rights.

Included in the foregoing arrangements are local distributorships/export marketing agreements that involve the licensing of foreign trademarks, as well as retainerships of foreign firms or individual technicians for the rendering of management and/or technical consultancy services as part of the technology transfer or licensing agreement. All technology transfer arrangements are registered with the Technology Transfer Registry of the Bureau of Patents, Trademarks and Technology Transfer. Royalty payments are remitted through any bank authorised by the Bangko Sentral ng Pilipinas.

To be entitled to registration, foreign investors must meet the following conditions:

- The contracts must provide for a fixed term of not more than 10 years with no automatic renewal clause; renewal is allowed upon prior approval of the Technology Transfer Registry (TTR). An indefinite term may be allowed for royalty-free agreements and arrangements for the outright purchase of technology.
- The contract must not contain the restrictive business clauses identified under Section 12 of the Rules, one of which restricts directly or indirectly the export of the licensed products under the technology-transfer arrangement, unless justified for the protection of the legitimate interest of the technology supplier such as export to countries where exclusive licence to manufacture and/or distribute the licensed product(s) has already been granted.
- Royalties/fees not exceeding 5% of net sales shall be granted automatic approval provided the technology-transfer arrangement involves the transfer of technology through the licensing of patents and/or know-how and trade secrets. Royalty rates higher than 5% may be approved subject to a determination of the reasonableness of the requested fee.
- The contracts must also contain requisite provisions as provided in Section 13 of the Rules, which among others provide that the laws of the Republic of the Philippines shall govern the interpretation of the contract and in the event of litigation the venue shall likewise be the Philippines. Withholding taxes on all payments relating to the contract would be for the account of the licensor. A bonus royalty of 2% of net foreign-exchange earnings may be allowed if the technology supplier assists the technology recipient in the export of the licensed product(s).

ESTABLISHING AN OFFICE

A business enterprise must complete the following steps before it can start operations:

- Apply for registration of the business name with the Bureau of Domestic Trade;
- Register with the Securities and Exchange Commission if a partnership or a corporation;
- Apply for permits from the *barangay,* the lowest unit of governance, and from the mayor to operate in a chosen locality and secure a municipal licence (EPZA enterprises excluded);

- Register with the Bureau of Internal Revenue to obtain a tax account number, value-added tax registration number, and individual residence certificates for owners/incorporators;
- Register employees with the Social Security System, Medicare, and Department of Labor and Employment.

The essential forms of business organisation in the Philippines are sole proprietorships, partnerships, and corporations. Other less common business forms include joint-stock companies, joint accounts, business trusts, and cooperatives. A foreign entity, depending upon the nature of its intended activity in the Philippines, may establish and register any of the following: a branch, a subsidiary, a licensing and franchising agreement, a joint-venture agreement, and a regional headquarters.

SELLING FACTORS/TECHNIQUES

There are several invaluable sales tools that suppliers should employ to maintain market leadership. Foreigners should exercise diligence in selecting their local distributors, agents, or representatives, since they are important market links. After selection, suppliers must provide full support to their local representatives. Suppliers should visit the Philippines at least once each year to keep abreast of developments in the industries they are serving, to show support for their local representatives to discuss problems or devise marketing techniques, and to visit customers. There should be a strong emphasis on regular customer calls by local representatives in order for them to identify sales targets or opportunities. Training programs for customers and distributors, advertising and product promotion support, and participation in trade fairs, exhibitions and product seminars are also important for suppliers to maintain leadership in this highly competitive market.

ADVERTISING AND TRADE PROMOTION

The Philippines is a brand-conscious market. Advertising plays a significant part in promoting the sale of most goods, particularly non-durable consumer goods. Most of the 178 advertising agencies have patterned their organisations after American agencies. Advertising expenditures in 1996 exceeded US$500 million, a huge jump from the roughly US$400 million spent in 1995. Television took a 65% share, with print (24%) and radio (17%) trailing behind. There are nearly 400 radio stations, 25 daily newspapers, and 55 consumer magazines in the Philippines. Of the various television stations, six are terrestrial, five are UHF, 120 are cable operators, and 75 are cable channels. There are televisions in 48% of Philippine households.

More than 20 national daily newspapers, all published in Manila, provide domestic and international news, as well as an expanding standard medium for advertising. The widest-circulated paper is the *Manila Bulletin*. Other widely-read newspapers are the *Philippine Daily Inquirer*, *Philippine Star*, *Business World*, *Today*, and *Manila Standard*. The widest circulated tabloids are *People's Journal*, *People's Tonite*, *Abante*, and *Balita*. Business journals include *Mining & Engineering Journal*, *The Energy Manager*, *Computer Times*, *Computer World*, *Garments and Textiles Association Journal*, *Construction Industry Association of the Philippines Newsletter*, *Metalworking Newsletter*, and *Philippine Business*.

PRICING PRODUCTS

In most instances, price is the primary consideration in the purchase decisions of Philippine buyers. However, in some cases the quality of the product as well as the after sales service/support and availability of spare parts supersede price as a primary criterion. End-users prefer American-made products if they can afford them because they are well known for high quality and durability. While the reliability of products works to the advantage of suppliers, they should nevertheless be concerned with cheaper prices of third-country competition. Manufacturers and suppliers need to be flexible in their prices and, where appropriate, should be prepared to provide end-users in different income brackets with alternative products.

AFTER-SALES SERVICE/CUSTOMER SUPPORT

Next to price, after-sales service and support are extremely important factors to marketing success in the Philippines. It is imperative for vendors to provide this support during and after the warranty period in order to satisfy their customers. The proximity of Taiwan, Japan and other Asian nations works against the competitiveness of North American and European firms.

SELLING TO THE GOVERNMENT

The Philippine Government itself is a large direct importer (usually through competitive bidding) of many essential products, including road-building and maintenance equipment, cement, machinery and equipment for various government projects, and military and defence equipment.

Government agencies pattern regulations and procedures after those of the Bureau of Supply and Coordination of the US Government's General Services Administration. Government purchasers include the National Power Corporation, National Electrification Administration, National

Housing Authority, National Irrigation Administration, Local Water Utilities Administration, Metropolitan Waterworks & Sewerage System, Department of Transportation & Communication, Department of Public Works & Highways, and the Department of National Defence. Defence Department purchases usually require an offset commitment from the foreign supplier.

Philippine Government procurement regulations permit a foreign company to bid on government procurement only if it maintains a registered branch office or a registered resident agent in the Philippines. The first step in obtaining government business is to be placed on the Bidder's Mailing List of the agency with which the applicant is interested in doing business. This is done by sworn application accompanied by certified copies of the company's application for the Certificate of Registration issued by the Philippine Bureau of Commerce, articles of incorporation, a receipted franchise-tax bill, an up-to-date financial statement, and other attachments as required. Application forms of the various procurement agencies are the same in most respects.

All procurement of the Philippine military agencies are undertaken directly from manufacturers, except in the following cases:

- When the manufacturer's marketing policy does not allow direct sales to its customer, the Philippine Government may procure from the sole or exclusive distributor of the firm's products.
- Foreign procurement may be undertaken through a duly licensed local representative of the foreign manufacturing firm. However, procurement from agents, brokers, import-export firms or any intermediary that has been engaged for the express purpose of making any particular sales will not be authorised.
- Government-to-government transactions require registration and accreditation of manufacturers and suppliers. A list of accredited suppliers is published annually and updated quarterly. In addition, foreign contractors are allowed to participate in the construction of only internationally bid and foreign-financed/assisted projects in the Philippines. For this purpose, foreign contractors must apply to the Philippine Contractors Accreditation Board (PCAB) for a special licence, which is issued on a project-by-project basis.

PROTECTION FROM IPR INFRINGEMENT

To protect products from intellectual property rights infringement, manufacturers and suppliers should register their patents, trademarks, and brand names with the Bureau of Patents and Trademarks located on the 5th Floor, Department of Trade and Industry Building, Sen. Gil J Puyat Avenue, Maers.

They should nevertheless be concerned with cheaper prices of third-country competition. Manufacturers and suppliers should be flexible in their prices and, where appropriate, be prepared to provide end-users in different income brackets with alternative products.

SIGNIFICANT INVESTMENT OPPORTUNITIES

By October 1996, the Asset Privatisation Trust had disposed of 253 assets identified for privatisation. The Medium-Term Public Investment Program covers the following: agro-industry, infrastructure and human development, and disaster mitigation. Infrastructure projects under this program include construction of airports, roads, ports, light-rail transport and railroad systems, water supply, power, telecommunications, and information technology. The projects are financed by the government and the private sector, under the (BOT) scheme and its variants, as well as by multilateral development banks and foreign government assistance.

APPENDIX A

BUSINESS TRAVEL

BUSINESS CUSTOMS

Office hours for business firms and the Philippine Government normally are from 8.00 a.m. to 5.00 p.m. It is best to attempt to accomplish business objectives in mid-morning or late afternoon. Many business deals are completed informally during meals, entertainment, or over a round of golf. Offices generally are closed on Saturdays and Sundays. Summer-weight clothing normally worn in temperate zones is suitable for the Philippines. It is acceptable for businessmen to conduct calls in short- or long-sleeved shirts and ties without a coat. The native *barong tagalog*, a light-weight, long-sleeved shirt worn without a tie, is ordinary business attire for businessmen. Light suits and dresses are appropriate for women. Tailors abound, and laundry and dry-cleaning facilities are widely available.

TRAVEL ADVISORY AND VISAS

In the United States, up-to-date travel advisories are available from the US State Department's Philippine desk officer in Washington [tel: (202) 647-2301; fax: (202) 736-4559]. Foreign nationals desiring to enter the Philippines for business purposes are permitted to enter and remain in the country for specific time periods as non-immigrants under provisions of Philippine immigration law.

General provisions

Persons may enter and stay in the Philippine for business, pleasure, or health reasons without a visa for up to 21 days and are exempt from payment of immigration fees and charges. This visa waiver may be extended for another 38 days. Thereafter, those wanting to remain may apply for regular monthly extensions for a maximum stay of one year and 59 days.

Temporary visitors who have been allowed to stay in the country for more than six months may apply for an Alien Certificate of Registration and a Certificate of Residence as a Temporary Visitor. This is done at the main office of the Bureau of Immigration or at its sub-ports that have territorial jurisdiction over these aliens.

Special provisions

Special investor's resident visas may be issued to aliens, their spouses, and any unmarried children if such persons invest US$75,000 or the equivalent in other foreign currency. This allows them to reside in the Philippines while the investment remains. Holders of this kind of visa are required to secure an Alien Certificate of Registration, Certificate of Residence as a Temporary Visitor, Emigration Clearance Certificate and Special Return Certificate. They must also pay all the required alien and immigration fees.

Citizens of countries that have treaties of commerce, trade, amity and/or navigation with the Philippines may apply for an international treaty trader or international treaty investor visa provided they have substantial investments in the Philippines or they conduct substantial trade with the Philippines or its nationals.

Foreign business people may be admitted under prearranged-employment status; however, foreign technicians are admitted on this basis only if they possess skills not available in the Philippines. Prearranged-employment status entitles a visitor to stay for a period of one year. The stay may be renewed annually with the Commission on Immigration and Deportation (CID). An alien who is admitted as a non-immigrant may apply for permanent resident status without departing the Philippines.

HOLIDAYS

All offices close during the following public holidays:
- 1 January, New Year's Day;
- Easter Holidays, which include Maundy Thursday and Good Friday;
- 1 May, Labor Day;
- 9 April, Bataan & Corregidor Day and Heroism Day;
- 12 June, Independence Day;

- 28 August, National Heroes Day;
- 1 November, All Saints' Day;
- 30 November, Bonifacio Day;
- 25 December, Christmas Day; and
- 30 December, Rizal Day.

Manila Day is observed on 24 June only in the City of Manila, while Quezon Day is observed on 19 August only in Quezon City. In addition, special public holidays such as Election Day and EDSA Revolution Day may be declared by the president.

THE CLIMATE

The Philippine climate is tropical. December, January and February generally are considered the most pleasant months. The hot season, or Philippine summer, is from March to June. The rainy season, punctuated by typhoons, lasts from June until November.

LANGUAGE

There are two official languages in the Philippines: English and Pilipino. English is widely spoken and is the major language used in the Philippine school system, as well as the usual language of commerce. Pilipino, based on Tagalog, is the national language and is required by the Philippine Government to be taught in schools. Relatively few Filipinos speak or use Spanish, although Chavacano, derived from Spanish, is spoken in and around Zamboanga in Mindanao.

GETTING AROUND

One can travel comfortably to any part of the Philippines. An extensive road network links much of the archipelago. The country has 86 serviceable airports. Of these, five are international airports (Manila, Cebu, General Santos City, Clark, and Subic) and three are alternate international airports (Laoag, Palawan, and Zamboanga). The 78 domestic airports are subdivided into 11 trunk lines, which include the Manila Domestic Airport, Bacolod City, and Iloilo City Airports; 42 secondary airports; and 25 feeder airports.

Accredited hotel taxis can be arranged with hotel doormen. These are recommended over taxis that are hailed on the street because they charge a flat rate for travel to specified locations. Car rentals also are available, with or without a driver, but the cost is much higher than standard US rates. US franchisees, such as Avis, Hertz, and Budget, charge higher rental rates than those of local firms, but they offer better quality vehicles.

HOTELS

Visitors to the Philippines have a wide choice of hotels and apartments for short stays. Sixteen deluxe hotels operating in Metro Manila. The Westin Philippine Plaza, Traders Hotel, Hyatt Regency Manila, Holiday Inn Manila Pavilion, Hotel Sofitel Grand Boulevard, Manila Diamond Hotel, The Manila Hotel and The Heritage are located in the Bay area. In Makati City, the business district, one will find the Hotel Intercontinental, the Manila Peninsula, Mandarin Oriental, The Dusit Manila Garden, Shangri-La and the New World Hotel. In the Greenhills area are the EDSA Shangri-La Hotel and Galleria Suites Condotel.

An additional 64 accredited hotels are located outside Metro Manila in such cities as Baguio City, Tagaytay City, Cebu, Davao, La Union, Subic, Cavite, and Angeles City. All hotel rates are quoted in US$, exclusive of a 10% service charge, a 10% value-added tax, and a 3.5% government tax.

For expatriates staying for longer periods, well-appointed houses, town homes and condominium units are becoming expensive and increasingly harder to locate.

GOING TO SCHOOL

The Philippines has the largest number of educational institutions in Asia. It has several international schools and a number of private schools for American, British, German, French, and Japanese children in the primary and secondary grades.

PERSONAL NEEDS

For personal needs, supermarkets, malls and smaller shopping centres, fashion boutiques, and a variety of shops are in abundance.

STAYING HEALTHY

There are several modern and well-equipped hospitals and medical facilities in Metro Manila. Doctors with US experience and other medical professionals are abundant. Medical fees are reasonable and pharmaceuticals of all types are available.

However, sanitary conditions in the Philippines are not up to western standards. Uncooked food and unboiled water should be avoided. The air in Metro Manila is heavily polluted, although other areas enjoy better environmental quality.

HAVING FUN

For entertainment, there is a wide choice of movie houses, theatres, and social clubs. Personal services such as fitness clubs, beauty salons, and others are easily obtainable. There are numerous restaurants offering a variety of cuisines. Business entertainment normally takes place in restaurants. Similarly, sporting facilities such as golf courses are abundant and varied.

THE MAIL

Surface and air mail are provided and include a postal money-order service, plus registered and special-delivery mail. Airmail letters between the Philippines and the US usually are delivered in seven to 10 days. Courier services, such as DHL, TNT Skypack, Federal Express, and UPS, are readily available and recommended to transmit important documents to and from the Philippines.

APPENDIX B

BASIC DATA

1996 population, in millions	72
Population growth rate, %	2.32
Religions:	Roman Catholic, 83%; Protestant, 5%; Islam, 5 %; Aglipay, 3%; Iglesia ni Kristo, 2%
Government system:	Presidential form, headed by a president. Government affairs undertaken by three branches: the legislative, executive and judicial.
Languages:	Various dialects, dominated by Tagalog, 28%; Cebuano, 24%; Ilocano, 10%; and Ilongo, 9%. English is normal business language.
Work week:	48 hours

Source: *Philippine Yearbook* (National Statistics Office)

Table 1. Domestic economy

	1996	1997	1998
	Actual		Projection
GDP, current prices, US$ millions,	83,776	83,210	NA[d]
Real GDP growth rate, %	5.7	5.1	2.0-2.5
GDP per capita, US$/person	1,193	1,289	1,392
National government spending as percentage of GDP[a]	18.4	19.2	19.3
Inflation, %	8.4	5.1	8.0-9.0
Unemployment, %	8.6	8.7	7.8
Foreign exchange reserves, US$ millions,	11,745	8,768	NA[d]
Average foreign exchange rate (pesos/US$)	26.22	29.47	40.00
Foreign debt, US$ millions	41,875	45,433	NA[d]
Debt service (% of exports of goods and services), %[b]	12.7	11.3	NA[d]
Interest rates, % Average T-bill rate	13.01	13.30	NA[d]
Average bank loan rate	14.82	16.22	NA[d]
US government economic assistance[c]	62.3	57.3	51.0

[a]National government's cash disbursements as percentage of GDP; 1997 and 1998 projections based on preliminary programmed levels.
[b]Ratio of principal and interest payments to export income. Export income refers to sum of goods and services exports; 1997 figure refers to approved level and 1998 figure to requested level.
[c]1997 figure refers to approved level and 1998 figure to requested level.
[d]Not available.
Source: National Trade Data Bank and Economic Bulletin Board, products of STAT-USA, US Embassy, Manila; National Economic and Development Authority; Department of Finance; and Bangko ng Sentral, Manila.

Table 2. Merchandise trade, US$ millions[a]

	1996	1997	1998
	Actual		Projection
Total country exports	20,543	25,228	29,769
Total country imports	31,885	39,200	46,650
US exports	5,911	7,928	NA[b]
US imports	6,966	8,815	NA[b]

[a]Philippine data, fob.
[b]Not available.
Source: National Trade Data Bank and Economic Bulletin Board, products of STAT-USA, US Department of Commerce.

Investment Statistics

The Securities and Exchange Commission, the Board of Investment, the National Economic and Development Authority, and the Bangko Sentral ng Pilipinas each generate their own direct investment statistics. Because of the confusion created by these different sets of data, the government has initiated a project to generate a standard set of investment numbers based on internationally accepted coverage/definitions.

For now, Bangko Sentral data, which is readily available in US$ terms and broken down by investor country and by industry, is used widely as a convenient and reasonably reliable indicator of foreign-investment stock and foreign-investment flows. The data reflects foreign-investment remittances registered with the Bangko Sentral or a designated custodian bank. Registration is required to enable foreign exchange sourcing from the domestic banking system for profit-remittance and/or capital-repatriation purposes. Tables 3 and 4 (foreign direct investment by investor country and by industry) give cumulative investments registered with the Bangko Sentral from 1973 to the dates indicated. Table 5 provides annual inflows registered with the Bangko Sentral.

Table 3. Cumulative foreign equity investments by investor country[b]

	US$ millions, as of			Distribution, %, as of		
	1994	*1995*	*1996*	*1994*	*1995*	*1996*
United States	2,013	2,069	2,362	38.2	34.0	32.1
Japan	960	1,204	1,676	18.2	19.8	22.8
Netherlands	722[b]	751	804	13.7	12.3	10.9
Hong Kong	334	570	646	6.3	9.4	8.8
United Kingdom	320	372	435	6.1	6.1	5.9
Singapore	108	183	203	2.0	3.0	2.8
Switzerland	108	108	116	2.0	1.8	1.6
South Korea	74	83	112	1.4	1.4	1.4
West Germany	56	72	100	1.1	1.2	1.3
Australia	77	96	99	1.5	1.6	1.3
Taiwan	43	50	97	0.8	0.8	1.3
France	53	59	70	1.0	0.9	1.0
Malaysia	14	41	59	0.5	0.7	0.8
Canada	55	57	58	1.1	0.9	0.8
Total	5,271	6,086	7,367	100	100	100
Total FDI stock as percentage of GDP				8.2	8.2	8.8

[a]Sum of annual foreign investments from 1993 up to the year indicated.
[b]Over US$500 million from a Dutch subsidiary of Saudi Aramco for the purchase of 40% of the Philippine Government's share in an oil firm (Petron).
Source: Bangko Sentral ng Pilipinas

Table 4. Cumulative foreign equity investments by industry[a]

	Levels, in US$ millions, as of			Distribution, %, as of		
	1994	1995	1996	1994	1995	1996
Banks/financial	548	638	1,151	10.4	10.5	15.6
Manufacturing	3,012	3,349	3,827	57.1	55.0	51.9
Chemicals	571	607	659	10.8	10.0	9.0
Food products	373	384	403	7.1	6.3	5.5
Petroleum & coal	785[b]	829	829	14.9	13.6	11.3
Basic metal products	205	229	291	3.9	3.8	4.0
Transport equipment	197	250	286	3.7	4.1	3.9
Textiles	123	135	137	2.3	2.2	1.9
Other metals[c]	68	207	364	1.3	3.4	4.9
Mining	938	980	983	17.8	16.1	13.3
Petrol/gas	780	803	804	14.8	13.2	9.6
Commerce	231	325	410	4.4	5.3	5.6
Wholesale trade	129	157	188	2.4	2.6	2.6
Real estate	82	119	171	1.6	2.0	2.3
Services	310	340	375	5.9	5.6	5.1
Public utilities	147	365	486	2.8	6.0	6.6
Communications	92	109	166	1.2	1.8	2.3
Agriculture	54	55	56	1.0	0.9	0.8
Construction	31	33	78	0.6	0.5	1.1
Total	5,271	6,086	7,367	100	100	100
Total FDI stock as percentage of GDP				8.2	8.2	8.8

[a]Sum of annual foreign investments from 1973 to the year indicated.
[b]Over US$500 million from a Dutch subsidiary of Saudi Aramco for the purchase of 40% of the Philippine Government's share in an oil firm (Petron).
[c]Includes machinery and appliances.
Source: Bangko Sentral ng Pilipinas.

Table 5. Annual foreign equity investment flows by investor country,[a] US$ millions

	1991	1992	1993	1994	1995	1996
United States	75.1	56.1	35.6	76.0	55.8	292.7
Japan	188.7	154.4	46.2	69.8	244.5	471.5
Netherlands	3.6	5.3	13.5	547.7[b]	29.8	52.9
Hong Kong	32.7	37.8	21.7	48.7	235.6	76.3
United Kingdom	15.2	2.1	153.2	34.4	52.7	62.9
Singapore	8.6	8.4	9.4	60.2	75.5	19.6
Switzerland	8.4	8.1	15.0	0.7	0.4	7.5
South Korea	35.6	13.1	3.7	6.1	8.2	29.3
West Germany	5.5	7.5	8.2	1.8	16.2	27.7
Australia	1.5	3.1	0.6	5.0	19.3	3.2
Taiwan	6.1	2.8	4.1	2.4	7.4	47.3
France	1.0	5.4	0.5	2.8	6.3	10.7
Malaysia	0.3	0.4	2.1	0	27.2	17.9
Canada	1.0	1.0	0	1.6	1.2	1.0
Total	415.3	328.0	377.7	881.9	815.0	1,281.0
Annual FDI flow as percentage of GDP	0.9	0.6	0.7	1.4	1.1	1.5

[a]Annual inflow equivalent to the difference of year-to-year stock figures.
[b]Inflows in 1994 were from a Dutch subsidiary of Saudi Aramco for the purchase of 40% of the Philippine Government's share in an oil firm (Petron).
Source: Bangko Sentral ng Pilipinas.

APPENDIX C

THE STOCK MARKET

By Robert Katz

The Philippine stock market is one of the oldest in Asia. There used to be two stock exchanges—the Manila Stock Exchange (MSE) and the Makati Stock Exchange (MkSE). The MSE was established on 8 August 1927 by five American businessmen. It was originally located in downtown Manila, then transferred to Pasig in 1992. On 27 May 1963, the MkSE was organized by five businessmen, but because there was opposition to its creation operations did not begin until 16 November 1965. It was located in Makati, the financial district of Metro Manila.

Although the two exchanges remained as separate entities, they basically were trading the same listed issues. The idea to unite the two exchanges and have it managed by a professional group became a compelling vision of the government of Fidel V. Ramos, elected president in May 1992. The idea was to develop a more efficient capital market. The initiative put forth by President Ramos to attain this vision bore fruit with the incorporation of the Philippine Stock Exchange Inc on 14 July 1992. To consolidate logistics and to hasten development, the leaders of both bourses agreed on 23 December of the same year to unify under the banner of the Philippine Stock Exchange (PSE).

The Securities and Exchange Commission granted the Philippine Stock Exchange Inc its licence to operate as a securities exchange on 4 March 1994 and simultaneously cancelled the licences of the MSE and MkSE. Reflecting its history, the exchange operated from two trading floors, one in PSE Plaza on Ayala Avenue, Makati, the other in PSE Centre, formerly Tektite Towers, on Exchange Road, Ortigas Center, Pasig. By May 1998, the exchange had 184 members, 119 in Makati, 65 in Pasig.

On 20 March 1993, the first election of the PSE Board of Governors was held during the second general membership meeting. Of the 15 elected governors, 14 are member-brokers of the exchange. The 15th slot was reserved for the PSE President, who is a non-broker. Eduardo C. Lim was chosen as the first chairman of the Board and Eduardo de los Angeles as the first president.

Since its establishment, the PSE has worked in concerted effort through its member-brokers and with its counterparts in government to become a world-class exchange and a leading proponent of economic growth and stability. Early on, the exchange took the necessary steps to establish the modern infrastructure needed to satisfy the stringent requisites of being a leading bourse in the Asian-Pacific region. The PSE continues to develop and implement rules and guidelines to provide investors an efficient, fair, orderly and transparent market.

One of the major steps was the installation of a computerised surveillance system, which enhanced the powers of the exchange to detect, document and prosecute trading violations in order to protect the investing public. The system has enabled the exchange to detect and investigate the causes of day-to-day anomalies and aberrations in the market, deterring abuses such as listing violations, price manipulation and insider trading. Publicly listed companies are monitored closely for adherence to strict disclosure requirements.

In October 1995, the PSE marked another milestone in its young existence when it was accepted as the 37th member of the Federation Internationale Bourses de Valeurs. Becoming a full-fledged member of this prestigious international body of stock exchanges enabled the PSE to attract more foreign investors into the domestic market. This contributed significantly to the development of the Philippine capital markets as an open, attractive and transparent investment option for major international players.

Eventually, the Unified Trading System (UTS) was installed successfully, fully integrating the trading between the two floors through implementing a single-order-book system utilising sophisticated trading software so that all orders are posted and matched in a single computer.

Efforts were further focused on increasing the investor base of the equities market. The PSE started to intensify its public awareness outreach through seminars in Manila as well as in the business centres of key provinces around the country. To accommodate more market players, the exchange, through the support of its members, sought to increase its present number of off-floor trading sites and provincial trading satellites. By the end of 1995, 50% of the total number of brokers utilised off-floor trading, while 10 brokers established provincial satellites. Some exchange officials had also embarked on international road shows to promote the PSE in the United States and in other Asian countries to attract more serious, sophisticated investors—foreign as well as Filipinos based in foreign countries.

To assist its investors, the PSE widened the scope of its library collections and PSE publications to provide timely, accurate and relevant data. Studies to modify the PSE Composite Index were undertaken to establish a more accurate measurement of market performance. Special studies on the Initial Public Offerings (IPOs) also were undertaken to create a more effective, rational, and transparent distribution system for future offerings.

Not only has the PSE been an important catalyst in developing the Philippine capital markets, it also has proved to be a responsible corporate entity by engaging in community and social activities. The exchange initiated a relief fund drive to help lahar-stricken victims in Central Luzon. Recently, the Exchange has been able to point with pride at the establishment of the PSE Foundation, its highly responsible social arm. The first major beneficiaries of the foundation were the Mother Theresa Project for the Poor and the Tuloy sa Don Bosco project.

With the attainment of these milestones, the exchange is energised to move forward at an accelerated pace to further promote the integrity of the capital marketplace and enhance the image of the Philippines as a sophisticated financial centre in the heart of Asia. By setting an aggressive pace during its early years, the PSE has demonstrated competence, savvy and sophistication. On this foundation, it is looking forward optimistically to a brightening future wherein the Philippines is expected to take a leading position within the region as the ASEAN countries leap beyond the current economic turbulence. The exchange has initiated numerous major improvements and plans to respond more effectively to the demands of a rapidly recovering economy.

The main thrust of the PSE is to spearhead the development of the Philippine equities market towards the growth of a capital market consistent with the projected development of the nation's economy. Although trading decreased amid regional economic troubles in late 1997 and early 1998, trading in 1998 is averaging about 40 billion shares a day, with the value of daily turnover ranging from one to two billion pesos. As the regional recession persisted, the value of a seat on the exchange declined from about 80 million pesos to about 60 million pesos, but almost none of the members wanted to sell. Given the remarkable accomplishments of the past few years, the PSE will soon achieve its mission of becoming a recognised, world-class stock exchange.

THE EXCHANGE IN DETAIL

The following information is edited from the Philippine Stock Exchange web site, http://www.pse.com.ph

PUBLICATIONS

PSE Monthly Report

A summary of transactions traded for the month. Notably, it highlights the trading statistics for all listed issues, dividend and stock rights declarations for the month, new listings, market capitalisation for the month for all listed issues, 20 most active companies by value turnover and market capitalisation, and top 20 gainers and losers. Selected financial accounts for all listed companies are likewise featured such as authorised capital, shares outstanding, stockholders' equity and net income. The publication also features selected economic indicators, special block sale transactions and a summary of the stock rights for the past three years.

PSE Investments Guide

A compact, easy-to-use reference manual that provides key investment information on listed companies in the Philippine stock market. It is a compilation of corporate profiles with financial highlights and major financial ratios for the last five years. It includes trading statistics such as market prices, volume traded and value turnover, dividend history and the latest top 20 shareholders.

PSE Fact Book

An annual publication that contains stock market trading activity in terms of sectoral indices, volume traded, value turnover and market capitalisation. It also includes statistics on listed companies, new listings and public offerings along with dividend and rights declarations. It contains combined historical data on the Philippine stock market since 1987. Also included is basic information on the Philippine Stock Exchange—history, organisation and management, operations, and summaries of the rules on trading, membership and listing.

PSE Weekly Report

A report that features stock market highlights for the week in review. It includes a write-up on the market's performance, ranking by value turnover and by market capitalisation of all listed issues, summary of corporate announcements along with technical charts of all stock price indices.

Corporate Review

A weekly publication that provides a brief study on a listed company. It features pertinent and up-to-date information and statistics for reference or to help the reader evaluate investments. The study contains company information and highlights, recent developments, programs and plans, financial performance and stock market performance.

PSE Annual Report

This publication reports the overall performance and operations of the Philippine Stock Exchange on an annual basis. A summary of what transpired during the year is the theme of the 'Message of the Chairman and the President'. Aside from the presentation of the Financial Statement of the Exchange, it also discusses the stock market performance supported by relevant statistics and charts.

The Exchanger

A bi-monthly newsletter which chronicles recent developments, new policies and personnel movement.

RELATED ORGANISATIONS
Securities and Exchange Commission
The securities industry is regulated by the Securities and Exchange Commission (SEC). It is a quasi-judicial government agency whose primary role is to protect the investing public from fraud and deception in securities transactions. It derives its regulatory powers and functions from Presidential Decree 902-A (as amended), the Revised Securities Act (RSA), Corporation and Partnership Laws, Investment Company Act, and Investment Houses Law.

The commission is a collegial body composed of the chairman and four associate commissioners. Its policies, rules and regulations are implemented through the various departments and extension offices whose activities are coordinated by the Executive Director.

Philippine Central Depository Inc
The Philippine Central Depository Inc (PCD) is a private institution that has been organised to implement a book-entry system which will greatly improve the operations of securities transactions. A book-entry system would reduce, if not eliminate, a lot of paperwork involved under present practices. Those who participate in the system would need first to open a security account with PCD and deposit their securities into the account. Any transfer of a particular security (ex. stock) from one participant to another may conveniently be effected via book-entry, that is, by debiting one account and crediting another without the need to handle the physical certificates or documents. The records of PCD would show what each participant beneficially owns in a particular security. The securities that are eligible in the book-entry system of PCD are equity securities (stocks listed in the Philippine Stock Exchange) and debt securities (treasury bills and treasury bonds). There are two types of transactions involving equity securities, namely, those transacted at the Exchange and those outside the Exchange. Transactions that do not pass through the Exchange are settled directly between two counter-parties, such as equity transactions between brokers and custodians and transactions involving debt securities. The book-entry system is practised in many capital markets around the world. The Philippines has been implementing similar operations and PCD is spearheading this project.

Benefits to participants include:
- Facilitates transfer of ownership of stocks and funds thereby reducing settlement risks;

- Allows prompt distribution of stock and cash dividends as well as interest and maturity payments enabling beneficial owners to immediately realise the fruits of their investments;
- Provides for immediate updating of portfolio records immediately settling the seller's and buyer's legal liability;
- Supports the scripless trading in the government debt market;
- Facilitates the process of pledging securities;
- Provides infrastructure to handle peak volumes; and
- Eliminates risk associated with physical certificates (i.e. lost certificates or forged signatures).

Securities Clearing Corporation of the Philippines

The Securities Clearing Corporation of the Philippines (SCCP) is a private institution organised as a clearance and settlement agency for the depository-eligible trades executed in the PSE; and also to manage and administer a Trade Guarantee Fund (TGF) for these very same trades. The specific functions of SCCP are:

- Establishing the liabilities between members;
- Synchronising the settlement of funds and transfer of securities;
- Guaranteeing the settlement of trades in the event of a member default; and
- Administering the appropriate risk management functions to facilitate the preceding.

The Philippine Stock Exchange has 51% holding in SCCP and the remaining 49% is held by Philippine commercial banks. The Company has submitted its draft rules and procedures to the Securities Exchange Commission (SEC) and is presently awaiting the issuance of its licence to operate.

Securities Investors Protection Fund Inc

The Securities Investors Protection Fund Inc (SIPFI) is a non-stock, non-profit corporation organised for the main purpose of creating, maintaining and administering a fund for the interest and promotion of the securities industry, and for aiding and protecting investors in securities and members of the Fund.

All persons registered and licensed as brokers or dealers by the SEC, under the RSA, are members of the SIPFI.

Philippine Association of Securities Brokers and Dealers Inc

The Philippine Association of Securities Brokers and Dealers Inc (PASBDI) is an organisation of all licensed stockbrokers and independent securities brokers and dealers, as well as investment houses in the Philippines. It serves as the voice of the securities industry vis-a-vis the public and the government in all matters affecting the members.

The PASBDI is tasked to undertake projects for the development of the securities industry and to protect its members whenever their interests are affected by certain factors, i.e., proposed government measures, which may have an adverse effect on the securities industry.

PSE Foundation Inc

The PSE Foundation Inc (PSEFI) is a private non-stock, non-profit corporation engaged in social welfare, charity, culture, business, education, science and research projects. PSEFI seeks to assist several cultural, academic and charitable institutions. PSEFI supports projects that generally promote the well-being and development of society; improve social and economic conditions; heighten youth involvement in productive activities and encourage self- sufficiency and self-reliance.

Among the Foundation's beneficiaries are the Interact Pamilya Foundation, the Missionaries of Charity, Tuloy sa Don Bosco, UNICEF, Foundation for Adolescent Development and the Clean and Green Foundation.

RULES AND REGULATIONS ON TRADING (abridged)
Trading Hours

Except for Saturdays, Sundays, legal holidays and days when the Bangko Sentral ng Pilipinas Clearing Office are closed, or if a computer problem cuts off the communication link between the two trading floors (Ayala and Tektite), the PSE trading hours are:

- Playing of the National Anthem, 8:45 a.m.;
- Pre-open period, 9:00 a.m. to 9:30 a.m.
- Calculation of open price/market open, 9:30 a.m.
- Regular trading period 9:30 a.m. to 12:00 noon
- Closing time 12:00 noon

Trading Booth

An operating member shall be entitled to one booth in either trading floor (PSE Plaza Ayala or PSE Centre Tektite). The booth shall be maintained and manned during trading hours from 9:30 a.m. to 12:10 p.m. by at least one user but not more than 10 authorised trading floor personnel composed of either the member or nominee, an authorised trader, or telephone clerks.

The personnel assigned in the booth must be capable of and actually be doing trades. The staff assigned to operate the computer terminal(s) must be certified by the Exchange as a MakTrade user. In case buying and selling orders are received on the trading floor directly from the clients themselves, the staff receiving the orders must be licensed by the SEC. Failure to appropriately man the booth shall subject the broker to a fine of P1,000 per day of violation. If client's orders are simply relayed from the broker's offices, the receiving staff need not be SEC-licensed. To be able to trade, at least one of the authorised trading floor personnel must be a Maktrade-certified user. If brokers will have to assign only one staff who will do both order entry and receiving orders directly from the clients themselves, then the staff must be both a certified Maktrade user and SEC-licensed.

Opening price calculation

The opening price for each security shall be computed by the System based on the pre-open postings and its last closing price. The computation shall include a determination of all prices which have possible matching and volumes that could be matched at each of the prices. The opening price is that price which offers the maximum number of shares matched. This is provided that, if the prices have the same volume that could be matched, the price closer to the previous close is taken as the opening price. It is provided further that, if the prices have the same volume that could be matched and are equidistant from the previous close, the highest price is taken as the opening price.

Special block sales

All special block sales should first be approved by the Floor Trading Arbitration Committee. The transaction value of the subject of the block sale shall not be less than five million pesos. A transaction is defined as one entry to the system. However, a block sale involving one listed issue to be done at two different prices shall be counted as two transactions. Each of the transactions shall be more than the minimum amount to qualify as a block sale.

Board lots and price fluctuations

Trading of shares shall be in terms of fixed minimum amounts called board lots depending on the stock price range. Also depending on the stock price range, prices may change only in fixed steps called price ticks or price fluctuations. For purposes of easy trading, the Exchange shall fix the board lot for each listed issue and set the table of board lots and make the necessary amendments if warranted by the circumstances. Board lots shall be automatically updated every end of the day based on the closing price of that particular issue and in relation to the existing schedule of board lots to be made effective the following trading day. Whenever board lots are updated, it shall be the responsibility of the brokers to update their affected GTC orders.

Cancellation of matched orders

There shall be no cancellation of done or matched trades except in computer errors or evident mistakes. The Floor Trading Arbitration Committee, indicating the reason(s) for the request for cancellation and a confirmation that the two parties involved in the transactions have agreed to the cancellation. This is provided further that, in the case of a transaction involving two brokers, the letter request shall be co-signed by the two brokerage's authorised signatories indicating that their respective clients and/or themselves have both agreed to the cancellation. It is also provided that the intended cancellation in both cases shall not violate any PSE or SEC rules and regulations. The following paragraphs outline the procedure for requesting cancellation.

A request for cancellation shall be submitted for the approval of the Floor Trading Arbitration Committee which shall determine if the cause for the request exists and to impose a penalty if warranted by the circumstances. Requests for cancellations require signatures of three committee members.

After securing the needed signatures, the letter-request should then be sent to the Exchange Management through the Market Regulator Terminal (MRTerm) staff on each of the trading floors for verification of the signature of the Floor Trading Arbitration Committee members and the authorised signatories of the requesting brokers. For this purpose, specimen signatures must be submitted. Cancellation requests with defects in the signatures submitted shall not be acted upon.

To ensure that the daily quotation shall no longer include the trades to be cancelled which otherwise would have distorted it, requests for cancellation shall reach the exchange management (the chief operating officer or, in his absence, the department head of the Information Technology Department) not later than 2:00 p.m. of the same day.

In cases of emergency where the letter-requests with the necessary signatures cannot be presented but trades need immediate cancellation, the concerned brokers may call the chief operating officer or the head of the IT Dept. to report the trade cancelled. However, the brokers shall make representation that they have already gotten the verbal conformity of at least three members of the Floor Trading Arbitration Committee. The appropriate letter request should be submitted to the management within 24 hours from the time management acted upon the request.

Requests for cancellation after 2:00 p.m. of the same day shall be incorporated the following day.

Responsibility of members on all orders

A member shall be responsible for any order entered into the system through his/its terminals, including any liability that may arise out of the entry.

Identification of orders as principal or client

Each order made by the dealer and/or principal must be identified after inputting such order. Brokers through Order Entry Window must set up the default flag to either P (Principal) or C (Client). Consequently, orders that are not specifically identified will follow the default flag. In case there is a need to change the P/C flag of a done deal, the broker concerned shall submit a written request addressed to the chief operating office indicating the reason for the change(s) not later than the settlement date. After this date, no changes shall be allowed.

If approved, the Information and Technology Department shall print a corrected Daily Transaction Report (DTR) indicating clearly in the title that it is an amended DTR. This amended DTR shall replace the old DTR print-out and shall be kept for reference and file by the broker. A fee of 100 pesos shall be levied for every amended DTR.

The DTRs for the week may be included as an attachment to the broker's regular remittance of transaction taxes to the BIR.

Identification of orders in terms of foreign ownership

All orders entered into the MakTrade and in their own broker system (for those equipped with the Communication Front End [CFE] must be identified whether the order is for a foreign or local client. Orders for the principal account (P flag) should also be identified as foreign or local depending on the nationality of the brokerage house. Similar to the P/C flag, the F/L flag may also be assigned a default value by the broker to facilitate order entry.

This monitoring system intends only to advise brokers on a real-time basis the extent of foreign ownership level of each listed issue. MakTrade cannot stop a trade if it is about to breach the foreign ownership limit and brokers shall thus decide for themselves whether to push through with their foreign client's buy order or not. Prior to entering a foreign buy order, brokers are advised to refer to the Stock Information (F4).

To maintain the integrity of the system, brokers shall advise the Exchange (c/o Clearing and Settlement Department) of any error or change in their F/L flag by using the same form as in the change of P/C flag.

Trading band and price freezing

Except for special block sales, a price band shall be set at not more than 50% up and not more than 40% down on a particular day, reckoned from the last closing price or at last posted bid price, whichever is higher. In cases of issues that were not traded for the last six months, the last special block sale or a negotiated sale price, shall be considered the last traded/ closing price. Whenever the price of a security falls outside the trading band, it shall not be accepted by the trading system.

Trading halt in relation to price movements

Whenever an issue reaches its ceiling or floor price limits during a particular trading day, a trading halt shall be imposed by the exchange on the following day unless the issuer discloses the reasons why its prices moved towards the limits. Whenever an issue hits the limits, the Compliance and Surveillance Department shall formally ask the company concerned for an explanation of the unusual price movement and the reply shall be distributed on the floor for the information of all member-brokers. The exchange may cause the publication of the company disclosure and only when such disclosures are disseminated that trading will be allowed to resume subject again to the trading band rule.

The preceding paragraph notwithstanding, trading may be permitted at a price above or below the limits set forth above if the exchange shall have determined that its strict adherence will result in undue obstruction in the attainment of a liquid market for a particular issue or class of securities in the following cases:

- If a broker is waiting to post a price outside the trading band and after a period of at least one whole day no transaction was made, the interested trader may write the exchange through the Floor Trading Arbitration Committee to be allowed to trade outside the trading band provided that the trade shall include at least 10 board lots or 100,000 pesos, whichever is higher; and
- Where the common stock of an issuer corporation has been classified and either class of shares has not been traded for more than 15 calendar days immediately preceding the transaction.

Trading halt in relation to disclosure requirement

Voluntary trading halt

Subject to the approval of the exchange, a listed security may go on voluntary trading halt if material information is to be disclosed to the exchange that would affect the trading of the said security. The listed company shall notify the exchange in writing of its intent to voluntarily halt the trading of its security.

Involuntary trading halt

When disclosure of material information or announcement thereof is made prior to or during trading hours, a trading halt may be issued until a written confirmation of the disclosure or announcement is made, verified, and properly disseminated to the public. Additionally, in case of press releases, a trading halt may be issued if:

- The press release submitted to the exchange was not approved by the Securities and Exchange Commission (SEC) and in the opinion of the exchange contains material information; or
- The press release was made without prior submission of a copy thereof to the exchange and in the opinion of the exchange contains material information.

It is understood that a press release with the Securities and Exchange Commission (SEC) approval submitted to the exchange is considered proper disclosure.

In the foregoing instances, the exchange shall first determine the circumstances involved, (for instance, unusual trading activity or drastic price movement) prior to issuing a trading halt.

A trading halt shall be in effect until after one hour from distribution of the disclosure by the exchange to the public or the next trade day if the disclosure is circulated after trading hours. Without the disclosure, the trading halt shall continue to be in effect unless otherwise lifted by the exchange. In the case of a press release, the trading halt shall be in effect until after one hour from distribution of the SEC-approved press release by the exchange to the public, or the next day if the SEC-approved press release is received by the exchange after trading hours.

Correspondent broker trading and trading on one floor only

If for any reason one trading floor cannot operate, the chairman or the president can authorise trading to start on the other trading floor at 10:00 a.m. Whenever the start of the trading hours is delayed, the pre-open period shall be shortened to ten minutes. Subject to SEC approval on the extension, market will close at 12:30 p.m. followed by a 10-minute run-off period to execute orders at closing prices.

Under a one-trading-floor scenario, affected brokers may trade on the other trading floor through their correspondent brokers. Trades done this way shall be on a no-commission basis. Affected brokers may send their trade(s) to the booths of their correspondent brokers to assist. The correspondent brokers shall allow at least one of these trades in their trading booths.

Suspension of trading activity

When, for any reason, the communication link connecting the Tektite trading floor to the Central Matching Computer is cut, the following policies shall be observed to ensure equality on the trading floors in terms of the ability of the brokers to conduct trading activities:

- The IT Department is authorised to put an immediate halt to trading, which means there will be no trading on either floor. The IT Department shall do everything possible to restore the link. As soon as the link is restored, trading is to resume automatically.
- Depending on the length of time that trading was suspended, the exchange may decide to extend the trading within the period provided for in Section 1 of Article 1 of the rules of the stock exchange. The decision shall be announced on the two floors at the earliest possible time.

Trading equipment failure during trading hours

Members shall report immediately to the exchange any event of failure, error or defect in any of the trading equipment (computer terminals, host computers, etc.) installed by the exchange in the trading floor or member's booth. In any such case, the exchange shall have the discretion to assign, allocate or, if necessary, reallocate booths and equipment, where possible, to the affected member/s. The exchange shall not be responsible for any damage arising from such failure, error or defect in the equipment.

Conduct on the trading floor

Certain acts are considered detrimental to the interest of the exchange and are strictly prohibited on the trading floor. Bringing in food or drinks, horse-playing and improper attire constitute minor offences and are subject to penalties including fines and suspension.

Bringing in intoxicating liquor, being under the influence of liquor, bringing in firecrackers, inflammable materials and other pyrotechnics, bringing in guns and other deadly weapons, destroying, vandalising Exchange properties, disrespect to the flag, governors and exchange officers and members of the Floor Trading and Arbitration Committee, fighting, sexual harassment, stealing and repetitive minor offences constitute major offences. Any personnel caught committing any of the above-mentioned acts shall be subject to penalties including fines, suspension and expulsion.

Any member-broker, dealing partner or authorised clerk has the duty to exercise due care in operating and using all equipment at the member's booth inside the trading floor. Any damage caused to any of the equipment or fixtures or any other property shall be the sole responsibility of the member-broker, who shall reimburse the exchange for the cost of repairing or replacing the same. The exchange may impose whatever disciplinary action it thinks fit if it is proven that the member-broker concerned or any of his staff or authorised clerks, or any person employed by him, caused the damage intentionally.

RULES AND REGULATIONS ON CLEARING AND SETTLEMENT

Choice of clearing house

Clearable transactions shall be strictly limited to purchases and sales of stocks listed in the exchange by and between member brokers. Brokers may choose their preferred clearing house for issues that are still under the scrip-based clearing. At the end of each trading day, the brokers shall print their DTRs and ABCs. The IT Department of the exchange shall segregate the day's trading file by clearing house. Issues that are already under the book-entry system shall no longer be included in the ABC and DTR that will be submitted to the clearing houses. Scripless issues shall be settled through the Central Depository.

Unless advised to the contrary, the exchange shall continue with the present clearing house preferences. Brokers wishing to transfer to the other clearing house shall formally advise the Exchange, which shall in turn advise the IT Department and the two clearing houses. The letter should be received by the exchange at least three full days before the request takes effect to allow all concerned to be advised accordingly.

Payment to clearing houses

All regular transactions in listed securities, inclusive of issues under the scrip-based and book-entry system, must be paid or settled with the clearing house not later than 1:00 p.m. on the fourth trading day after the transaction date. Payments not received or remitted to the clearing house by 1:00 p.m. of the settlement date shall be penalised.

Deliveries to the clearing house

Certificates of stocks and/or stock assignments of issues that are not yet under the book-entry system of the central depository shall be submitted to the clearing house not later than 1:00 p.m. of the fourth trading day after the transaction date. In support of their sell transactions, brokers shall submit their Form E's for clearing accompanied either by stock certificate(s) or by stock assignment(s). In support of their buy transactions, brokers shall submit their Form D's for clearing.

Brokers shall see to it that the stock certificates delivered by them are endorsed in blank, indicating therein that all endorsements are guaranteed by them.

Direct/delayed deliveries

There shall be no direct and delayed deliveries. Direct deliveries refer to transactions done on the trading floor but are not coursed through the clearing house. Delayed deliveries refer to transactions done on the trading floor and are coursed through the clearing house but are made on a date later than the usual settlement date.

In the event that timely delivery cannot be made, the broker shall write the Floor Trading and Arbitration Committee for assistance, but no penalty shall be imposed if delivery is eventually made on the due date. The broker shall fill up a PSE letter of Assistance for the purpose. A prescribed letter form is set out in Form 4.

Without prejudice to the penalties provided, in the event of failure of the broker to make delivery on the due date, the Floor Trading Arbitration Committee may buy the shares for the account of the erring broker. In such event, the Floor Trading Arbitration shall inform the exchange management through its Trading and Settlement Department who shall likewise inform the clearing house about the delay in the delivery of the certificate(s) of shares.

Effect of suspension

In cases where a suspension is imposed under Chapter II of the rules, the suspended broker shall be prohibited from trading with or through any broker and from issuing confirmation receipts. The exchange shall freeze the broker's holdings by not allowing any lodgements and uplifting of shares at the PCD and advise the clearing houses not to allow the over-the-counter clearing of the broker's form and stock assignments. The suspended broker's holdings may be released only upon clearance by the exchange.

Number of offences

The number of offences a broker has made shall be reckoned from the start of the exchange's operations until the end of the year. Thereafter, the count shall start all over again.

RULES AND REGULATIONS ON FEES AND COMMISSIONS

Exchange fees

The Exchange shall collect from both the buying and selling broker an exchange fee of 1/200 of 1% of the total amount involved in every contract executed.

Commission rates

The brokerage rates of commission on listed and unlisted (that is, over-the-counter, common and preferred shares) shall not be more than 1-1/2% of the total amount involved in the contract excluding taxes and other fees. Brokers' commission is subject to VAT equivalent to 10% of the total amount and the VAT can be shifted to the market and investors. Brokers shall pass on the 10% VAT on commission to their clients. Therefore, brokers' confirmation receipts shall indicate the net amount of commission and then separately a 10% VAT.

Transfer fees payment

Member firms shall have 48 hours from receipt of a written notice from the transfer agent or the clearing house to pay the required transfer fees.

PCDI fees

Issues lodged into the scripless system shall be charged a PCDI fee based on the *ad valorem* rate of 0.0000834 without any maximum or minimum amount. This rate shall be applicable on both the buy and the sell side. PCDI fee is supposed to be in lieu of the transfer fee of 100 pesos plus VAT and the cancellation fee of 20 pesos plus VAT. Should a client buy a PCDI-cligible issue and still wants a stock certificate issued to his name, said client shall therefore pay the PCDI *ad valorem* charge, an upliftment/withdrawal fee of 25 pesos per request and 100 pesos plus VAT per certificate transfer fee. Similarly, a client who wishes to sell a PCDI-eligible issue and has still with him the stock certificate for delivery to the broker, said client shall then be charged the PCDI *ad valorem* rate and a cancellation fee of 20 pesos plus VAT per certificate. For clients whose shares are all lodged into the PCDI system, only the PCDI *ad valorem* rate will be charged. For the relevant procedures, brokers are advised to refer to the PCDI manuals. PCDI charges shall be passed on to the client and shall be made mandatory.

Payment of tax and manner of filing returns

A stockbroker who effects a sale has the duty to collect the tax from the seller upon issuance of the confirmation of sale, issue the corresponding official receipt therefrom and remit the same to the revenue district officer where his principal place of business is located within five banking days from the sale of collection thereof and to submit on Mondays of each week to the Trading and Settlement Department of the exchange a true and complete return, which shall contain a declaration that he made it under the penalties of perjury, of all the transactions effected by him and turned over to the concerned revenue district officer. The Trading and Settlement Department shall reconcile the same with the weekly reports of stockbrokers and, in turn, transmit to the revenue district officer on the first and 16th day of each month a consolidated return of all transactions effected during the preceding period.

RULES AND REGULATIONS GOVERNING MEMBERSHIP
Definitions

Exchange or PSE means Philippine Stock Exchange, Inc.
SEC means Securities & Exchange Commission.
Member means a natural or corporate person who has been accepted as a member of the exchange and who owns a seat in the exchange, including a nominee member.
Individual member means a member who is a natural person.
Corporate member means a member who is a corporate person represented by a nominee.
Nominee member means a natural person appointed by a corporate member.
Seat means membership in the exchange.

Seat ownership

Each member (other than a nominee member) shall own and hold and be entitled to only one seat in the exchange. There shall be only 200 seats in the exchange.

Rights of members

All members in good standing are entitled to vote in the regular and special meetings of the members and may be voted upon or be appointed to any position and exercise the rights and perform the obligations appurtenant to such position. All members shall have the right to participate in the assets of the exchange upon its dissolution.

Membership Committee

The Board of Governors of the exchange shall annually constitute and appoint a Membership Committee which shall be composed of at least two members. The members of the committee shall serve for a term co-terminus with that of the Board of Governors.

The committee shall have the following functions and powers:

- To develop specific rules and regulations to guide the conduct and affairs of the members, to include rules and regulations regarding reporting requirements, insolvency, investigation, suspension, expulsion and reinstatement of members;
- To investigate and make recommendations to the board on all applications for membership in the exchange, and for reinstatement of suspended members;
- To require that rules of the exchange regarding applications for membership are strictly complied with and to make recommendations to the board; and
- To compel interview of applicants for membership.

Posting and approval of applications

All applications for membership shall be circularised and subsequently posted on the bulletin board of the exchange for at least 15 days. All applications for membership must be approved by an affirmative vote of at least eight members of the Board of Governors.

RULES ON LISTING
Initial public offering

The applicant company shall engage the services of a duly licensed underwriter, who, among others shall firmly underwrite the entire issue. The underwriter may likewise act as the applicant's lead underwriter/issue manager. The applicant company may at its option, engage the services of another to act as its lead underwriter/issue manager to manage the issue. The lead underwriter shall warrant that it has exercised due diligence in ascertaining that all material representation is contained in the applicant's prospectus or offering memorandum, that their amendments or supplements are true and correct, and that no material information was omitted, which was necessary in order to make the statements contained in the applicant's prospectus or offering memorandum not misleading.

The applicant company shall engage the services of a stock transfer agent, which shall be duly licensed and certified by the commission and accredited by the exchange. The applicant company shall submit a certificate issued by the exchange certifying that its stock transfer agent has been accredited by the exchange. The applicant shall take full responsibility for all the acts of its transfer agent. The applicant shall execute and submit an undertaking holding itself jointly and severally liable for all the acts of its transfer agent in relation to the issue.

The following may be grounds for disqualification from listing of securities in the exchange:

- If there exists a serious, adverse and imminent action or claim against a substantial or significant portion of its assets;
- If the applicant or any of its officers and directors have been declared insolvent or bankrupt or placed under receivership or has applied for suspension of payment of debts or voluntary insolvency or bankruptcy within the past five years and said order of insolvency, bankruptcy or receivership or application for voluntary insolvency, bankruptcy or suspension of payment has not been withdrawn, revoked, discharged or otherwise superseded;
- If the applicant is engaged in a line of business which is contrary to morals, good customs, public order or public policy.

First board listing

An applicant's suitability for listing in the First Board shall be based on the following factors:

- Generally, it must be in actual operation for at least three full fiscal years;
- It must have sufficient capitalisation;
- Its management and controlling stockholders must possess integrity and good managerial skills; and
- It has stability and stature in the industry or in the business community.

Track record

In general, the applicant shall have a proven track record of profitable operations for at least three full fiscal years immediately prior to the application for listing with a cumulative consolidated pre-tax profit of at least 50 million pesos and a minimum pre-tax profit of 10 million pesos for each of those three years. For purposes of this rule, pre-tax profit shall not include non-recurring and extraordinary income. The applicant must be engaged in materially the same businesses and must have a proven track record of management throughout the last three years prior to the filing of the application. Without prejudice to compliance with all the requirements set forth in the rules, there are the exceptions to the three-year track record rule.

Management

The applicant must be under a sound and competent management with a proven record of profitable operations in the same or related line of business and operations engaged in by the applicant.

Disclosure

The applicant company shall fully disclose any and all material information relative to the issue. The exchange may require disclosure of additional or alternative items of information as it considers appropriate and material in any particular case.

The applicant company must show its willingness to comply with the full disclosure policy of the exchange. If during the application, the applicant company fails to make a timely disclosure of material information or deliberately misrepresents material facts to the exchange, then the exchange may consider said actions as evidence of the applicant's refusal to comply with the full disclosure policy of the exchange and on the basis thereof reject the application.

Applicable fiscal year

The applicant company shall be prohibited from changing its fiscal year if the purpose of the change is to take advantage of exceptional or seasonal profits in order to show a better profit record.

Minimum number of directors and stockholders of company

Upon the filing of the application, the applicant company shall have a minimum of seven directors. After listing, the listed company shall, at all times, maintain, at least 1,000 stockholders owning shares equivalent to at least one board lot.

Lock-Up

The applicant company shall cause its existing stockholders who own an equivalent of at least 10% of the issued and outstanding shares of stock of the company to enter into an agreement with exchange not to sell, assign or in any manner dispose of their shares for a minimum period of 180 days after the listing of the said shares.

If there is any issuance of shares (for instance, private placements, asset for shares swap or a similar transaction) or instruments which lead to issuance of shares (such as convertible bonds, warrants or a similar instrument) done and fully paid for within 180 days prior to the start of the offering period, and the transaction price is lower than that of the offer price in the initial public offering, all persons who availed of the shares shall be subject to a lock-up period of at least 365 days from full payment of the aforesaid shares.

In order to faithfully observe the lock-up provision, the exchange shall require the applicant company to enter into an escrow agreement with the trust department of an independent and reputable financial institution that is acceptable to the exchange in order to have the subject shares physically delivered to the escrow agent for deposit and safekeeping during the lock-up period. The agreement shall contain, among others, the following points:

- The company shall physically deliver the stock certificates to the escrow agent for deposit and safekeeping;
- The escrow agent shall notify and seek prior approval from the exchange before the subject shares are removed from its custody;
- The escrow agent shall immediately inform the exchange if in its sound judgment, it perceives that there is a potential violation of the agreement; and
- The escrow agent shall make a final report to be submitted to the exchange within seven calendar days after the lapse of the period stipulated in the agreement.

The applicant shall furnish the exchange a certified true copy of the agreement at least seven calendar days before the start of the offering period.

In cases where the applicant company has more than 100 shareholders and either the exchange or the provisions of these rules require a lock-up of all existing shareholders of the applicant, the exchange may, at its discretion, accept other arrangements or agreements executed by the applicant for the purpose of complying with the lock-up requirements; provided that said arrangements or agreements may be availed of by the applicant company and accepted by the exchange only if the following conditions exist:

- The applicant company has successfully placed 98% of its shareholdings under lock-up through an escrow agreement as described above;

- The applicant company must show that the alternative arrangements and agreements adopted by the applicant company for the lock-up are effective means of locking-up the shareholders and have substantially the same effort or in case of contracts, the same provisions required under said escrow agreement; and
- The shares of stock of major shareholders and shareholders who are project proponents or officers and directors of the applicant company and their immediate family, must be locked-up by means of an escrow agreement as described above.

Upon the commencement of the operation of the central depository system in the trading and settlement of securities in the exchange, the lock-up of the subject shares shall be implemented by blocking off said shares in the central depository system to prevent the sale and transfer of the same during the lock-up period.

In both cases, the applicant shall cause the recording of the shares subject to the lock-up in the books of the company. The applicant company shall furnish the exchange a sworn corporate secretary's certification stating that the subject shares are duly recorded in the applicant company's books at least seven calendar days before the offer period.

Red-herring prospectus

The applicant company shall submit its red-herring prospectus to the Listing Department at least seven calendar days prior to its presentation to the Listing Committee.

Within seven calendar days from the receipt of the notice of approval from the Board of Governors of the application, the applicant company shall furnish all the member-brokers of the exchange a copy of its red-herring prospectus.

Offering prospectus, press releases and other similar documents

All offering prospectus, primers, subscription agreement forms, newspaper prints, advertisements, press releases and the like in connection with the IPO shall first be submitted to the exchange for review and approval before they are printed or disseminated to the public. The newspaper prints, advertisements, press releases and the like shall contain all facts that are considered as material by the exchange. If the newspaper prints, advertisements, press releases and the like came from an unauthorised source, the exchange reserves the right to require the applicant to issue its own advertisement or press releases either confirming, disclaiming or rectifying the same.

Qualifications and responsibility of directors and officers of the issuer and lead underwriter

No person convicted by final judgment of an offence punishable by imprisonment for a period exceeding six years, or a violation of the Corporation Code committed within five years prior to the date of his election or appointment, shall qualify as director, trustee or officer of any applicant.

Directors and officers of the applicant are required to accept responsibility for the information that the listing application and all documents submitted to the exchange contain, including its prospectus. A statement to that effect shall be incorporated in the prospectus. Moreover, the last page of the prospectus or offering memorandum shall contain the following:

- A statement that the applicant company and the lead underwriter/s have exercised due diligence in ascertaining that all material representations contained in the prospectus or offering memorandum, their amendments and supplements are true and correct and that no material information was omitted, which was necessary in order to make the statements contained in said documents not misleading; and
- The name and signature of a majority of the members of the board of directors of the applicant company and the chief executive officer/ chief operating officer of the applicant company and the lead underwriter/s.

Chainlisting

A subsidiary will not be considered for listing if its holding/parent company is already listed in the exchange and it accounts for a substantial portion of the holding/parent company's average profits. Conversely, a holding/ parent company will not be considered for listing if one or more of its subsidiaries are already listed in the exchange and one or all of those listed subsidiaries accounts for a substantial portion of the holding company's average profits. For purposes of this rule, 'substantial' shall be an amount greater than 50%.

Minimum capital requirements

At the time of filing of the application, the applicant shall have a minimum authorised capital stock of 100 million pesos, the subscribed capital stock of which a minimum of 25% must be subscribed and fully paid.

Track record

A new start-up venture with no track record may be considered for listing if it meets the following criteria:

- It needs funds to finance a projected or to develop a new product, which through extensive research is proven to be highly feasible;
- It has a management that is an expert in the industry where the new venture is operating;
- It shows a strong commitment to implement the venture;
- It provides a realistic and achievable feasibility study and work program; and
- It shows that it has a potential for exceptional growth.

Property appraisal reports

The applicant shall engage the services of two independent appraisers duly accredited by the exchange in determining the value of its assets.

Offer price of shares

The offer price of the shares applied for listing in the Third Board shall be equal to its par value.

No secondary offering of shares

The applicant company is prohibited from offering secondary shares to the public.

Lock up

The applicant company shall cause all its stockholders to enter into an agreement with the exchange not to sell, assign or in any manner dispose of their shares for a minimum period of 365 days after the listing of the shares.

Minimum number of directors and shareholders of company

Upon the filing of the application, the applicant shall have a minimum of seven directors. After listing, the listed company shall, at all times, maintain at least 500 stockholders.

Transfer to First or Second Board

Upon application and showing that it has already met the requirements for listing in the First or Second Board, the applicant may, upon written request, be elevated for listing in the First or Second Board.

Offering and listing

Offering period

The applicant is prohibited from selling or in any manner disposing of its shares to the public, both locally and abroad, before the start of the offering period. The exchange shall have the right to revoke the approval of the listing application if it finds that the applicant violated the aforementioned rule.

The period within which to offer the shares to the public shall be determined by the applicant, which shall not be less than eight trading days.

Minimum offering to the public

Unless otherwise provided by law or government regulation, the minimum offering to the public for initial listing shall be based on a schedule determined by the exchange.

Distribution system

It shall be the objective of the exchange to distribute to the investing public the securities sold through its member-brokers. To attain this objective, the exchange shall undertake to promote the distribution of securities to small domestic investors and arrange with the applicant companies and the lead underwriters and/or issue managers for the sale and distribution of securities through the exchange for the purpose of distributing the shares as widely as possible to the investing public.

Delivery of selling kits

The applicant shall deliver to the exchange for distribution to the brokers sufficient selling kits, which shall contain, among other things, the following:

- Five copies of the offering prospectus and any amendment or supplement thereto if any;
- A minimum of 150 subscription forms;
- Signature cards;
- Computer diskette; and
- Instruction sheet for use of computer diskette.

The selling kits shall be delivered to the exchange at least two trading days before the start of the offering period. Failure to comply with the aforementioned requirement shall be a ground for the deferment of the offering period.

Rejection or reduction of shares

The applicant shall have the discretion to reject or reduce an application to subscribe/purchase its shares, provided that the same is exercised in accordance with the law and the rules and regulations set forth by the exchange. However, the rejection or reduction shall not in any way be used to reduce the allocation to the exchange.

In exercising the right of rejection, the applicant company shall be guided by the following:

- It shall serve notice of rejection or reduction to the applicant/subscriber within ten banking days after the end of the offering period; and
- It shall refund to the applicant the whole or part payment, as the case may be, for the rejected or reduced subscriptions/applications within the same 10-banking-day period.

Delivery of stock certificates

Stock certificates shall be issued and delivered to the subscribe/purchaser not later than three trading days prior to the actual date of listing. However, in case of secondary offering, stock certificates shall be delivered to the applicant/purchaser not later than one trading day prior to the actual date of listing.

Actual listing and trading of shares on the scheduled listing date shall take effect only after submission by the applicant company of a sworn corporate secretary's certificate stating that all stock certificates had already been delivered within the prescribed period.

The exchange reserves the right to require the applicant to register its shares for IPO in the Philippine Central Depository Incorporated (PCDI)

Submission of list of stockholders

The applicant shall submit an undertaking committing itself to submit to the exchange not later than 10 days after the end of the offering period a computer diskette containing a complete and updated list of its stockholders and a copy of the top 1,000 stockholders of the applicant company.

Reservation of listing date

In reserving the listing date, the basis for queuing shall be the date and time when the exchange receives the hard copy of the letter-request. The applicant company shall only be allowed to reserve one specific date. In the event that the applicant company abandons its reserved date, it shall forthwith file another letter-request which shall be subjected to the same basis for queuing.

Listing date and failure to offer and/or list

The offering period and formal listing of the shares shall be conducted within 60 calendar days from receipt of the notice of approval of the listing application. If no listing was conducted within the prescribed period, the listing application shall be deemed abandoned. On the other hand, if an offering was conducted, formal listing shall be made within 21 calendar days from the end of the offering period. If formal listing could not be made possible within the prescribed period, the applicant company shall be required to refund all subscription payments within 10 banking days from the lapse of the prescribed period. In both instances, the applicant company may file another application for listing, but it shall be filed only after 180 calendar days from the lapse of the 60-day period. Except for justifiable reasons as determined by the board, no requests for extensions shall be allowed.

Listing process for initial public offerings

Basis for queuing

For Listing Committee presentation, the basis for queuing shall be the date when the Commission's registration and licensing order and certificate of permit to offer securities for sale (licence/permit to sell) were issued and delivered to the exchange regardless of the date when the applicant submitted its listing application to the exchange.

Where two or more companies secured their registration and licensing order and licence/permit to sell on the same date, the date of submission of the complete listing application to the exchange would be the basis for the queuing.

Where two or more companies secured their registration and licensing order and licence/permit to sell, and submitted their complete listing applications on the same date, the queue shall be based on the date and time of submission to the exchange of a certified true copy of the registration and licensing order and the licence/permit to sell.

If the Listing Committee or the Board of Governors decides not to take action on the application until a particular condition(s) has been fulfilled, the applicant company may be relegated to the end of the present queue.

Processing of the application

The applicant company shall secure the necessary forms and file an application for listing, attaching all the necessary supporting documents and requirements. An application shall not be considered complete and thus cannot be processed unless the processing fee is paid and all documentary and other requirements shall have been submitted to the Listing Department of the exchange. The registration statement and listing application of the applicant company shall be filed simultaneously with the exchange.

The applicant company shall then make its presentation to the Listing Department. The schedule of the presentation shall be subject to the final approval of the Listing Department.

The Listing Department shall conduct an ocular inspection.

Upon submission of all the requirements, the application shall then be reviewed and processed by the Listing Department, which shall in turn, draft its report.

The Listing Department shall make the appropriate recommendation and shall then present its report to the Listing Committee.

The Listing Committee, in turn, shall review the application and the recommendation of the Listing Department.

If the application is found to be in order, the Listing Committee shall recommend to the Board of Governors the approval of the application.

The board shall take action on the application. The exchange shall notify the applicant in writing of the status of the application. The processing of the application by the Listing Department shall be at least 30 working days but not be more than 45 working days from the submission of all documentary and other requirements.

Appeals

Decision of the Listing Department

If the applicant company is found to be in violation of the Listing Rules and of the policies set forth by the exchange, the application shall be denied and the department shall inform the applicant of its decision as soon as practicable. The applicant company may file a request for reconsideration to the Listing Committee within ten calendar days from receipt of the notice. If the applicant is not satisfied with the decision of the Listing Committee, the applicant company may file a request for reconsideration to the Board of Governors within 10 calendar days from receipt of notice to the applicant company of the committee's decision. The decision of the board shall be final.

Recommendation of Listing Committee

If the application is found not to be in order, the Listing Committee may defer its decision to recommend its approval to the Board of Governors. The applicant company shall be notified of the committee's decision, stating the reason therefor. Within 10 calendar days from receipt of the committee's decision, the applicant company may file a request for reconsideration to the Listing Committee. If the request for reconsideration is denied, the applicant company may file an appeal to the Board of Governors within 10 calendar days from receipt of notice. The decision of the board shall be final.

On the other hand, in case the committee decides to deny or reject the application outright, the applicant, within 10 calendar days from receipt of the notice of rejection, may file a request for reconsideration to the Board of

Governors, specifying the reason(s) for its request. Only one request for reconsideration shall be allowed. Thereafter, the decision of the board shall be final.

Decision of the Board of Governors

If the Board reverses the favourable recommendation of the Listing Committee, the applicant company may file a request for reconsideration to the board within 10 calendar days from receipt of notice, specifying the reason(s) for its request. Only one request for reconsideration shall be allowed. The decision of the board shall be final.

APPENDIX D

COMMON ABBREVIATIONS

ADB	Asian Development Bank
AFTA	ASEAN Free Trade Area
AID	(US) Agency for International Development
APEC	Asia Pacific Economic Cooperation forum
APT	Asset Privatisation Trust
ARMM	Autonomous Region for Muslim Mindanao
ASEAN	Association of South-East Asian Nations
BAI	Bureau of Animal Industry
BAP	Bankers Association of the Philippines
BCDA	Bases Conversion Development Authority
BFAD	Bureau of Food and Drug
BLC	Bonifacio Land Corporation
BOC	Bureau of Customs
BOI	Board of Investments
BOP	balance of payments
BOT	Build-Operate-Transfer
BPI	Bureau of Plant Industry
BPS	Bureau of Product Standards
CBA	collective bargaining agreement

CBCI	Central Bank Certificates of Indebtedness
CBD	central business district
CDC	Clark Development Corporation
CENRO	Community Environmental Natural Resources Officer
CEPT	common effective preferential tariff
CIBI	Credit Information Bureau Inc
CISS	Globalised Comprehensive Import Supervision Scheme
CMO	Customs Memorandum Order
CP	commercial paper
CTRP	comprehensive tax reform package
DA	Department of Agriculture
D/A	documents against acceptance
DAR	Department of Agrarian Reform
DENR	Department of Environment and Natural Resources
DND	Department of National Defence
DOCS	Department of Transportation and Communication
DOE	Department of Energy
DOSRI	directors, officers, stockholders and related interests
DOLE	Department of Labour and Employment
D/P	documents against payments
DTI	Department of Trade and Industry
ECA	Environmental Critical Area
ECC	Environmental Compliance Certificate
ECP	Environmentally Critical Project
ED	Export Declaration
EDA	Export Development Act
EFF	extended fund facility (program)
EIA	environmental impact assessment
EIARC	EIA review committee
EIS	environmental impact statement
EMB	Environmental Management Bureau
EPA	Environmental Protection Agency (United States)
EPD	Entry Processing Division (of the BOC)
EPZ	export processing zone
EPZA	Export Processing Zone Authority
ERB	Energy Regulatory Board
EVAT	expanded value-added tax
EXPONET	Export Assistance Network
FBDC	Fort Bonifacio Development Corporation
FCDU	foreign currency deposit unit (loans)
FFW	Federation of Free Workers

FIA	Foreign Investment Act
FPI	Federation of Philippine Industries
FTZ	free trade zone
GATT	General Agreement on Trade and Tariffs
GEM	Growth with Equity in Mindanao program
GIR	gross international reserves
GDP	gross domestic product
GNP	gross national product
HLURB	Housing and Land Use Regulatory Board
ICFTU	International Confederation of Free Trade Unions
ICSID	International Centre for the Settlement of Investment Disputes
IFC	International Finance Corporation
IMF	International Monetary Fund
IPO	initial public offering
IPP	Investments Priorities Plan
IPR	intellectual property rights
JICA	Japan International Cooperation Agency
JUSMAG	Joint United States Military Advisory Group
KMU	Kilusang Mayo Uno (1 May movement)
L/C	letter of credit
LGU	local government unit
LLDA	Laguna Lake Development Authority
LRTA	Light Rail Transit Authority
MAV	Minimum Access Volume (certificates)
MEPZ II	Mactan Export Processing Zone II
MIGA	Multilateral Investment Guaranty Agency
MNLF	Moro National Liberation Front
MSE	Manila Stock Exchange
MkSE	Makati Stock Exchange
NCMB	National Conciliation and Mediation Board
NDF	non-deliverable forward (contracts)
NEDA	National Economic Development Agency
NFA	National Food Authority
NGA	non-governmental agency
NPC	National Power Corporation
NTC	National Telecommunications Commission
NWRB	National Water Resources Board
OBU	offshore banking unit
OECD	Organisation for Economic Cooperation and Development
OECF	Overseas Economic Cooperation Fund
OFW	overseas Filipino workers

OPIC	Overseas Private Investment Corporation
OPSF	Oil Price Stabilisation Fund
PCAB	Philippine Contractors Accreditation Board
PDCP	Private Development Corporation of the Philippines
PDS	Philippine Debt Securities (Market)
PD	presidential decree
PENRO	Provisional Environmental Natural Resources Officer
PEZA	Philippine Economic Zone Authority
PEC	Philippine Environmental Code
PEP	Philippine Environmental Policy
PEZA	Philippine Economic Zone Authority
Philea	Philippine Industrial Estates Association
PHIVIDEC	Philippine Veterans' Investment Development Corporation
PIA	PHIVIDEC Industrial Authority
PIDS	public-issued debt security
PIE	PHIVIDEC Industrial Estate
PLDT	Philippine Long Distance Telephone (Company)
PNR	Philippines National Railways
PNS	Philippine National Standards
PPP	purchasing power parity
PS	Product Standard
PSE	Philippine Stock Exchange
RAIC	regional agri-industrial centre
SBMA	Subic Bay Metropolitan Authority
SEC	Securities and Exchange Commission
SEZ	special economic zones
SGS	Societe Generale de Surveillance SA
TRM	(Inter-Agency) Tariff and Related Matters (Committee)
TUCP	Trade Union Congress of the Philippines
USTDA	United States Trade and Development Agency
VAT	value-added tax
VQC	Veterinary Quarantine Clearance
WTO	World Trade Organisation

INDEX

enterprises
    ecozone types, 52–55
    free-trade, 52, 53, 54–55
    incentives, 44
    operational requirements, 49–50
    ownership requirements, 40–41
    private, 58–59
    registration, 48–50
    setting up, 208–209
    types, 42–43, 209
entertainment, 217
Environment and Natural Resources (DENR) Department, 88
environmental compliance certificate (ECC), 85–86
Environmental Impact Statement (EIS) System
    businesses/projects under, 86–87
    exempt projects, 87–88
    steps, 85–88
    targets, 84
environmental legislation, 83–89
Environmental Management Bureau (EMB), 88
environmentally critical areas (ECAs), 87
environmentally critical projects, 87
EPZs *see* export processing zones
equity participation, 39
exchange rate, 19–20, 35
Eximbank, 169, 170
Export Development Act (EDA), 153
export enterprises, 52, 53, 54
Export Processing Zone Authority (EPZA), 51, 53
export processing zones (EPZs)
    described, 52
    facilities, 128–129
    location, 8
    PEZA program, 123
    use of, 2–3
exports, 21
    controls, 110–112
    documentation, 112–113
    financing and insurance, 169–170
    investment incentives, 153
    marketing support, 58